Third Wave

Third Wave

The New Russian Poetry

Edited by Kent Johnson and
Stephen M. Ashby

Introduction by Alexei Parshchikov and Andrew Wachtel

Afterword by Mikhail Epstein

Ann Arbor

THE UNIVERSITY OF MICHIGAN PRESS

1995   1994   1993   1992   4   3   2   1

Library of Congress Cataloging-in-Publication Data

Third wave : the new Russian poetry / edited by Kent Johnson and
  Stephen M. Ashby ; introduction by Alexei Parshchikov and Andrew
  Wachtel ; afterword by Mikhail Epstein.
        p.   cm.
    Translated from Russian.
    Includes bibliographical references.
    ISBN 0-472-09415-7 (cloth : alk. paper). — ISBN 0-472-06415-0
(pbk. : alk. paper)
    1. Russian poetry—20th century—Translations into English.
I. Johnson, Kent.   II. Ashby, Stephen M., 1953- .
PG3237.E5T47   1991
891.71′4408—dc20   91-42069
                                                        CIP

To Nadia Burova, Arkadii Dragomoshchenko,
Alexei Parshchikov, and Dmitri Prigov—
Спасибо

Preface

AS WITH SO MUCH ELSE in the Soviet Union over the past decade, poetry has undergone an accelerated process of exploration and change. Indeed, the spirit of linguistic and conceptual experiment that has characterized a new generation of Soviet poets may be seen as approaching a "paradigmatic" moment in Russian literature, analogous in significance with the avant-garde surge of the early century and the poetic revival that accompanied the liberalization of the 1950s and 1960s. It is in this sense that Soviet critics have begun to speak of a "third wave" of literary iconoclasm and innovation building at century's end—one that anticipated, and now parallels, the remarkable social and cultural revolution that unfolds.

A noteworthy feature of this new poetry is that nearly all of its representatives are in their thirties or forties. But more significant than generational criteria is the fact that these writers share a self-consciously oppositional stance toward the established literary culture, publishing almost exclusively, up until the past few years, through the underground channels of samizdat. What is opposed, as Mikhail Epstein explains in his afterword to this book— and as do Alexei Parshchikov and Andrew Wachtel in their introduction— is not only the stultifying legacy of "socialist-realist" aesthetics, but the bardic, oracular style that has typified the dominant mode of "second-wave" verse since the 1950s. As Epstein, with an ironic twist, put it in an unpublished essay sent to us in the early stages of this project, the new poetry realizes "the ideal of mystical communism . . . in the sphere of linguistic practicums, as the expropriator of sign systems from all epochs and styles, enacting the destruction of their value hierarchies . . . [and] the abolition of lyricalness as a relic of ego and humanism."

Such a synopsis is not meant to suggest that this collection was begun with a privileged purview of its subject. In fact, the beginning of this book was an incredibly fortuitous encounter. In early 1988 the fifteenth anniversary issue of Michael Cuddihy's renowned journal *Ironwood* had appeared and featured poems by Arkadii Dragomoshchenko and Alexei Parshchikov. We were stunned by the work and intrigued by the mention, in the contributors' notes, of an active current of young, "experimental" poets in the Soviet Union working in open contempt of the official literary establishment and affiliated in two major groups called the Poetry Club and Club 81. It seemed to us that such a development—particularly in light of the last sixty years of Soviet literary history—was of some consequence. Certainly, we thought, an anthology of some of this work in English translation would be a timely document and make for an excellent book.

A few days after seeing this work for the first time, a leaflet came into our hands announcing the annual Edward Lamb Peace Lecture at Bowling Green State University: Dr. Nadia Burova, president of the Center for Creative Initiatives in Moscow, was to speak the next day on the topic "Building Bridges of Cultural Understanding." Her professional title suggested that she might be able to provide us with some advice on proceeding with such a project—or at least perhaps give us a clear indication that the idea was folly. Following a great many phone calls that evening and the next morning to the organizers of the visit, we were granted a five-minute audience with Dr. Burova, before a luncheon in her honor with, as we were told, the university president, members of the board of trustees, and local congressional representatives. Thus, we were hurried to a conference room and solemnly introduced. Talking as quickly as we could against the clock, we told her of the poems we had seen and of how it seemed to us that a collection in translation would be most appropriate given the growing spirit of glasnost and warming cultural relations between our two countries. Did she, by any chance, know about any of these new poets? And was there anyone in particular who would be appropriate to contact?

She laughed quietly and leaned forward to say something fairly close to the following: "Do you know that my husband is Dmitri Prigov, perhaps the most famous avant-garde poet of Moscow and one of the founders of the conceptualist movement and the Poetry Club? If you would like, he would gladly contact almost all the important new poets of the Soviet Union for you." At Dr. Burova's insistence our meeting was extended for close to an hour, causing the luncheon to be canceled, but allowing us to arrange the first essential details for the anthology. About three months later we received from Dmitri Prigov a mailing of original manuscripts from a number of Moscow poets, many of which are included herein.

A second crucial meeting took place a few weeks later at the Detroit Institute of Art, where Arkadii Dragomoshchenko and his translator Lyn

Hejinian were making their last stop on a national reading tour. Both received our idea with enthusiasm, and their cooperation over the last three years, like Prigov's, has been generous and invaluable. With Alexei Parshchikov, they were instrumental in arranging for our attendance at the "Language, Consciousness, Society" conference in Leningrad in August of 1989, where we were able to meet a number of the poets and collect new materials of relevance to the project.

The collaboration between Dragomoshchenko and Hejinian, which dates back nearly ten years, is primarily responsible for the significant and multifaceted exchange that continues to develop between this generation of Russian poets and American poets who are concerned with linguistic and formal experiment. In many ways this book can be seen as yet another outgrowth of that fruitful collaboration.

Third Wave: The New Russian Poetry, while constituting the most representative collection of the new poetry to date in English, is far from exhaustive. There are poets whose work might have been represented here, and it bears pointing out that, to Soviet readers, some of the omissions might be notable: Andrei Karpov, Mikhail Sukhotin, Iuli Gugolev, Oleg Khlebnikov, Marina Koudimova, Alexandr Soprovsky, Igor Irtenev, Maria Avvakoumova, Evgeni Daenin, Konstantin Kedrov, Vladimir Kucheryavkin, Elena Katsyuba, I. Pivovarova, and Ludmilla Khodynskaya, would be only a partial list. In addition, poets like Gennadi Aigi, Vsevolod Nekrasov, and Viktor Sosnora, though of the 1960s generation, are major figures whose formal innovation and refusal of any form of accommodation with the cultural establishment has strongly influenced a number of these younger writers. The work of all these poets awaits further translation and critical discussion in English.

The invitation is certainly there. As the prominent Moscow critic Viktor Erofeev wrote to us in a letter accompanying the first poems sent by Dmitri Prigov, "Here you have poets who are published rarely in the USSR, and some who have not published at all in the USSR. But the young people of Moscow and Leningrad love them (and often know them by heart). Perhaps American readers will be offered a chance to get into the atmosphere of the newest Russian poetical festival, not just as observers, but as participants— Let's invite one another to dance."

Acknowledgments

WE WOULD LIKE TO THANK those who have made significant contributions toward bringing this project to fruition. We must first thank the translators of this book, who endured, with magnanimous patience, the delays and logistical complexities of this project. If we did our best to keep all the loose ends together, we know that we were far from always successful.

A like thanks goes out to LeAnn Fields, of the University of Michigan Press. Her interest and belief in this project were immediate, and along the labyrinthine meanderings of its course we have come to value her friendship.

John High and J. Kates, whose translating roles have been instrumental to us, have also gone out of their way numerous times to help in maintaining contact with a number of the poets. In particular, both ferried materials and communications back and forth during trips to Moscow and Leningrad in the past two years. Dr. John Schuck of the Department of Psychology at Bowling Green State University was extremely helpful in facilitating our early contact with Nadia Burova and Dmitri Prigov.

A thanks goes to Jane Burbank, William Rosenberg, and Laurence Goldstein of the University of Michigan for inviting us to write about and preview some of this work in the special issue of the *Michigan Quarterly Review.* "Perestroika and Soviet Culture" (Fall 1989).

And two very special mentions must be made: It has become almost a commonplace for Marjorie Perloff, professor of Comparative Literature at Stanford University, to be thanked in the prefaces of books. We have no choice but to do so too, and with the greatest degree of appreciation. Her warm, continuous support and keen criticism from very early on in this project has been, quite simply, essential. Equal thanks go out to Lyn Hejinian; her contributions have been touched on above, but the importance of the many instances of her help and counsel to this anthology are inestimable.

It is fairly de rigueur, of course, for authors or editors to "lastly, but not leastly," thank their spouses. Convention in no way dictates the simple and heartfelt gratitude we express here to Deborah Elzinga and Patricia Ashby.

Acknowledgment is made to the following publications, in which some of these translations originally appeared:

Tatiana Shcherbina: "Still-Life," *Minnesota Review;* "The Thousandth Anniversary of the Christianization of Rus," *Michigan Quarterly Review.*

Alexei Parshchikov: "Address to an Assumed Interlocutor, "Two Women Make-up Artists," and "Flight," *Five Fingers Review;* "New Year Verses," *Ironwood;* "Mud-flats," *Michigan Quarterly Review.*

Arkadii Dragomoshchenko: "Synopsis/Syntax" and "Nasturtium as Reality," from *Description,* by Arkadii Dragomoshchenko. © Arkadii Dragomoshchenko, 1990. Translation © Lyn Hejinian and Elena Balashova, 1990. Reprinted by permission from Sun & Moon Press, Los Angeles.

Nina Iskrenko: "To Beat or Not to Beat," "Still Life," "To talk with you is like burning in the marsh," "Polystylistics," "Talking to my crested hen," and "You're hungry," *Five Fingers Review;* "Fugue," *Talisman.*

Dmitri Prigov: From "Reagan's Image in Soviet Literature," *Berkeley Fiction Review;* "Forty-ninth Alphabet Poem," *Michigan Quarterly Review.*

Sergei Gandlevsky: "A lynch law of unexpected maturity," "To Dmitri Prigov," "To Aleksey Magarik," "To Aleksander Soprovsky," "Ah yes, the lilac this May. Bulging clusters," and "The dawn came late. The blanket slid," *Berkeley Fiction Review.*

Olga Sedakova: "A Boy, an Old Man, and a Dog," "The Figure of a Woman," "Two Figures," "Mistress and Servant," "Pitcher. Tombstone of a Friend," "Child Playing," and "Inscription," *Berkeley Fiction Review.*

Lev Rubinshtein: "From Thursday to Friday," *Michigan Quarterly Review.*

Ivan Zhdanov: "The Personage," "The Walker," "A City Tune," "Home," "I'm not the branch, only the prebranchness," "But already sensing terror," "Portrait," and "I'll always take stock in," *Five Fingers Review;* "Table," *Poetics Journal.*

Pavel Pepperstein: "The daring dreams of willful admissions," *Michigan Quarterly Review.*

Elena Shvarts: "Statement," *World Literature Today;* "On the 'Four Elegies to the Corners of the World,'" and "Four Elegies to the Corners of the World," *Berkeley Fiction Review;* "Animal-Flower" and "Voyage," *Bomb.*

Viktor Krivulin: "some few of all the voices," *Michigan Quarterly Review;* "into the fluting of the spinal cord," "all the spring walls crumble into powder," and "flight to egypt," *Poetry World* (England).

Yuri Arabov: "I'm introducing it as a hunchback," "Windy," and "A Monument," *Five Fingers Review.*

Aleksandr Eremenko: "Twelve Years in Literature," "A horizontal country," "And Schubert on the water, and Pushkin living on rations," "Igor Alexandrovich Antonov," "Pieter Brueghel," "I look at you from such deep graves," *Five Fingers Review;* "Philological Verse," *Five Fingers Review* and *Michigan Quarterly Review.*

Contents

Introduction

ALEXEI PARSHCHIKOV
ANDREW WACHTEL

IN 1834 NIKOLAY GOGOL CALLED the Russian poet Aleksandr Pushkin "an extraordinary and perhaps unique manifestation of the Russian spirit: this is a Russian man in his mature development, which he will perhaps achieve in two hundred years. In him the Russian nature, the Russian soul, Russian language, Russian character have found a reflection of such purity, such unalloyed purity as only a landscape can achieve when reflected on the convex surface of a magnifying glass." And although for the rest of the nineteenth century it was to be prose writers (Turgenev, Tolstoy, Dostoyevski) and not poets who dominated the cultural arena, the turn of the century saw a rebirth of Russian poetry and a new recognition that the poet was indeed the bearer of the nation's language, spirit, and essence.

The first two decades of the twentieth century have come to be called the Silver Age of Russian poetry, in apposition to the Golden Age of Pushkin. During the Silver Age the lyric replaced the novel as the leading literary genre, and educated readers were treated to a dizzying array of constantly shifting poetic schools and movements, from decadence to symbolism to acmeism to futurism. But while the movements may have been ephemeral, the best poetic work was not. This period saw the first publications by poets who are the glory of Russian twentieth-century literature—Anna Akhmatova, Aleksandr Blok, Vladimir Mayakovsky, Osip Mandelstam, Boris Pasternak, and Marina Tsvetaeva. And although by the 1930s most of these poetic voices had been suppressed (none of these poets met the standards of socialist realism, and, as a result, their poetry was almost unpublishable in the USSR between 1934 and the late 1950s), the poems lived on: memorized, passed from hand to hand in manuscript or typescript, and recited clandestinely. For the twentieth-century Russian reader (and practically all Russians are readers) the poems of Akhmatova, Blok, Mayakovsky, Mandelstam, Pasternak, and Tsvetaeva served as signposts, markers of the age. The cruel fates suffered by so many of them—Mayakovsky and Tsvetaeva committed suicide, Akhmatova and Pasternak were hounded and harassed, and Mandelstam died in a prison camp—came to symbolize the agony of an entire nation. Their poetry did not merely express the nation's soul, it *was* the nation's soul.

From the 1930s until after the death of Stalin in 1953 no new unsanctioned poetic voices appeared. But with the gradual coming of the so-called thaw of the 1950s a new generation of poets came to the fore: Bella Akhmadulina, Josef Brodsky, Yevgeny Evtushenko, Andrei Voznesensky. They formed a kind of bridge, linking contemporary Russian literature with the poetic traditions of the 1920s: Voznesensky was befriended by Pasternak, Brodsky by Akhmatova. These were the new individualists; after the collective fog of the Stalinist years their voices rang out plangently with uncontrolled and almost uncontrollable romantic individuality, a poetic pose that captured the hearts of their Russian audiences, as the packed halls to whom most of them read attested. In the public mind they stood for free expression, political and personal, outside of party control. They seemed to be larger-than-life figures but were nevertheless perceived as speaking for their generation, expressing the yearnings of all but in a vibrant and individualized idiom.

They were also the first generation of Soviet writers to make contact with and to be influenced by American literature. Evtushenko, Voznesensky, and Akhmadulina all came to the United States for the first time in the early 1960s, and all of them eventually returned home filled with stories of the life of the American upper class and with poems by the Beat poets. Indeed, it is not surprising that the raw antiestablishment voices of the Beat generation should have appealed to these Soviet romantics.

Gradually, however, as the thaw shaded off into the Brezhnev freeze, these poets lost the authority with the broad public they had originally had. They did not give up their public roles or their literary privileges, and, particularly in the wake of the Soviet invasion of Czechoslovakia in 1968, they took on, fairly or unfairly, new symbolic roles. In the public mind Evtushenko came to symbolize complete capitulation to the new order, a kind of poetic prostitution. Voznesensky took on the role of the doubting and ineffectual intellectual, unable to take a strong stand either for or against the regime. Akhmadulina withdrew from the fray almost entirely and slipped into silence, only rarely making appearances or publishing. Finally, Brodsky (who had always been the most private of the poets of this generation) was separated from his public after his arrest and trial in 1964.

At the same time by the end of the 1960s and into the 1970s new poets were appearing, but given the atmosphere of stifling conservatism that characterized the Brezhnev years, they were almost unable to publish. It is this generation, poets now in their thirties or forties, who are represented in *Third Wave*. Unlike their immediate predecessors, the poets of this new generation shied away from public and universal pronouncements, meetings in large halls, and public readings. In part, this was because such opportunities were not available. But in part, and perhaps even more important, this was an aesthetic choice, a conscious artistic reaction to the excesses of the previous generation. These new poets produced chamber music in contrast with their predecessors' symphonies.

How did the poetic generation of the 1970s get its start? Although publication was almost entirely out of the question for new writers, it was still possible for poets to meet frequently, circulate their poems in samizdat (meaning literally "self-published"; a writer would type his work together with ten or so carbons and this was the entire "edition"), and read their works to each other in what writers of the time called "studio contacts." Information and new works of literature were exchanged among groups of initiates in closed circles, and a dedicated literary underground sprang up. The anthologies published through the University of Texas under the title *The Blue Lagoon Anthology of Modern Russian Poetry* will give the Russian-speaking reader a sense of some of these groups. This concept of small-group society was not limited to the poets of the underground; it was a characteristic model for Soviet life in this period in general, and for intellectual life in particular, from the salons of the literary elite in the town of Peredelkino outside of Moscow to the miniconferences on semiotics at Tartu University in Estonia to the unknown reading groups of underground poets in tiny Moscow apartments.

This form of social and literary exchange left specific psychological marks on all the poets who began to write in the 1970s and separated them in three important ways from the writers of the previous generation and from their own contemporaries who attempted to produce work for publication. First of all, they were able to avoid worrying about the extraordinarily complicated and subtle system of Soviet censorship. Any writer who wished to publish poetry in the Soviet Union knew reasonably well what would or would not pass, and, therefore, official and semiofficial poets started to censor their own work, in effect doing the Soviet censor's job for him. Since the poets of the underground were not writing for publication, the only kind of censorship they faced was personal. They never had to distort their words and ideas in order to make them acceptable to a potentially hostile outside reader.

Second, the Soviet literary system was arranged in such a way that the only possible path to publication lay through the good offices of one of the recognized stars of Soviet poetry. The system encouraged young poets to apprentice themselves, as it were, to a recognized master, whose letter of introduction would potentially allow a younger poet to be published. For a wonderful description of the psychological damage that such a system can do, the reader is encouraged to look at Aleksandr Eremenko's "Twelve Years in Literature," which appears in this anthology. Although many of the poets in this volume were tempted by the system, in the end they refused its blandishments, and this eschewal provides another important link between them, despite all the differences in their approaches to poetry.

Third, there was one other standard method of getting one's foot in the literary door: translation. Of course, throughout the Soviet period poets had turned to translation when other avenues of creative work were denied them; one might recall Pasternak's Shakespeare translations, for example. But the situation in the mid-1970s was somewhat different. In this period young poets were encouraged to translate not the classics of Western literature but the poetry of writers from the various Soviet republics. This was a dangerous thing for a young poet to do, however, for two reasons. First of all, the young poet ran the risk of being considered primarily a translator and not a poet. Having fallen into this category, one lost all hope of publishing original poetry. Second, one faced a loss of respect because most of the poets who were being translated did not themselves wish to be published in Russian, seeing in the translation efforts of the Soviet literary bureaucracy a veiled attempt at the Russianization of Soviet literature. Young Russian poets who were willing to produce translations of these poets ran a real risk of being seen as prostituting their talent in the service of the literary and state bureaucracy. With only a few exceptions, the poets in this volume avoided translating, and so they were able, at the cost of practically never seeing their work in print, to preserve their independence.

It should not be assumed, however, that all of the poets of this new generation formed a homogeneous group. Within the poetic underground a number of more or less distinct groupings appeared. Those who can be classified as conceptualists (see the afterword by Mikhail Epstein) started with the recognition that they were Soviet men and women through and through. Their task, they felt, was to use the special resources inherent in this position to describe the world around them. This meant, first and foremost, the use of the vocabulary of signs (visual or verbal, for most of these poets are also visual artists) of a standard Soviet observer, for in their view the individual's semiotic field defines his world. Although they did not know the works of Roland Barthes, they would have agreed with his formulation "my Japan, a system of signs I call Japan." They decided to explore the connection (or lack of connection) between this semiotic system and the world around them.

The result, of course, is a kind of grotesque parody that grows out of the inevitable clash of a vocabulary that was initially invented to describe the rose-colored world of the "bright socialist future" with the reality of life in the Soviet Union. Most of the early conceptualists' readings took place in conjunction with unofficial shows of their visual art. The earliest publications of the conceptualists appeared in the unofficial journal *A-Ya* (A–Z), which was published in Russian, French, and English, despite constant harassment from the Soviet State Security Commission (KGB).

If the conceptualists took the signs provided by the external world as the source of their inspiration, most of the other innovative poets of the 1970s tried to work with imagined worlds and avoid any conventional uses of language. Each and every thing or situation was renamed: Adam's task was taken on anew. Indeed, it is significant that this loosely connected group of poets felt a tie to the Russian acmeists (through the work of Mandelstam and Arsenii Tarkovsky), a group that was originally dubbed "Adamists" by one of its founders, and had also attempted in their poetry to rename the concrete external world. Thus, what these young poets valued most of all was the idiosyncratic world produced by the poet's language—his or her personal world.

At the same time the poets of this orientation were fascinated with the specifically poetic arsenal of the past and present. While the conceptualists worked with everyday Soviet language, these poets often employed an exaggeratedly literary idiom. This approach can be traced, in part, to their educations. Most were students at the Gorky Literary Institute in Moscow, the only full-time institution for the education of future creative writers in the Soviet Union. Although most of the courses were fairly banal, the atmosphere was one of high culture, and samizdat editions of Russian, European, and American poetry circulated freely among the students and were avidly discussed.

In the end, then, at base most of the disputes between the conceptualists and the nonconceptualists concerned language: Should one borrow and infuse new life into preexisting language, or should one invent an entirely new one? The former led inevitably to a parody of the existing world, while the latter led to its avoidance and to the romantic dream of the creation of an entirely different world. Both groups, however, could agree in their disdain for the existing order in the Soviet Union and in their dislike of the remaining poets of the 1960s, who were now seen as apologists for that order.

Thus, by the late 1970s the poetic scene in Russia was in crisis. Russian poetry, which had held the nation together for generations, had broken into two seemingly irreconcilable camps. On the one hand, there were the representatives of "palace" culture: the "official" poets who got their start during the first Soviet thaw—Evtushenko, Voznesensky, Akhmadulina. On the other hand were the younger members of the poetic underground. To the outside observer it seemed that the gap separating these groups was unbridgeable. The official poets could publish, read their poetry in public, and travel abroad. The underground could, at best, organize tiny readings in private apartments, but publication and travel were out of the question. Their respective poetic voices were, in many respects, equally far apart.

The differences between the poets in this anthology and their immediate predecessors in Russian literature can be brought out anecdotally through a description of an attempt by the main Russian literary newspaper, *Litera-turnaia gazeta,* to bring these groups together in 1984. Over a period of four months the newspaper published a series of articles devoted to a half-hearted discussion of the new "complicated" poetry. Eventually, the editors of the newspaper decided to invite the leading members of the poetic underground to read and discuss their work in front of an audience consisting of the staff of the newspaper, literary critics, leading representatives of official poetry including Evtushenko, and selected foreign journalists. The evening was designed to unite the younger poets and the older, serious poets against the looming threat of naked Russian literary nationalism. The hopes of the evening's organizers, however, were not to be realized. A poem by Aleksandr Eremenko on Mayakovsky's suicide so enraged Evtushenko that he came to the microphone and began to dress his younger colleague down. The younger poets present sprang to Eremenko's defense, hissing down Evtushenko, who left the hall crying "Discotheque hippies!"

Nevertheless, when censorship ceased to exist in the middle of the 1980s and publication became possible, many people began to realize that the differences between the generations of the 1960s and 1970s were not as great as they had seemed. For one thing, it turned out that there had always been a fair amount of personal contact between them. A particularly important indication of this contact was the preparation of the almanac *Metropol* in 1979. *Metropol* marked an early attempt to reunite the official writers and the underground, and, although it was doomed to failure (the almanac was banned immediately), the government's harsh treatment of its participants, both official and unofficial showed that in vital matters all Soviet writers were in the same position. Another analogous example was Andrei Voznesensky's sympathetic article on the new poetry (he called it "prepublication poetry") entitled "Muki muzy" ("Tortures of the Muse") that appeared in *Litera-turnaia gazeta* in 1977.

More important, however, with the relaxation of censorship starting in about 1985, the system of "us" and "them," which had played such an important role in the consciousness of Soviet writers, began to break down. For all their differences the poets of the 1960s and those of the 1970s had had the same enemy. The disappearance of the common external enemy of censorship forced a complete reevaluation of the poetic map, a reevaluation that is still in progress. There are, however, a number of results of this process that are already clear. For one thing, it became obvious to all that the categorical division into poets of the 1960s and poets of the 1970s was not an adequate classificatory system. It turned out, for example, that writers like Akhmadulina were, in their poetic thinking, much closer to many of the former underground poets than they were to Evtushenko or Voznesensky. On the other hand, the divisions that separated the underground poets themselves came to the surface, and it was noticed that they did not form a unified block in any meaningful sense.

If one were to propose a different classification, one that might more truly get at a real difference between groups of poets, then one might suggest a division between those poets who have a monologic and those with a pluralistic worldview. The classificatory system being proposed here has nothing to do with the value or quality of the poetry, it is merely a heuristic device and is advanced to help readers approach the poetry in this anthology. The poetry of the monologic writers (Aizenburg, Gandlevsky, Iskrenko, Kibirov, Krivulin, Pepperstein, Prigov, Rubinshtein, Shcherbina, Shvarts, and Turkin) is characterized by the presence of a strong and well-defined lyrical "I." In almost all cases these are poets who like to read their verse in public and who do so well. They work off and against a clear enemy. For the conceptualists (and all of the conceptualists belong to this group) the enemy started out as the Soviet bureaucratic state and its language, but the movement has branched out recently and has begun to subvert any and all linguistic and cultural systems, including those of Western Europe and the United States. For poets like Shvarts and Krivulin, the central fact of existence is personal experience, and that experience (which may be quite broad) becomes the central factor in their work.

All of these monologic poets parody what might be called the idiocy of daily life by treating that idiocy as something incredibly serious and important. In this regard one sees connections between their poetic thinking and such earlier Russian models as Sasha Cherny, Kozma Prutkov, and Igor Severianin. Intellectually, this kind of thinking is in tune with the systematizing approach of the great Soviet semioticians and scholars of the 1970s: Sergei Averintsov, Viacheslav Ivanov, Iuri Lotman, and Boris Uspensky. Their great collective work, the encyclopedic two volume *Myths of the World's*

Peoples, can be seen as a paradigmatic text for many of the monologic poets, who seem to be writing a kind of personal and sociological mythology.

Although the poets of this group tend to reject any comparison with non-Russian poetry, claiming that they are ignorant of foreign schools and that the Soviet situation makes their own poetry unique, a few poets and American schools that seem to have some similarity to the work of the poets whom we have lumped together here can be mentioned. Through the central importance of the experience of the lyrical "I" and its almost desperate need to express itself, these poets seem similar to the poets of the Beat generation of the late 1950s and early 1960s. In their more complex gestures to bracket mass culture in ironic and parodic terms, however, they can be likened to some of the poets of the "New York School" of the same period (Padgett, Berrigan, and Coolidge) and pop artists like Andy Warhol and Roy Lichtenstein. In all of these cases we see a strategy of subversion by incorporation: the linguistic or physical objects of popular culture are fully recognizable, but their automatized presence is undercut.

The other block of poets in this volume are those who, in one way or another, attempt not to think in monologic categories at all. That is, they reject binary oppositions such as "us" and "them" or the lyric "I" and the outside world. Once again it should be noted that we are not trying to identify any specific poetic "school" here. The poetry varies tremendously.

The poets in this second group reject the importance of real-life experience (a recognition of the importance of which links the monologic poets with such predecessors as Evtushenko, Voznesensky, and even Solzhenitsyn) in favor of internal, linguistic experience. For these poets language is more important than society, and, if the group of poets mentioned above believes that parody of specific idioms is needed in order to renew debased language, the poets of this second type try to renew language by foregrounding the resources inherent in language itself, by allowing and encouraging a free play of meanings and linguistic connections unfettered by conventional, quotidian usage. Since for these poets contemporary usage and linguistic behavior carry no more value than any other kinds of literary or linguistic fact, they are free to pick, choose, and combine material from any and all periods, schools, and movements. This freedom gives their work a distance from real-life experience and a free-associating macaronic quality that makes them seem quite "postmodern" to a Western reader.

As far as actual influences of Western poets on their work goes, the poets of this group can claim a large number of sources: Rainer Maria Rilke, modern Greek poetry (Seferis and Kavafis, for example), and Dylan Thomas (all in translation). They admire Rilke for what they call his discovery of the ontology of things, the Greeks for their ability to link the past and the present and for their connection to the Eastern Orthodox tradition, and Dylan Thomas for infusing things of the world with purely poetic passion. More recently, many of the poets in this group have discovered a strong affinity with the American "Language School" poets. For both groups the source of poetic production is found in language itself, and it is with this group that, for the first time, the former underground poets have entered into active poetic dialogue. It will be noticed that some leading Language School poets figure as translators in this volume (Jean Day, Lyn Hejinian, and Michael Palmer), and in the last few years these contacts have increased as the Soviet poets are actively translating and being translated by their newfound American poetic soulmates.

After many years in the literary underground the poets in this anthology were able gradually to come out in the open during the early stages of Mikhail Gorbachev's glasnost. Interestingly enough, the fame of the poetry represented here was initially fed by a strange kind of accident. Like practically all other Soviet organizations, the Writers' Union recognized the fashion for democratization. To show off their new democratic credentials the literary establishment turned to the former underground writers and began to allow them to read in public and to participate in conferences. But in 1987 some of the journals controlled by the resurgent Russian nationalist literary establishment decided to "expose" the new poetry in a series of vitriolic attacks. In articles with titles like "Citizens of the Night" (*Literaturnaia rossiia*), these "complicated" poets were accused of immorality and an absence of spiritual qualities and national feeling. The result of this criticism, however, was not quite what the attackers had in mind. Suddenly the names of the new poets became well known, and a widespread demand to read their work appeared. In response to this upsurge in interest, and in order to polish their "democratic" image, these very same journals found it necessary to publish the younger poets, expecting, presumably, that audiences would reject them. Thus, it happened that the first journal publications for many of these poets came on "enemy territory," on the pages of such nationalist organs as *Molodaia gvardiia* and *Moskva*.

At the same time the most famous literary periodicals in the Soviet Union (*Novyi mir, Oktiabr, Druzhba narodov,* and *Literaturnaia gazeta*), those same journals that would not publish the underground poets before 1985, have, by and large, refused to publish them since. The reasons for this are varied: a desire to bring out the great works of Russian literature, which had been suppressed for many years (*Doktor Zhivago,* and *The Gulag Archipelago,* for example); an orientation toward prose fiction and essays rather than poetry; and a simple aesthetic dislike of experimental poetry. Building on their newfound and unexpected popularity, however, a number of poets represented here realized that it had become possible and practical to publish independent literary almanacs, at first under the aegis of larger publishing houses and later independently; *Molodaia poeziia* '89 (1989), *Vest'* (1989), *Zerkala* (1989), and *Laterna Magica* (1990) were the result. Most of these almanacs published both monologic and pluralistic poets under a single cover together with contemporary prose fiction, drama, and essays.

As for books, a few poets represented here (Krivulin, Sedakova, and Shvarts) were lucky enough to have Russian-language editions of their works produced by émigré publishing houses long before it was possible to think of Soviet publication. For others (Kutik, Parshchikov, and Zhdanov) the first book-length publications were in translation (Danish editions of their works came out as early as 1987). In the last two years, however, now quasi-independent Soviet publishing companies have issued books of poetry by many of the writers represented in this anthology (Dragomoshchenko, Eremenko, Kondakova, Kutik, Parshchikov, Prigov, and Zhdanov). These are small paperbacks of about one hundred pages, but they are published in what would be gigantic runs for poetry in the United States: Ten thousand copies is standard. The fact that these editions have sold out completely is an indication that there is still an avid audience for poetry in the Soviet Union.

Many of the writers represented here have also been able to reach out to the international audience for poetry through anthologies that have appeared in book or magazine form. Collections of contemporary Soviet poetry in translation have been published in the last five years in Denmark, France, Finland, Germany, Sweden, and Yugoslavia. *Third Wave: The New Russian Poetry* is the first attempt to assemble a significant number of contemporary Soviet experimental poets under one cover in English. Naturally, a Soviet reader with an encyclopedic knowledge of the contemporary literary scene would notice certain biases. All the poets here live in Moscow and Leningrad, and thus provincial poets (Nikolai Gudonets, Vitali Kalpidi, Sergei Solovev) and fascinating non-Russian language Soviet poets (Lev Berinsky [Yiddish], Igor Remaruk [Ukrainian], Muhamad Salikh [Uzbek]) do not appear. In addition, the editors have consciously focused on various types of experimental poetry, although there are quite a few contemporary "traditional" poets whose work is worthy of notice (Nikolai Kononov, Vladimir Salimon). Nevertheless, what the editors of this volume have done is to select a broad and representative collection of the most interesting new poetry being written in the Soviet Union today.

And what of the future? Naturally, for underground writers who come out into the wide cultural world there are both advantages and pitfalls. On the one hand, there is the possibility of publication, travel, contact with a broad audience, and a feeling of security. On the other, the closed intimate circles of producers and lovers of postmodern art have broken down to a great extent. The hermetic environment in which most of the work in this volume was produced no longer exists. In the past the underground writer could be sure that his or her small circle of readers would recognize and appreciate every nuance, every citation, every reference, and many poems depended on the existence of this kind of reader. Now many poets are afraid that they will find it necessary to readjust in order to become comprehensible to eager but uninitiated readers. Aleksandr Eremenko, for example, was horrified to learn that the publishers of *Ogonek* were planning to print one hundred thousand copies of his first book. As he put it, "no one will take a book that comes out in that quantity seriously."

In addition, some of the writers who appear here are now living abroad; others spend much of their time traveling. This distance from the Soviet Union obviously leads to an even greater separation from the intimate circles that originally nurtured their talents. Should the economic situation in the Soviet Union continue to worsen, one can expect that more poets will, at least for a time, leave the country, thus further diluting the literary atmosphere of Moscow and Leningrad. Finally, a wider range of works is being published in the Soviet Union, and, therefore, consumers of literature have more choice. Books of poetry now come out not in samizdat editions of ten but of ten thousand, and, as a result, acceptance must be won in broader and sometimes hostile circles. Although the pressures of the literary and cultural marketplace and heavy competition from more popular forms of entertainment have not yet made themselves felt strongly in literature, they are probably inevitable as the Soviet economy lurches toward a market economy.

Still there is cause for optimism. Unquestionably, the vigorous production of poetry and the favorable response that younger Soviet poets have elicited both in the Soviet Union and abroad indicates that the grand traditions of Russian poetry are still very much alive. In the voices represented here one can catch echoes of Akhmatova, Lermontov, Mandelstam, Pasternak, Pushkin, and Tsvetaeva. In spite of all the changes and dislocations of the Soviet period, the Russian poet is still a reflection of, in the words of Gogol, "Russian nature, the Russian soul, Russian language, Russian character."

Tatiana Shcherbina

TATIANA SHCHERBINA was born in 1956. She has published two books in samizdat, *Still Life with Transformations* and *Null Null* (1987), and is active with the "independent" cultural movements in Moscow. She has received "official" recognition with publication in *Druzhba naradov* and elsewhere, and she broadcasts regularly on Radio Liberty. All selections here have been translated by J. Kates.

Foreword to *Null Null*

Nothing-Nothing: This is a tabula rasa, a table with room on it for anything that fits. To put more on it is only to duplicate what's already there—to put more into nowhere: only a second stratum, which means—once again—to duplicate. So Nothing-Nothing is everything and nothing. Doubled. Nothing-Nothing is the summit of culture and the point of its falling off, as well as the flatland, *style neutre*. A subjective whim, an individualistic assault for or against: this is just what it is not. More accurately, it's there like a pattern, the bend of a sine curve.

"For" is plus one, plus two, plus forty.

Any more than that is too high a burning, and a death redeeming Nothing-Nothing into time only when, together with all the dials of the world, suddenly a new circadian rhythm starts up: Nothing-One. And there will be still other laws. A new life, a new heaven—and that moment, known to everyone who isn't asleep at midnight, will be near.

"Against" is minus one, minus forty,

and a permafrost from which we'll draw out a hero someday, the way we draw out mammoths, to play his own particular role.

In this space-time-Nothing-Nothing—the human creature Nothing-Nothing will not be called forth by its name, but by the magic of the picturesque tension of culture composed about him. The magic will all be in the vision of cunning that stretches behind into artless simplicity.

Letter from Rotterdam

Universalism of consciousness and of the means of expression is the "glue" of a fragmented world in which humanity stands on the edge of the third millennium of the Christian era. If there is to be no new creative program for the future, in the way that Christianity presented a program for the last two millennia, the world will perish.

I make use of all levels of the Russian language, from classical literary diction to fashionable contemporary slang, including international words and my own neologisms. By counterposing these levels, cross-building them in relation to one another, I compose my own contribution to world culture from this particular vantage point, to keep our history from dying out.

Right now we are at a point of bifurcation. And all the time I conjure the end, I do not close my eyes against whatever is painful to know or see. For me it's important to proceed from reality. I cannot forget that we live in this three-dimensional world, but neither can I forget that I inhabit the cosmos. In my own dreams I travel on a journey of logic and a journey of magic, trying to answer logic with logic, magic with magic.

From my point of view it was classical art that acknowledged objective things, established their connections, and inserted "man" into a social context—a structure now complete. All of the possibilities of "man" in a common manifestation are settled in literature.

At the beginning of the twentieth century the avant-garde presided over the change from classical art with slogans that everything was possible. It upset the hierarchy of minor and major, of important and trivial, of moral and immoral. After the avant-garde and semiotics, a postmodern sensibility succeeded to the collapsing stereotypes and systematizing of culture.

Now, at the end of the twentieth century, all the old oppositions— ethic versus aesthetic, romanticism versus realism, subjectivity versus objectivity, etc.—have been rearranged into distinctly different conscious meanings. In general, I speak through my work about the end of the culture of binary opposition, about the first dim glimpses into a four-dimensional expanse where life passes at the speed of light.

And about those of us in the first wave of the third millennium.

The Garden

Language stifles, like a body—hang it—get out of language.
Verses are like people, fingers tremble on the rhythm,
                              the delicious, invisible longing.
The street of home, the garden of giving birth,
an apricot light.
The mature garden is fatty with brazen toxic dyes
only the black waterfall of night,
                              (to its shame) washes away
the siren's damp fur, the silk of tulips, and so on.

What's there to say about the Beautiful, an air innocent of deodorant!
No better irony—nothing not to have been ashamed of.
Language-land. A feather's gleam turns into a shepherd's crook,
and rakes away the autumn leaves. Wanders off, in full view.

In this garden, in the aroma of flowers and manure,
Give me the strength not to drone like a bee, and not to reek like a rose,
pushing a cumbersome body of speech to its conclusion.
Always this apricot glow—snow,
                              making even the road spin.

Concerning the Limits

Cicadas, my Ramses, cicadas are singing.
Wing your circuitous way to me, Socrates.
Swing to the Central Committee—please?
No way, soul brother. Soul am I and will not.

Look at the building, my idol, look at the building.
Don't we turn into insects and fling
our bodies down on unoccupied bunks in the hive
and hang up our rags on stiff-legged chairs they provide?

Open, Columbus, open up quickly,
your offspring sweated out laborious lives.
Where will it lead the impoverished Jews,
how indicate the way to our wretched refuse?

My friend, my soft-shelled genetic sport,
my crazy colleague whom nothing can thwart!
We reach our limits at puke, diarrhea:
Here they are. Take a look, we've arrived, my dear.

Still-Life

Zing—Boom—Snap:
drop here and there drop
the seed senses the ground like a greedy trap.
Whether it needs to fall, it needs to stay put
as the uttermost prophetic white grasslet in the air
and kafka, with golden inks a crazy engraver
writes: "The seed succeeded, conceived immaculate."

The seed Zing—Snap—Boom:
sets out at random
either toward this mother or that mother
or swimming orphaned toward a leeside cutter:
hurrah, an oasis! hurrah, an oasis!
And all of it a mess!

Snap—Boom—Zing:
my mother's a sun descended from yellow melons,
father a boomerang of moons a lunar elk,
between them a euclidean parallel:
il mirroring *il, elle* mirroring *elle.*

The seed, mothlike, like trout
knocks knocks against the lantern's light
locked behind a glass door . . .
Still-life: pitch dark on market day.

No Smoking!

Program for tomorrow: Stop smoking, no smoking, quit.
Maybe in the face of the state you are impotent,
deep-water and blue-veined,
but you are the smith of your own health,
and as much as poets are poppy and hemp,
they drug and drug. Recall, recall:
A single line is an eternal high,
so think about it . . . think of all the people.
Program for tomorrow: learn English.
"U-ni-ted States," how much in that sound
for a Russian heart—in that Esperanto
it doesn't croak like the native frog.
Somehow I'm not forced to struggle
with insufficiencies or catastrophes,
everyone struggles, but see how I sit here,
against cowardly health I oppose
the soul's audacity: I smoke.
But I don't parade my purity,
I know that a drop of nicotine can be a horse,
and I gallop headlong horseback.
God forbid you should be worrying me again
with the reproach of impossible health,
with the twit and swindle of the country's future.
The end of the cigarette-break is my program
            for tomorrow:
a cigarette an hour, cutting down to ten a day.
You, Russian literature, have fallen that low!
See how you fly off in all directions and light up again,
although only. . . .
Only that Grandma taught me Russian and good
manners, Grandpa read Pushkin, Yesenin, Blok,
and Mama said: Put your toys away
and still says: Stop smoking.
Only that I wrote up a program for tomorrow,
            and that was yesterday
but I continue to write for tomorrow, otherwise not only
            haven't I really lived
but also I will not know that living was imperative

and I will come to die without confidence. That life
          exists on Earth.
That it has its God. That we are not alone in the universe.
This lore, evidently, could still come in handy.
—The Voice of America, dateline Washington. Excuse us for this
     interruption.
—That's okay. We'll interrupt all of you, if you interrupt us.
Thus spake Zarathustra.

They all say no one can be saved, but I think some can. Those who don't
drink, don't smoke. . . . Stop smoking. So, how can you smoke even for a
minute now, when nuclear threat hangs over the world!

Program for tomorrow: Learn English. I'll do that first, a step in extending
the hand of friendship to the United States of America, I'll start talking to
them in their own language. Maybe then they will understand, and that will
be what Earth needs. And I'll smoke, because a person ought to have a
weakness and some kind of pipe-dream. Listen to the program broadcast
tomorrow and you'll hear the same thing.

     The title is in English in the original.—Ed.

Icarus

They said: He'd never fly to Thebes,
too painful to fall from such a height,
the clouds
spreading their wings all across the sky . . .
But the cliff below, again the cliff and
a river running over stones,
May, plums splitting open
and the hand
pulled to pieces, like a branch in the light.
Now where is Icarus?—later—Icarus!—
Flown off, like a raucous black cry,
and Dædalus on a campstool stiffened,
head buried in his hands—old,
too old, to have his children die.

My ideological antagonist,
my foreignpolitical whim,
you there, where tropical downpours
wash scampering rats off the pavement,
you there, where the Oval Office
is built with a secret corner,
you all over this planet—
sweetheart!
You might be a captain in Star Wars,
you might be a stellar hunk,
but let me live here in peace
laying out odes for you swerving
along the dangerous curve,
I am the one at risk
traversing the path of empire—
my people hold to their creed:
in the dark past, darkness—and in you.
Triangles aside, what gleams
for me is naming Vega, standing by Betelgeuse.
A Catholic constellation,
the Southern Cross has been given
for you and yours to stare at
but for me to dream on.

The Mermaid

I make my way as a mermaid,
as they wrap themselves in raincoats and plunge into
        the shower,
I always go out in my golden scales on the shore.
They will say: here's the moonlit sea splash-flashing
        under my tail
The thousand-eyed will see its likeness in me.

City, city, you are old and you barely fill the eye
how the air congeals, like a bird and a lion

and how it strips scales from off my scaly skin,
how brave and tender I stand in the light
    of the world.

And the scales float onto a merchant vessel
     from Thebes.
The wind is long and comely, slow in its flight.
They drift like snowflakes, like tea leaves—
     my stiff attire.
They will say: Look, the sea sparkles and gulls hang
     in the air.

Sappho and Alcaeus

Could a lovely woman, the poet Sappho,
ever love her own rival, Alcaeus?
Suspended on a closet door
she stuck her little mirror before her,
embarrassed, when it showed small faerie lips.
In front of her stretched the glass, paler,
yes, against the pallor, like Zeus with Amalthea.
Under the fast-lane scrutiny of a lens
she started sweating. Where Orpheus went silent,
there Sappho sang, and never missed a beat:
"Reflecting, you admire what you see;
see, we are the fairest of them all!"
It glinted back at her: "Big deal, Alcaeus
was praising me, not you, above all others
with his 'Oo la la! What a heavenly silhouette!'"
A mirror's mutiny, a meaningless prick,
but Sappho threw herself off the nearest cliff.
That necrophile, Alcaeus, cried after her, "Sappho!
What do I care about this cupboard door,
and what fun can I find in the armoire?
To mirror you alone, Sappho my own,
see, I've invented these alcaic stanzas."
"Alcaeus, I loved only you, and if
you truly love me"—came from far away—

"master instead my sapphic measures,
make them more popular than yours."

Letter to a Contemporary (D.A.P.)

You pack into a trunk
all the torments of cast bronze
like little theatrical costumes,
parts of speech and crumbs.
You keep looking into the trapdoor
of its marble breast,
and from that we get a metro
luxurious with urban slums.

I am adding a role for you
like a creator god in a play—
no text, but lines to say,
inconvertible into print:
"Open Metro," we'll put in. Voilà,
Hey, that's you, Ali Baba.

An energy crisis. Not a soul.
Potential lies locked in a box
They shoved you into: hold on!—
It's time you took the gods for a stroll.
You ride it out like Noah,
and people, no sweat,
gave the words a second thought
to provoke, at last, a yawn.
O monuments of tears, urine,
slobber—all our bodily functions!
And they told you: shhh—here
poetry is being written.

It's time to look at you
as a hero, a protagonist
in a play that's no set piece,
that I can write you letters in.
Yay, we're alive—good for us!

But the play being written couldn't
be kept on course by playwrights,
only by prototypes.

The Thousandth Anniversary of the Christianization of Rus

I play my typewriter like a dulcimer.
From *SU*[1] to the reflecting *US*
as the Pope rides his airliner
to the Vatican, and here's what's sad:
ars longa, vita brevis, and on the Boulevard
the trolley crawls, but the reflecting *US*
demonstrates its jazz and blues,
and you are mirrored in it, my Russian,
my little tongue-exhibitionist
erect-eject-soloist,
great indweller of the mouth,
lover of lips, invader of slackjaws,
the airplane came back here to us
and into our homeland's heart shot Cupid's dart
(not what ars will ravish from museums—
companies and regiments can't get it out).
My printer, zither, on its fretless staff,
by night and summer, vita shorter by a dot,
and I roam with somebody in the hermitage combine
around the staff, where lines don't live,
but just what I consider important,
Kuryokhin, Vinogradov, and Sorokin.
The homeland, frightened by immune deficiency,
isn't hurrying to give into them,
and two tongues in Earth's mouth,
the changing sound of wood to heavy metal,
drove at the old man in the Vatican
with an explosive wave, but he witted not at all.

---

1. Words in italics are in English in the original. Kuryokhin, Vinogradov, and Sorokin are
   contemporary artists in music, visual arts, and literature.—Ed.

Alexei Parshchikov

ALEXEI PARSHCHIKOV, born in 1954, is one of the most influential poets of the new generation. His book *Figures of Intuition* was published in 1989 in Moscow to substantial critical discussion. He was a founder of Club 81, and he is presently a doctoral candidate at Stanford University. The essay that follows is included in *August on the Dniepr*, a collection of Parshchikov's poems. The title "Conversation between an Editor and a Poet" refers to Pushkin's 1824 title, "Conversation between a Poet and a Bookseller."

Conversation between an Editor and a Poet

—Have I been writing long? I started late; but if one were to talk about one's actual beginnings, then, I was born into a doctor's family in the Far East, lived in Belorussia, and later in the Ukraine. I graduated from secondary school in Donetsk. I had intended to become an agricultural scholar in Kiev but suddenly during my third year at the academy I took up writing and A. Mikhailov, the critic, accepted me into his seminar at the Literature Institute. It was with this unexpected turn of events that my contact with the world of serious writers began. I was introduced to the reading public with the publication of my narrative poem "New Year Verses" in the journal *Studying Literature*—the poem serving as the backbone of this book. Its publication was followed by a dispute over "complex" poetry in the *Literary Gazette*, which is where the poem was later discussed.

—Yes, I do want to share my perception and understanding of surrounding reality with my readers. Naturally I want to be sure that all of our social and ethical questions, the entire complexity of the social world is not overlooked in my work. I also think that in our times, it's important to imagine and create images within which reality's richness is not lost. And things, for instance, like viruses, our heredity, computers—they're equally important for you and me. But what was the material world, say, for Homer? The coast, some fleet, a fortress, the chariots, or in the sky—anthropomorphic gods. And Homer depicted everything according to the human scale. But we have to know how to imagine expanses within bacteria, you see! We have meta-galaxies, contemporary politics, the formalization of information, our own "weirdos"—or on the other hand, the typical human cliché types—approx-imations won't explain any of this. We're not the ones changing, but rather—it's the people's movement, their language, the signs of the times that are changing. These things constitute the varying quantities of our cosmos. The constants are the commandment of good and the reaction of the heart muscle to adrenaline. The complex, spatial metaphors, which saturate the young poetry so close to me, originate here. This is why I want to be plugged into the search for a new descriptive language.

—What do we do with the "old" language? For a poet such a question probably doesn't exist. It seems to me that there is no "old" language, only the discovery of new ways, only the growth of language. Is it even possible to imagine poetry without growth, without language's movement?

—Yes, I do understand you: a conversation with a poet, even a beginner, will always touch upon his ideals. So I'll also do my best at answering you here.

It's easy for me to talk about the literary hero. You know, for me he's not quite what one might call "poetic." I do want an individual personality behind the poetry, one who prefers initiative, efficiency, truth. It's all good and well if the poetry contains this. Youth doesn't forgive reticence, the absence of conflict, demagoguery. And yet if a poem works it retains its own secret, so I cannot give exact instructions on how to read it.

I often describe animals, the world of inanimate nature. Not only because agriculture is close to me. Man's contact with earth is oh so far from good-natured! Biochemistry is leading us into a world where the border between the living and the dead is washed away as with Professor Vernadsky's "Living Matter." And so I write about the concrete work on earth as well. The earth, it's elemental, just like coal—the Babylon of time and the ocean of labor. That is how I tried to convey her in "The Earthquake at Harbor Tse" and in the "Coal Elegy."

Man can always evaluate the progession of time through the measure of his own responsibility toward it. My hero constructs a scarecrow in his own vegetable patch, out of things belonging to the past. His farewell to the past is the same kind of carnival as a New Year's Eve celebration.

Once I was hitchhiking from Moscow to Kharkov and somewhere near Serupkhov I ran into a strip of bad luck: not a single truckdriver paid any attention to me. Bored and fidgety, I wandered along the highway until I finally saw in the near distance a farm with a large vegetable garden scattered with several scarecrows. These scarecrows were made of discarded clothes and old white gauzy window curtains which billowed in the wind, freezing like chunks of ice. This impression immediately spurred me toward two actions. I began to photograph the scarecrows. And while doing this almost automatic work I understood that I am a witness to what has survived, the entire departed epoch of the sixties, that is—simply put, I'm not so young anymore, I do have some experience. This is how my poem "New Year Verses" was started.

The path to poetry begins at a crossroads and then moves into an area without roads. What can we do about it? After all, poetry is not merely the ability to write what is called a good poem—that's the psychology of those who win medals. No, what is more important is to perceive and share the experience of creating.

Translated by John High with Katya Olmsted and Nina Genkin.

The Porcupine

Dark prophet porcupine in Saint Sebastian's suit
pulled from the skies above a square root.

Porcupine passed through a sieve to disconnect
His spine multitudinous.

Hiss at him—he'll deflate like a punctured balloon,
But away from your feet, just you wait, he'll come out of his swoon.

Porcupine's a locksmith's dream, a swivel-hipped old punkster
who wraps up all his fears in dissolving bathing trunks.

For women, his spines are quiet as pins in cushions
But they're stubble on sleepy masculine chins.

A disappearing porcupine makes a dry pop.
But when you're resurrected—shake! you're covered with needles.

Translated by Andrew Wachtel.

Flight

Dust. Sea-foam and dust. Slowly, the way
a crushed cellophane packet stirs
and expands, memory blurs. An airplane out of
sand descends—not even a plane.

At the start of the war of the worlds harsh wormwood takes command.
Preparing to set out, I was scraping bugs
from the radiator when a new fire torched
half the land, seeking but missing us.

Gas station's ashes. Sea-foam and dust. Nothing
around but this control panel in eternal malfunction.
Was a rider shimmering there, or was sand scattered
from the sky along the shoreline . . .

Flashing teeth and flying heels in the bar. The dance
fans out like a seine net in a turtle's claws. In vain
I search for you, not knowing who I am;
Maybe the earth dissolves us.

Translated by Michael Palmer.

Two Women Makeup Artists

I was lying dead near Syktyvkar
as large ravens picked at my flesh

then while lying on the Orsha Station tracks
the makeup artists approached from two different perspectives

with their combs behind their belts
they found my torso on the moon

one prepared me as a rock
the other served me on a plate

my thorax cut to limbs
they resembled hanging padlocks

and when the trumpet sounded at the feast
the first woman, who took hold of the primordial chisel—

this shining star of the pebble culture—
she was modeling my sculpture, admiring its nature

and sensing the split I weakened
as the heated pole broke away from me

a pole of black light that went its own way
sloping like a hermit-column

The title is a variation on Mikhail Lermontov's poem "In noon's heat . . .".
Translated by John High and Katva Olmsted.

New Year Verses

Me, the Snow Princess and a rooster on a chain
                              —meet the gang—
tour the land, at a fee, round the segmented
                              face of a clock,
a wedge sails away and abandons the circle.
                              At New Year
clocks quit their housing and spin off like
                              polka-dots over the sky.
The glued beard gnaws my cheeks, you're tired,
                              the hobbling rooster's done in,
we're a dog-eared card-pack that'll cut
                              at the king of spades,
doors open for us, kids are nudged in the back
                              —guess who's come!
Champagne rustles like shimmering poplars.
Who's come, who's stepped onto the freezing globe, making
                              nothing and changing no names?
We swap gifts for three slices of toast.
There's a sack on the floor like a sagging bust, like the rooster,
                              like you, like me,
The sack shifts and tries to copy the questioner's expression.
Kids hang around, muscles tense, ears looped in their specs.
Toys tumble out of the sack.

2

Stop going round in circles, let the toys do the running about,
                              let's announce them!
Humming mechanical creatures with keys in their backs
                              circle the new Jerusalem,
a toy sees the other side of the moon, but not ours,
                              one not yet risen,
circling the sandpit the toy chatters with Krishna:
our Galaxy will be split in two as if it had passed through
                              a conjuror's cabinet,
play again, it'll split again, time after time
                              for ever and ever.

Crawl out from the bottom of the sack into the world,
vulcanized rubber dragon,
two round Earths are reflected in its eyes—I'm standing on one
but who's that on the other?
Whatever their relation, brother or enemy, sister or commander,
instigator or servant,
they're all carried away on a wooden horse and—oh!—its neck curves
back from the nostril in a perfect arc.
A clockwork crow pecks at the earth's sphere with
the triangle of its gaping beak
but the sphere splits in two and the crow flies off in all directions.
The ship is smaller than the sabre, the sabre bigger than the town,
they're all smaller than me—talk about Gulliver!
A toy regiment. Three-phase footsteps. Raise your hands—
there's a lull in the battle.
The world divides into people, but it multiplies into the rest.
A child makes new games
by weaving a whirlwind from the fragments; the whirlwind sweeps up a
pearl— watch out,
if the rooster doesn't peck it up, it'll turn into the origin of your earring.

3

If the origin of time is ringing in your ears,
remember the taming of the beasts,
how they entered the waters of the flood, yet emerged:
a sheep brought the alphabet in a skin bag,
a to z in a fuzzy baalamb;

a horse as if baked in ice,
more graceful than man,
apostle of motion;

a cow descended from terrestrial orbit
but still there in thought;

a donkey—head in front,
otherwise, a back on little legs,
use it!

a pig stepped onto dry land
and gave the continents
stability;

a goat with gold eye-pupils
but itself unsightly;

a bee in profile approaching
the slit of a razor blade,
it's scary, and where is she, the honeycarrier?

a dolphin—a slice of the sea—
stayed at a distance
until the creation of an iron fleet;

a cat—live glass
smoked by hellfire,
its sinews will stand out in the dark, then in the light places;

and the camel?
and the dog?
and the hen?—
all holy!

4

I can see you sitting, polite and stiff-bearded
                                    at the celebration,
you're thinking: mummy, where's your prewar smile,
                                    the joy of a solution
to what the future may bring; the elementary melon
                                    is sliced up and served
and if you compare the eye's longing to the sum total
                                    it'll work out right—
only objects will shrink as if pulled out of water,
                                    but others
will be slightly enlarged as if outlined in pencil: where are you now,
                                    strapped shoes
of the sweet young girls in their flowing dresses, the studious cigarettes,
                    the girls who were too assiduously fashionable?

I can see you sitting at the table, but you've been wandering,
                                    high on aggressive pep talks,
story-teller, tugging your hair toward the essential heavens,
                                    you took a joyride
on the number of fate—33—into musical darkness
                                    like a coin astride an eyelid.
You were youthful, you wanted to treat the stuck-up girls of the city
                                    like your god
and strip them of their stars and hairpins, chains and trinkets
                                    the tennis courts
where they practised their strokes, and the tubes of powder,
                                    hypnotic
pendants and magnetic tins of lotion and dog-
                                    whistles and their
dogs and hair-clips' ellipses and the perpetual
                                    hoop round their necks,
fur coats and dresses, shirts and bras, slips,
                                    the midnight,
their tablets and whatever shoes they needed for dancing and skiing,
                                    the process
of walking through seething mirrors, seeing that you
                                    yourself are Narcissus
and confused a knife with a mirror, sliced a fish with a mirror,
                                    posed
in front of the blade for longer than a slit apple
                                    takes to go rusty.
You heard more than you saw but whatever flew into
                                    the cornea
took place: light won't bend and the dark doesn't straighten out:
                                    everything distorted
before the eyewitness, just as a wheatfield
                                    shifts in the wax stage
from silver to darkness, like the flaring
                                    shower-bath door
where you'll no longer recognize her, who wove herself for you
                                    into a cage
one bright Sunday, elbow behind knee, elbow
                                    behind knee.
Each of us at the beginning inhales a heavenly pledge
                                    but gives in exchange

our own life for a strange one, for liquor, for a waterlily in a creek
                                        —to Elena—
this resource disappears and you are the princess of picnics,
                                                curiosity's bait,
you plunge under an island afloat in the lake
                                to cool off
but get lost in the darkness: over the diver
                                        a tangle of sunk roots
sways and swells with each throb of the pulse
                                        into a thunderhead
where a clock tower rises and copper hands on the dials
                                                are gaping,
you hear whistles and footsteps and lean back against this new
                                                firmament.
What is to be done? stamp your feet? who can help?
                                        what's trailing behind you?
make money? become a provincial highbrow? a lily?
                                        There was an allotment
so scavenged by birds you'd have thought they were going to bleed the
                                black earth white,
bindweed didn't abound there, nothing ran wild;
                                        a trio
of scarecrows—you concluded—would be able to protect
                                        this patch from the petty thieves.
You chopped three poles for the stems
                                and three smaller ones for the arms.
As a shattered Christmas-tree ball
                                leaves a bauble of slivers in the mind
so in dreams this bundle of sticks
                                got mixed up with the skeleton plan
of a sliverworld and you split them
                                into three lots of crosses,
bound twine round the sticks, not tightly but with play,
                                        the scheme is simple:
brave bird lands on scarecrow's arm, shoulder swings up and
                                        —wallop!—
horizon tips, horns blare, scales
                                tilt into terror,
bird streaks away; so three points of the fenced
                                        rectangular plot

were planted with the frames of the future scarecrows—
                                                    trapezoidal
for the one with the piercing whistle, pyramidical for the spherical one
                                          with the regular rattle
and for the dumb one q.v. the sketch plan: the trunks
                                         hungered for heads.
Made from the fingerboard of a guitar with screws
                                     like Lomonosov's wig,
one head bears a windvane, one a gaping propellor to mask its features
                              and one has a spike for a head.
The Lomonosovite strikes the thief with his similarity to the famed
                                 glorifier of mirrors,
the weathervane-windmill effaces the distinction between full-face and
                              profile —a burden
on any eye, and the third scarecrow's pike is
                            simply a peril.
You'd hardly capped them with heads when the sky cleared,
                            cabbage took heart
and a dark cloud rose and broke over the allotment
                          and garlic sprouted!
Winter coat and raincoat and ancient jeans and jackets
                          and everything
that you could remember you once might have worn
                          not flaunting white shirts
but the uniform of progress—of the plastic decade
                        of five-story blocks
where a meditating Buddha was crammed into polymer
                    like a molecule of buddhas and molecules,
you hauled those capes out of the shed and draped them over the masts;
                          humankind
finds a monument dreadful when it's hooded and the tarpaulin
                        creaks in the wind,
dreadful the shame of a rigid body, laid out
                    in a formal suit,
your beard will jut out of the coffin, from a distance
                    you'll look like a jackplane,
thus you remembered carpentry and the connection
                    between heaven and diapers.
Become a scarecrow?—never! The corpse demands resurrection.
                    For a bird it's another matter:

what's a scarecrow to a bird?—just a test of your luck,

                                        you can learn,
bind their wings, with a hop or a skip they'd appear

                                        on the top of its head,
and the band would gasp: bravo! What then?

                              You set three foolproof traps
on the heads of the scarecrows, let resemblances remind the birds

                                                as us
—of images: let the birds bewail the example of a hero

                                        split in two,
let them divide into two hordes and let the dolls go into battle,
let those killed in the trap cry out to them—die

                                        then we can embrace!
The figures were left standing—not racketeers plotting

                                        on holy ground
and not, of course, saints, but scarecrows as if laid back

                                        under an imagined
sunshade and leafing through books while ruminating on

                                        magnetic tape,
and you walked off down the path to the beach.

                              They guarded the allotment from crooks.

5

But what's the sea? It's a rubbish dump of bike-wheels

                                        earth rolled out from underfoot,
the sea's a dump of every dictionary, but the firmament has swallowed

                                                language.
And what's sand?—it's clothing without buttons,

                                        it's the limits
of the chance of being chosen from similar milliards

                                        elements of a desert.
There's sand for the kids, let them build their walled cities!

        Translated by Michael Molnar.

Catfish

For us, it's as if he's excavating a trench in the water.
And above, surfacing—his wave explodes about him.
Consciousness & skin compressed tightly together.
He's like a black passageway leading from the moon's bedroom.

So plunge your hand—into these underwater alleys
beginning to speak with you, predicting futures on your palm.
The kingfish thrashes about the sand, echoing,
freezing up, like a key growing thick in a lock.

> Translated by John High.

Mudflats

We trudge kneedeep through medicinal mud and never look back,
and the ooze sucks us down and its dead clutch is alive.

Draw a blank here, a joke, a ridiculous sack race
littering funnels of slime behind us like smokestacks.

As ever, my angel, I love the rustling at dusk,
as ever I will offer you heather and hides,

but this is all just a whim dreamt up by the mudflats,
golden in the morning, wooden as a pipe at night.

Frail stalks and dragonflies seethe with a velvet charge,
no route through the earth or sky, just a tangle of tracks.

Among these sickly waters that heave like a stretcher
there's no bridge or hill or star or intersection.

Just a rock like a thunderhead and both of them similar
to any point in a universe that's achingly familiar.

Just the wrench of a vista heavy as a punctured ball,
just a hole in the ground or simply the lack of a hole.

> Translated by Michael Molnar.

Vladimir Druk

VLADIMIR DRUK was born in 1958 in Moscow. He is a member of the Writers' Union and was also a leader of the "Poetry Club." His work has appeared in numerous publications in the Soviet Union and abroad. In 1989 his play entitled *Gluki* was staged in Moscow and in cities in Europe and Canada to wide acclaim. He visited San Francisco as a participant in the "Crossing Boundaries" festival in 1991.

From **The Full and Unfull Out**

Out—/Eng. for *vn'e/* the position of the ball in competitive sports when it is out of play, flies beyond the bounds of that area designated by the rules of the game.

POSTREALISM. The lyrical "I" of postrealism is a mutant or an AIDS patient, a telemaniac-zombie game technician or programmer. Literature is like a weather report or ANAMNESIS—a history of illness. I am a plastic piston, an artificial valve in the cheery heart of Russia.

Radicals pose the question of creating Accelerated Classes for the In-Depth Study of Civil Self-Defense (ACISCS).

The society of developed socialism is like a fruit of literary fantasy. The collective author, positive and negative heroes, myths, laws, the state are like literary phantoms. The socium is like a text.

The culture of the twentieth century is a curio cabinet. The calculated conclusion of all civilization, all preceding culture, allowing, giving birth to this unimagined up till now, unique in its massivity COLLAPSE, the entropy of all its institutions.

The rust-colored forest. Unpunished poaching.

Many people say it's early yet for you to know about this, or that it's not needed in the first place. Is that so?

The informational society. The right to information. The power of information. The struggle for power—the struggle for information.

Head-bangers bang heads. Vacuum cleaners clean vacuums...

Parentheses, signs of replacement, of the variant—fundamental signs, always in use, never finally comprehended. TEXT. METATEXT.

Roland Barthes and Derrida. From rough draft—from parenthesis—to the line-by-line translation, the text as a line-by-line translation.

What kind of socialist realism is it we need?
We need a good socialist realism. A very good one.
We need a very good socialist realism.
We need socialist realism with a human face!
We need communist realism!

I write with my left foot dipped into cold water and the right in hot sulphuric acid. This is very helpful for the head and kidneys.

WE HAVE NOTHING TO HIDE BUT OUR CHAINS

Pa-pa-pa-pa-pathos!!!! /as P-p-p-prigov, Dmitri Aleksandrovich would say. /

I am the inspector general. We know, we know! I have come to you incognito—we know, we know! I have come to give you freedom!

The aesthetics of a radio receiver. Strolls with CHAOS. The self-destruction of tongues.

Formerly, in drama, there was the confrontation of two logics, two tactics—today's tragedy lies in the impossibility of even one logic. The self-destruction of logics.

The Myth of the Tower of Babel. One interpretation: the lord was afraid lest, having conquered ONE, universal tongue, and having agreed on everything, foolish mankind should come to catastrophe.

The unanimity of people of a single tongue with harmful proclivities can lead them to a fatal SINGLE-MINDEDNESS.

Texts: utopia, fortune-telling, horoscope, the SPORTSOUTLOOK.

The theater of imagination. The theater as the possibility of theater. Utopia in the theater. Utopic space. Poetry as theater.

Radicals pose the question of mass production of individualized bunkers and shelters. A good man is a dead man. (DM)

Instead of clean, white writing paper, we could use pages of the newspaper, directories, the phonebook, contour maps, and the like.

POST realism is the first to understand global, deep-rooted questions of being a person in a world in which the person is not.

Postrealism describes the world AFTER the person, the world where the person already is not /not yet/. The world in the OUT.

POSTREALISM DESCRIBES THE TYPICAL MUTANT In TYPICAL
CIRCUMSTANCES
—MAOOoo

The government is run by a mafia. Don't touch Grishin, he knows too much!

A bureaucratic coat.

Bandaid

Don't touche me, touche!

A PLAY. Stalin /loudly/: I am Lenin! Lenin /firmly/: You are not Lenin, you are Stalin! Stalin /stubbornly/: No, I am Lenin . . .

The new paganism. A bare television.

TEXT as an open system. Strolls through the valley. An unlocked text, in which you can stroll.

The image of the enemy. The artistic image of the enemy. The high artistic image of the enemy . . .

Three Nazis, three fun-loving friends, the crew of a fighting machine . . .

Tell us, now, Dad, it's not for nothing, after all, that you were once an un-official, but I belong to an-other.

TEXTS with notes, echoes, words on the side and alongside. A text with words in the OUT. A text with excess words. The tragedy of the excess word.

From dead souls to the living corpse. A trip.

Turn your attention to the fourth page, third paragraph from the top. Turn your attention to the fourth wall in poetry.

The disappearance of words and languages.

It has been said: the Poet in Russia is more than a poet. It has been said: the Poet in Russia is less than a poet.—The Poet in Russia is not poet at all, but a member of the Writers' Union.

The doctor took all the medicine, the cook took all the compote.

The reader is smarter than the text. Apologia of the line-by-line translation.
Through the text, besides the text, in spite of the text, above the text—we enter into a secret and luscious pact.
Motion, the striving of the verse, the text—to the line-by-line. A small, green katydid of meaning. The doer of its own meaning. The verse is only an excuse for poetry, its possibility, but not poetry itself.
The fabric of verse, the fabric of the text—the marks, lapel pins, signs, signposts, props—paths in the valley.

The TEXT as a line-by-line translation of another text. The world as an unclaimed text—that is, a line-by-line translation. Variants of translations. Authorship. Monopoly.

Roll, Gingerbread boy! Now's the time!

Wild animals go barefoot in nature. Between me and god there are only I and GOD.

Come back, stagnation, come back la-la right away!

"Literature" is the sum of cultivated devices for fooling the reader, subjugating him to the authorial will and manipulating his behavior. One only has to take apart these devices, shake them out like the parts of a construct, turn them inside out, and the myth, the illusion, the captivating illusion disappears, man remains alone with himself. There arises a fear of the abyss. And there begins SPEECH. The discovery of the device, the broken device. Clearing of the speech field. White threads. White Poetry. OUT.

Flatness of everyday language. Flatness of rigid linguistic layers. *Exposure and arrest of the device,* its denuding gives a breakthrough into the volume, the multidimensional space of SPEECH.

A word is a red rag in the hands of a matador. A verse is the dance of the matador before the nose of the enraged bull of everyday speech.

From closed, elite, monopolistic, and monologic literature, the literature of "-isms" and any kind of aesthetics as a last resort of the tricksters, adventurists, and charlatans—to a literature that is open: to open, bare texts that live only in the presence-absence of reader and author, only through their participation-nonparticipation, assuming and giving a chance to express its natural capacity for imagination. This is a literature of silence, of pauses, this is a literature of overcoming silence, this is a literature of contradiction, of primodiction. Can music be recorded by notational signs? The TEXT is a harmonic of speech.

Hail, Caesar, Out!

Translated by Anesa Miller-Pogacar.

Telecenter
A Stereopoem

*"My idle hours I spend
before the TV screen..."*

I'm just a natural scientist   I
I'm no ham radio operator   one ah
in my bean I've got a record stylus   two ah
in my belly a woofer and a tweeter   my flight's a laugh
                                              frequency of lines
and then there's arms or legs to boot   frequency of cadres
and then maybe a valve or piston   squeaky clean cadres
I've been sitting totally tuned out   cadres decide all
not croaking like a frog, just sitting   am I in the cadre?
                                               grain allotment
policemen and the underaged   short circuit
have been stirring up subversive centers   with their own hands
I plunged by chance into the epicenter   Ave, Caesar, our Dose!
the hum had cooled, I walked out on the stage stand straight, hands on the
                                             shoulders broader, hands ex
on me the gloom of night is focused   what's your will, golden fish?
along with other photoelectric cells   I don't want to be a crimean
ramakrishna, galich, and korotich   tartar
waited for this moment a long, long while   I just want to be a
                                                             tartar
I want to talk such utter crap   Nos. 186–187
and put on such a disgusting face   mon tu mon tu tu tu
that people who'd never heard me blab   7:00 - sunrise
would run and rat on me to the police   7:15 - yesterday's news
                                             7:47 - still early
I want to lapse into such disastrousness   it's late!
a phase that would earn me such a dosage
that I'd go straight into metastasis
passing metamorphosis narcosis   ab ovo
                                              here we are and
I'm just a natural scientist   I run run run
prepared to labor and defend the motherland don't take care of myself
or penetrate a girl's birch-tree curliness   in india
                                                   in america

my room and board is fully covered and

if you're not a member of nato
if the authorities don't have you listed
we can live in the same accommodato
where they use a self-financing system

despite the limits they get plastered there
drying out on bunks that couldn't be harder
where they're as gaga as crimean tartars
with a pass to the hotel angleterre

my rectifier won't straighten me out
but the transformer transmogrifies
a drunk tank gets to be a pretty full house
when the stabilizer's been neutralized

every baddy or every bawdy
hari krishna or hari rama
everybody who's free has got it
the whirling cinematic panorama

—colossally sized sizes—
—colossally scaled scales—
—highly scientific sciences—
—deeply vicious vices—

—scarcely effective effects—
—reinforcedly concrete concretes—
—far-reachingly idealistic ideas—
—multiply millioned multimillions—

o god yes propmen and costumers
where the hell's our buttermilk-kefir?
where are our masquerading homers?
tell me where the secret addresses are

whoever's a hostage to what happens
is hostage to the utopian temperament
tsarevich dmitri's peacefully sleeping

on color televisia
from A follows B
from B follows C
thus it follows
from A follows C!
words from a song aren't
he viewed himself himself
a long long time
without suspecting
he fell into pure ether
a long time ago
13:00–14:00 - lunch
1/6 of the end of the world

I love you, Brrring!
which of course on its own

my flight is mighty
broadchested
of it of course I
make use
I blow foam from my lips
and from my nostrils
I send forth rings
Ave, Caesar!
what's your will, golden fish?
I don't want to be their agent
that is, tass's
I want to be the agent
of the masses
I don't want to be doctor
hyder
I want to be ilya
glazunov
children from kisses
hairdressers of the world
totalitarian left-liberal
16:30 - military coup
direct transmission
17:47 - at the tone the exact

right through the european championship

I'm just a natural scientist
I'm not at all a radio ham
find what the common denominator is
and a common substitute will also come

you're my electroquiz-hour
you're my connection still unclosed
you're like snowball berries, just as sour
and slimmer than antennas on radios

why are we sardines in tomato sauce?
why aren't we berries in a bowl of fruit?
at work I've never had a boss
as high-minded as you in your birthday suit

in this hour of nocturnal plasticine
I close the circuit of son and father
darling, let's produce a rattlebrain
a pinocchio or cheburashka

darling, let's produce a blockhead
so he'll come sooner from the fog of mystery
so he can pull his hand out of his pocket
so he can yank the cord that says
  "emergency"

I'm healthy, but homozygous I'm not
just like a slaughtering scientist
I can get high as a kite on Aeroflot
but stain remover gets me just as pissed

I love my air base, it's one of those
where the clerks are calm at the px
where my marasmus always finds Rx
where they teach me to think in prose

how much effort's wasted on rituals!
how much effort's wasted on procedures!

time
at the epicenter of world rumor
at the epicenter of world terror
the axis of coordinates:
all named
and all destroyed

march 9 tuesday 17:30
while life
how do you look
surrounded by cold attention
what a drunk tank!

thirty cops appealingly
blowing whistles
run after me
from ennui
and I run after them
john's running after me
so is lennon
and thirty-two kilos
of codfish
demons and dumb ones
herbicide pesticide
karabakh barabakh

forward, foolish duryemars!
pinocchio to the rear!
stalingrad
stalingrad
stalingrad
no!
no!
no!
world war three
will conclude as a worldwide
television show!

man is a ruby

how many of those sokurovs and arabovs?
how many of us arabovs and sokurovs?

life's closed like an electrical switch
but open like a cannon port
the censor's made "death" a banished word
for the rest, a toxic, sewn-in preventative

and there's still a shkattle-hertle
and there's still a pudromentle
and there's still Jonnon or there's Lennon
and there's still the mutter or the vater

we will construct a new accelerator
and achieve complete decomposition
and from the last parade on television
erase the television's last spectator

man is a record
man's a horizon
that's our man
but now I am filled with
electrolyte
fluids run through me
and agitate
this is me running
and maybe that one too
who's on your television
running
r. reagan - 493 points
f. mitterand - 607 points
m. canadiens - 703 points
sorley - 917 points
23:15 - the next-to-last news
23:55 - the last news

oo hours   oo minutes
end of the world
god! I'm Your nomenklatura!
god! I'm Your nomenklatura!

00:07 - end of the
world on videotape

Translated by Paul Graves and Carol Ueland.

Evening Check

Ivanov—I!
Petrov—I!
Sidorov—I!
All accounted—also I!

Unfortunately—I
so it seems—I
so many it seems—I

Telephones—I
megaphones—I
headphones—I
stereoheadphones—I
colortelevisions—I

In the best wise—I
otherwise—also I
not so wise—again I
here—I, present—I
at your service am I

Rabindranath Tagore am I
Conglomerat Bagore am I
Dikhloretan Cagore am I
Saint Vasilisa, if I'm not mistaken, am I

Where you're not—am I
where I'm not—am I
the last lullaby
the long lullaby

I shoot the bull's-eye
I join the trade union
and the country is proud of me

I-I—hoop-de-doo
I-I—woop-de-woo
and I can be seen from the window

Beginning from the right is I
and ending from the left is I
so del-i-cately I
and overr-i-pely I
so sl-i-ghtly I
and not d-i-aphonously I
so girly wh-i-tely I
so melanchol-i-ly I

My I flies
no i, can't fly!
with i, high
high into the sky

But I'm another I . . .
I'm seven times eight I . . .
I'm eight times seven I . . .

You can't compare with me
the forests or the fields
peaceful folk am I
armoured train 14–69 am I

and Vesuv-i—us
and Virgil-i—us
and Vasil-i—us

And I'll tell you it's no lie
Mr. Twister also am I

The more so I
the less so I
nevertheless—I

What about you?
my, you're so cold
my, you're so handsome
my, you're so bold
to a t like me

say, I'm the fitting image
say, I'm the flitting image
say, I'm the spitting image
say, I'm the splitting image
forgiven, forgotten, forbidden am I
a good guy and a very good gal am I

Do you speak English—aye
Do you speak English—aye

Do you speak English—aye
an eye for an eye
I die, I die!
in the sweet bye and bye
WHO ELSE IF NOT I?
I ELSE IF NOT I!

Resistance don't try,
for it's I
who arrived . . .

                    Translated by Gary Kern.

Phrase Book-86

Hello!
Good day! Good evening!
Good two o'clock 18–19–20–21 minutes!

It's my first time in your country.
Milosti prosim—Welcome.
It's my first time in our country.
Milosti prosim—Welcome.
Your country is our country.
Our country is your country.
Milosti prosim—Welcome.

In our group are three people, five people, twenty eight-nine-
ten people.
Are there earthquakes in your country?

Where went Masha?
Masha went to sleep.
Don't weep, Masha!

Are you married? I am a bachelor.
I have a husband. I do not have a husband.
We do not have a husband.
We divorced our widow.

Whiskey is divorced in the proportion of one to three.
Bitte, two poor portions of your proportions!

Do you have children, brothers, sisters?
I have no children, brothers, sisters.
I have one, two, three children, brothers, sisters.

Do you speak Russian, English, Spanish, French?
I understand it, but cannot speak it. Do you understand me?

I do not understand you. Please speak more slowly!
Ple-e-e-e-z-z
Z-z-zank you . . .

What you study? Do you work? I do not work.
Whom do you not work?
I am a locksmith-assembler, veterinarian, engineer technician,
teacher, teacheress, poet in the feminine gender . . .
We are colleagues.

In our country we have freedom of religious belief.
I am a catholic protestant,
orthodox atheist
sectarian fireworshipper
and member of the British congress of trade unions.
When is checkout time in our hotel?

In my room there is no cold water, ashtray, bath,
magazine stand, bed, cinema, happiness
and sensation of profound
force of gravity.
In my room it is hot, in my room it is cold and the lamp burned out.
I request that you regulate and replace all the disrepair.

What is your name, Masha?

My name is Masha.

Where can one exchange currency? What is the rate of USA dollars,
pounds sterling, marks, drachmas, tugriks, pesetas and tsarist pennies?

I am disturbed by the metre of your pension.
I am disturbed by the size of your poem.
I will kill you, I will slit your throat, I will rape you, I will eat you.
Can you break fifty dollars down into fives
and smaller?

No, this is a kiss by military air.

Earthquake is a kind of transport...
Earthquake is a kind of transport which...

A bun, a bun with a hot frank, a continental breakfast,
halibut in white sauce, pike perch in white wine, yorkshire pudding,
kentucky-fried chicken, cow-cow...
Please bring another chair, table, pepper shaker, wine glass,
shot glass, cook, microscope, woman and two more of the same!

How are you doing here, Masha?
I am doing here like here, Masha!

I lost my way. This is wayward.
I lost myself.
How do you phone the lost-and-found?
If I am found, please phone!
So I can locate myself.

Khau mach do ai pyei? Khau mach do ai pyei? Khau mani rublei?
Briefink-bloomink-pressink-ticklink-snorink-suppink-strainink.
Khappenink!
Do you have a self-teacher of Russian?

How do you translate this? Train from Biryulevo. Freight car
to the Biryulevo-Freight platform?
How do you film this: "Please clear the coaches"? I demand they
be cleared! Clear! The coach! Make the coaches clear!

Doctor, what's wrong with me? Is it catching? Is it a good catch?
Can I show it to a therapist, neuropathologist, stomatologist,
gynecologist,
patholoanatomist?

I have a cough, cold, boil, infection, tumor,
stroke, fit, constipation!
I dislocated, broke, wounded, bruised and rubbed sore!
Doctor, write me a prescription and please give me a filling!

Earthquake is a kind of transport which
performs the most general tasks.

Lovely Masha! Comrades! Mister Chairman! Dear Friend!
Glad to see you, not to blame you, I do not object, this suits
me fine, excuse me.
Excuse What, excuse Where, excuse How
Who? when? what for? why? from where? how much? what way?
Who is it?
Who is this man? Who is this woman?
Who is he? Who is she? Who are they?
Who are you? Who am I?
Who's there?
Masha? . . .
Who's there?
Masha?
Where are we?
Is that true?
Did I understand you correctly?
Do you understand me?
Did I understand you correctly?
Do you understand me?
What does this word mean?
I understand me!

       Translated by Gary Kern.

Ilya Kutik

ILYA KUTIK was born in Lvov, Ukraine, in 1960 and educated at the Gorki Institute of Literature. His work has appeared widely in Europe, and a collection of his poetry appeared in 1990 in the Soviet Union. He presently lives in Lund, Sweden, where he works for the British Broadcasting Corporation. All selections here have been translated by Andrew Wachtel.

Odysseus's Bow

I

Somewhere, although I'm not sure that this is right, I read that a poetic text as a whole is a necklace from which the string was pulled out, and the pearls (we'll call them pearls) remained in place.

For me the creative process (as in meaning and "duration") is that place in *The Odyssey* which describes the competition among the suitors: stringing Odysseus's bow, warming up the bow string, rubbing it with fat, and before that, a sacrifice (otherwise where would the fat have come from?) . . . And then, all at once, His appearance. He comes up, hunched and in tatters, his calves beset with cramps—a goddess's anesthetic; but then he straightens up from under the ether, thunder (a sign from Heaven), on his cheekbones and muscles the tattoo of "rosy-fingered" Strength; he concentrates, and the bow bends!, the arrow passes through the rings in all twelve ax heads that had been placed into the earth. It touches none of them and flies straight to the target. There you have creation, an act. O, Penelope.

And for me, *that* is a poem. It is that arrow from Odysseus's bow which passes untouched through all the parts (each strophe is a ring) and hits the target.

2

This stringlet of ring-shaped meanings is like a metaphysical thread. And in its path the arrow pulls that thread, which gradually melts into the "sky" of the subconscious, in the same way that the vapor trail of a jetliner becomes invisible as the arrow-flight hurtles forward.

3

The rings Comprise ALL cultures—Hellas, Rome, Judea, Byzantium . . . "Air" (limited by the surprising? hermeticism of a "ring"), like an arrow, is taken from each of them; it's joined to the sharp air-whistle of flight. Like a funnel the flight-movement pulls the air into itself and carries it away, while still remaining in the same place. The deflowering of an absent hymen.

An example (the best one) is an eight-line poem of Mandelstam. An attempt (a personal one) is my Ode.

This (in the Ode and in general) is for me a solution to the problem of the Whole, of nostalgia in an epic key.

4

Poetry as a Game.

My pseudo-intellectualism (but pseudo with a plus sign, "in the spirit" of T. Mann, T. S. Eliot, Borges, and E. Poe) is the ONLY way to create myth: to tell (or speak) with SUCH an intonation that it all IS and WAS. According to Pasternak, poetry is the cognition of one's own rectitude; but it would be better to say it's CREATION! From "romanticism" we know that an utterance is irreversible. That's why Mandelstam said that poetry is power.

5

With his poetics, Aristotle arrested all of old European culture.

With the loss of "norms and rules," the post-folkloric epoch of the Whole as such disappeared forever.

6

"Neo-classicism" was the last attempt to resurrect—create the Whole— at the cost of the loss of the depth of images. I translated Alexander Pope's "An Essay of Man." He writes:

What's fame? a fancied life in other's breath,
A thing beyond us ev'n before our death . . .

(4th epistle, 237–38)

But in my version he says:

What's fame? a wind we only know about
from curtains that come billowing out.

In the first instance (Pope's) there is only an utterance. In the second
there's an utterance and an image simultaneously. As a "fragment," the first
gives no more information than it contains, while the second ALREADY behaves
like a Whole, even with nothing else. Pope is the *pointillist* of the 18th
century—he creates his whole out of aphoristic point-utterances. But that is
not flight, but knitting.

7

A yearning for the epoch of the Whole can be felt in the epic tones
of Shelley's "Ozymandias": in the desert bits and pieces of something—
arms? legs?—and the echo of the Whole is the Voice. Do we reader-
Stanislavskians believe him? Yes, a breath of cold air, like an arrow, forces
its way through the air, but the quivering of its tailfeathers, like the skeleton
of an extinct animal, leaves an impression in stone.

8

Does that mean that something whole (that is, wholer by itself) is
ALREADY a residue (a fragment as a "loud-speaker" of the whole) if the
ENTIRE strength of what is missing is hidden in it? . . . The part is greater
than the Whole. A principle of the baroque? Yes. Or, perhaps, it is classicism
from the point of view of a paleontologist for whom the skeleton of a dinosaur
is more important and meaningful than the "monster" itself?

What has remained of, say the *Annals* of Ennius—lines, a few verses
and parts of verses . . . But THAT is the same as the "result-residue" of all
"anthology poets," outsiders to THAT culture (to use a contemporary term).
The lesser have turned out to be "equal to" the greater. It's almost a Borges
poem.

9

The WHOLE must be such that EACH of its FRAGMENTS is SELF-
SUFFICIENT, but that taken together they form a kind of metaphysical UNITY.
That is my principle.

10

According to Shpet, poetry is strength + turning. Aigi interprets it to mean the ability at any speed ("strength") to control the wheel (to write yourself into your turns). But this is just a "game" with the Whole. Rocks or splashes (lines) fly off the tires. And what will you do with them?

11

I write "Jesus whose piscine scales. . . ." There's a line. Without any continuation. Poetry's a desert of sounds, but it's not every one engenders a whirlwind.

Sosnora, who is deaf, was told that in the U.S. they could do an operation after which he would be able to hear everything, but only in a continuous way—that is, without being able to differentiate separate sounds.

The poet hunts for sounds from just this kind of "chaos"—in strophes and lines, and only later does he "write in" everything that fills the space between them. For example, I hear the following:

................Litti's madonna
....
........like a person who's on Soma
with eyes more still than stillness, and
....

And then, for example, between the first and second line I could insert "under Leonardo's hand," or something like that. The profession is the unavoidable "profanation" of space. The beginning of "craft."

12

I believe, yes, I believe that Faulkner (was it only he?) hung pieces of paper with a most detailed list of the events of each hour/day/chapter of his latest novel on the walls.

For me the poetic text is movement from strophe to strophe, "hung" in the subconscious and conscious mind, from sound to sound.

But the principle of collage, of montage, is outdated: from Shershenevich (poetry) and Eisenstein (film) to Rauschenberg (painting).

What remains is the principle of the "fragment," "the craft," of Odysseus's arrow. Or, as Pasternak says:

The game and torture
Of achieved triumph
Is the drawn bowstring
Of a taut bow.

But I'm not sure that I won't "renounce" this principle. For if something is "achieved," then WHAT is Penelope for?

On your back I trace the letter A.
You must sense how my hand's caress
travels first along your spine,
from the uppermost vertebrae
to your waist, and then inclines
back again—in languid absent-mindedness
until that moment when the lines all intersect
and I create, with one sharp motion,
a cross of the type that in pre-Christian sects
evoked a). insanity and b). commotion.

Yes, I know that the body's a locked-up safe
and I search for its armor's alphabetical chink
in all epithelial directions—for the link of links
and the pick of picks—from O to A.
For it's just this way, twixt A and O
that one finds myth, just as Io
escaped from the fly. He first chased her
straight and then they backtracked
until, having endured manifold tortures
She completed a circle with him . . .
I trace that circle with my nail on your back
til O thrObs hOt Over all yOur limbs.

Like a blind safecracker in a bank vault
in the darkness I gathered all my strength
to the very ends of my fingers and at length
like Braille, the first martyr to touch, straining
I saw that the five points, whose strings
I draw are still one less than his gestalt.[1]

---

1. Louis Braille's alphabet for the blind is based on combinations of six points.

I'm surrounded by some overmuch
silly, long, and sticky spiderweb of touch.
I fully recognize the figures,
but fail to see how my five fingers
can direct it—since it seems its elevated ridges
comprise a tongue that needs six digits.

I do not know which of this language's signs
will make your skin resonate down the spine,
but I'm ready to try the whole alphabet
through all its permutations until I elicit
that festive plangent aria:
O-o! . . . A-a!

Each person's skin has its own special smell.
That's how, sleeping in the Alps, the elephants
of Hannibal discerned the smell of Hannibal
and of his soldiers and of his courtesans.
But when they raised their spyglasses of sniff
they couldn't sense the whiff
of battle's sweat, because it's only in the body's nodes,
from the battle of our spiritual armies
(that which the Hindus call Karma),
that this fine gunpowder explodes;
and after each explosion, that is, act.
We know sensations by their shadow flares,
a Yogi pushing up his stomach, lying on his back,
or through the gunsmoke—martial squares.

Yes, sensations must wander in a cycle
of transformations . . . that's why, small or large,
but for a truly excellent example,
enter the elephant, light or dark.
his ears—like o-va-tions of the hearing
to the sense of smell, while his seemingly naked midsection
and his entire body, covered with such tough protection
that each part of him should feel that same thing.

For we are always in a ring: our feelings closed
like fists all tight, under layers of mail or clothes,
we were stuffed like bombs with dynamite
well before Nobel invented it.
And when we open up, as when we count
to five—in any order—that's when
an explosion rings out, but it doesn't flay the flesh . . .
Behold—karma's calories, its chow.

I love to inhale your skin, and in a way
this intrigues as much as it entrances,
because, in addition to the skin's bouquet
there's one more unknown code and cipher.
Sensation's like a storm linking in some manner
thunder and ozone . . . and if the model's proper
then the storm's gong and smell belong to different zones,
but the latter can be sensed by elephants alone;
the Bodhisattva of feelings—on the path to Nirvana—
is found in a state of odor.

I lose myself in your skin. What am I to do!
Even so—although there are but five
of these lacy circles, and not Dante's nine,
I'm afraid I'll get lost and fall right through.
But the samsara of sensation—is still not the Cannae
of Hannibal: it's like a cincture
with five holes; allowing each without censure,
one after another, to try to fit the proper way.
And when the circle closes round the final one
to trumpet o'er the world with Elephant's Trunk . . .

From Ode upon a Visit to the Belosaraisk Spit, on the Sea of Azov

I
It's cloudless and the sea is rapt.
The heat encompassing has slapped
the clumpy sand upon the wheels

of what might seem a travelling theater.
Because there's not a breath of breeze
a farce they're going to provide
distorted, naturally—"I-frigg-enia in Tauride."
That first one chased a tidal wave through Marathon,
but here in heavy daubs the seas
In sleep can merely put their makeup on.

2

Through sleep external, Neptune's lair
beneath the Azov depths I spy:
our Aivozovsky puffs his gills down there
while on the other side
his storms of water roil the waves.
He drags out seaweed from beneath the glaze
as mirrors blacken from the back
and all the while his stormy water froths
and warms like furry jackets
devoured long ago by moths.

3

Though Ovid's not a fan of waters,
he slid into the depths so damp
and instantly became a clam,
a rhyme that's worth at most a quarter.
And there he lies, the shutters closed
on bottom like a worn-out box
that's relegated to the market square.
Now any sprout that's finger sized,
if its got nerve, can come up alongside
and touch the vulnerable locks.

4

There is a tie, for future reference,
that links the mollusks to the fish.
As once a year the shadows surface
like targets fully liftable,
within Bermuda's triangle,
from heights all covered up with sand
and here the ocean, gratis, belches out

both jellyfish and clams,
and her whole body shouts
from blows of hypothetical meridians.

5
Just like a germinating seed which twists
upon itself while puffing up below
until it's wound its insides
inside out around itself.
But here with midair hesitation
it's quickly caught inside a web,
a python wrapped around itself,
and pulling at the threads with all its might,
it telegraphs inspired thoughts,
it whispers into dictaphones.

. . . .

50
The fishermen were digging on dry land
In startling steamy humid air,
And feeling suffocated there
In fear they started off the strand.
But in amazement on the spot they froze,
As if they'd seen from right up close
Medusa's Gorgon face;
Their faces turned from this ordeal
To busts, on which a trace
Of sweat could make the gilding peal.

51–52
The wave began to move. And while,
Beyond the foamy bustle,
It's heavy train spread wide,
The sandy shelf took on a shade of russet.
And just as when you beat accumulated dust
Out of a blanket or a drape
The balcony starts shaking
Beneath the woolen weight
Whose sobs are mirrored by gyrations
Which flow away cascading

Upon the street, the yard, the town—
Thus did the air, already not itself,
But rent assunder by the water's moving shelf
Give off not boom, nor groan, nor roaring sound,
But rather sobbed. The water's strength
Just swept it up, and swirled it with the sand.
It happened once, and then a second time at length.
Then still more thickly, and with force so great
That when the air was covered by the brine
The atmosphere began to suffocate.

53
Dry land caved in beneath the force
of these two conjoined bodies. The boards
Slammed shut. The threads of heavenly orbs
Which held them like a tent
Above the beach were rent.
And now, in the whirlwind of the movement,
The air rose up into the sky
The sands collapsing in the void it spied
It tried their headlong rushing to avert
By grabbing at the water's skirts.

54–55
The avalanche caught up and took
Fish, fishermen, and jellyfish, and gulls,
Some buoys, bison, bishops, rooks,
And knights, and schooners, clanging bells,
And scraping of reptilian shells,
the wind in pennants of the fleet
A barracuda, sharks and dolphins;
And all these feathers and these fins
Were trying gamely to evade
The wall of water's wild cascade,

Until the wave which roiled up the sea
And turned the whole beach upside down,
In horror clad in stones all round
A skull had freed
From lower depths in seaweed wraps.

When finally it reached the cenotaphs
Belonging to the water's vestal virgins
In Northeast winds it drowned a version
Of prayers for them in jasmine serenades
By fishtailed, breasted siren maids.

56

In dolphin-ravaged Delphi
The flooded altar smouldered.
The wave engulfed the dead shelf
And slightly slowed by polders,
It turned in on itself, and in a ring
It closed around. And then it accidentally
Stepped on the edges of its train. Then suddenly
In all their starry fittings,
Through falling ochre plaster layers,
The heavens above were bared.

57–58

First the horizon fell, then came alive
Down where the jugs tsunami's train
emerging, narrowed down, contrived
to turn into dry land, that water'd overlain
just like a throne, and, starting from
the outlines of the seat, the wave's penumbra
receded, subsided round its legs and on both sides
encircled the Edenic contours
of still-damp Belosaraisk spit
which by this time had spread

some shrouds of sand to bake
the dawns. And to the right it left
the sea, while on the left
it placed Liman, a swampy lake,
all lemon-yellow in the view
of day. But when the winds
are blowing from the west, it changes tint,
and takes the brightest hues
of apricot, a fruit whose stone is harder
than its flesh, although it's clothed much softer.

59

And in the elemental battle,
the toothy fish's spawn
was hurled from far Seattle
to the banks of Ilion,
like a catastrophe of gooey lymph
which hardened into coral reefs
and clouded up the minds of sheikhs,
and farther on—a little strip
of blue by which, within the narrow slip
between the mollusks and the fish,
now lies the Belosaraisk spit.

60

And soon the heaven's curator
had cleared the sky, and by the morn
the tide, like Greece's orators
was putting pebbles in its mouth.
And now Calliope, the muse of epic song
emerges from the flood's blue waters
onto the shore, the leader of a throng
of muses, and leads them midst the boulders,
to where the whole procession can be viewed.
I think that I will follow too.

Prayer

O pendulum, o braid of time, during
the reign of which of the Friedrichs or Louis
did they let you grow out? You're harsher than "fire!"
and longer than slow-burning fuses.

O take me from the battlefield
ye Son of Father and of Time!
For hoplites smashing shields
Are more honest than its scythe.

Do not let me fall down beneath it, o Time!
For I—like a headless horseman—could
thrust my foot in the pendulum, as into a stirrup
no matter how high your rump.

But like the living flesh that covers up the body's damage
the clock face shines—without pauses or advantages.
But I can't fly on your cannon ball like Munchausen—
or gallop on your rump like Faust can.

For everything that has the weight of outlines
is too concrete; abstractions, like prostheses,
gradually fill the empty spaces
and they loose God.

So leave me the right to the battlefield!
Like the dumbell hidden in the middle of a razor blade,
emptiness—cannot be raised, and I can't squeeze out something
that besides its frame is lacking content or weight,
while the surroundings are always newer.

Time: a cannonball tearing meat from a body.
God's body: emptiness.

Arkadii Dragomoshchenko

ARKADII DRAGOMOSHCHENKO was born in 1946 in the Ukraine. In 1970 he moved to Leningrad and has lived there since. He was one of the founders of Club 81 and later of Poetic Function, a discussion circle of poets and critics that publishes a journal by the same name. His book *The Corresponding Sky* was published in 1990 in the Soviet Union, and his work *Description* has recently appeared in the United States, translated by Lyn Hejinian and Elena Balashova, who have also translated all of the selections that appear here.

SYNOPSIS / SYNTAX

All this is familiar; still it needs to be repeated. In its very essence the decorative grid of the Chinese interior is inexhaustible. Repetitions do not exist as long as there is time. Thus noncoincidence, deviation, residue, all requiring a different approach.

An ornament consists of holes or of transitions from one void to another. Where does the distinction between one void and another lie? Distinction is not a noun; location is impossible. Nothing changes, by changing itself. Wandering and wandering: "The goal of one is to observe the disappearance of the old, the goal of the other is to observe change" (Lao Tzu).

It is just as ridiculous to divide up a hole as for me to represent a poet with marble wings and a flaming mouth.

Does the imagination picture the way in which this particular tongue crumples itself in the living scale of saliva, is kneaded like fingers and like clay in the fingers, rises to the palate, hangs there for a moment waiting for the explosion to dissipate, turns away.... Does this "image" haunt the imagination when the hand goes from "wandering" to "wandering"? It's

67

Khlebnikov who comes to mind when we talk of the wandering furrow: minotaur of its own labyrinth, an overturned mirror under the Heavens, a mole (see Mandelstam) that has fallen into a trap of roots in search of the indivisible "particle" of speech, the center, Form, points of Being, the way physics fell into a linguistic trap in its quest for the indivisible particle. But we have to talk. Does the word exist?

One can assume from the preference given in ancient China not to the quantitative characteristics of number but to qualitative ones that the *I Ching* is not a handbook on aleatorics but the first research into syntax. Thus "language did not fall from the sky," "language is an activity" of society. I think of a pitcher because it's a cocoon. Revolving gave birth to ornament. On one hand the concept of a "person" forces me to talk about the sum of certain characteristics, more precisely about a bundle of them; on the other hand, I, based on experience, can imagine a person whose violence and suffering make him indifferent to his surroundings. Wherein lies the difference between a person and a rock? Self-expression requires a certain I which demands expression. Memory signifies only some other memory. We are born twice, the first time in the "separation" of self from the mother. Not signification but stratification. The second time, until death itself, endlessly to be born into the world—that is, in this infinite dividing. As the world creates itself, inscribing itself in me, I change it, abiding in the noncoinciding of birth and death. Seeing is a process of deferral. A process whose pace does not coincide with the speed of understanding. "To see—to create." The word *create* is a word with a "dual anchor." However, seeing is backed by blindness. What does language teach? I don't hear. I say that is not experience and not the expression of experience but an activity; language finding itself encapsulated by the transparency of representations opens itself to the future (all this is familiar, but still it needs to be repeated), to that which was never there (in experience?) but which is forever enclosed in it as a possibility— mobility within mobility!—

Poetry comes in the act of anticipating the fact of possibility. What did you say? The spatiality of silence is created by the temporality of speech. I know. The realization of meaning reveals itself in the muteness of this "nothingness" between sound and sound, sign and sign. Between you and me? Nonexistence is a result of coincidence. But poetry begins as unknowing. The sea in Homer was red. Meanings are necessitated by rising forth . . . to what?

There are two types of duration; the "duration" of a change in social consciousness and the "duration" of the change in meanings in poetry are incommensurate in their rate of transformation. As a result we are once again speaking of history. Language "piled up," language as "treasure," language not wasted by loss—by r-evolving it dies. Here begins the circle of Pushkin's small tragedies—"The Greedy Knight," if a circle can have a beginning. The law of the conservation of energy permits us to imagine a certain map.

Sanctioned by the Areopagus of lawgivers, a "uniquely correct language" (the importunate specter of agglutination) leads to homogeneity and fetishism, killing consciousness of an other. There is much that did not occur in front of our eyes, but we have repeatedly seen how language died and became a murderer, abandoning itself to soapy fantasies about basic values. Imagination differs from fantasy as the word *is* from the word *if.* The "avant-garde" is one of the death-bearing banalities.

Perception feeds the world. What existed before the digit? Invention is selection—from the unidentifiable. Imagination is the intransitive action of anticipation. The opposite is a yearning for nondifferentiation, for indifference: irresponsibility. An ornament represents a system of holes, of discontinuities. Emptiness is the core of bamboo. The source of the echo, an answer. There is no emptiness, but we talk about it. We talk about people, love, the line, poetry. Do all these things exist? Poetry is that state of language which in its workings constantly exceeds the actual order of truth. Who defines how our knowledge should exist, or how is the one who is supposed to identify it identified? And so forth. Here is Heisenberg's sentence, in which I have substituted one term: "In poetry are we describing something objectively more real, something that in a certain sense exists independently of human thought, or does poetry represent only an expression of the capabilities of human thought?" What term in this sentence is replaced with the word *poetry?* Or does "this vagueness pertain to the subject or only to the language in which we speak about it and whose imperfection we in principle can't disregard?" Here in this sentence there is no substitution.

An illusory I.

At the moment that language is immobilized the figure of the "enemy of values" arises. It seems that only negation allows us to talk about those things which can't be touched by language. Taste and geometry are two different things. The pendulum of rhetorics moves the course of the agonist. What do they ask the poet?

The encyclopedia's body can give satisfaction:

Dictionaries propose:

Psychology, sociology, political science, mythology, religions break open:

Literature offers:
Institutions of information fulfill the enthusiasm for solutions:

But poetry is always something else.

All this is familiar, but still it needs to be repeated. Without asking the poet anything, they ask, is it possible to ask about that to which no answer is possible—not asking, they ask: does such a question exist, whose absence gives birth to the same irresistible anxiety which quite naturally excites doubt about many things, and first about the fascination of the paternalistic relations between the holder of truth and its user. Or: can a person (not reduced to a stone's existence) eventually find (from) the possibility of being the question asked? And what kind of "answer" might it be, this pearl, locked around its shell? Responsibility is a mode of hearing. The shadow of a dead language turns into the specter of the universal, the one, quantitatively infinite: voracious.

But language cannot be appropriated because it is perpetually incomplete. Perfect action leaves no trace . . . Poetry is imperfect, unachieved, as it is. There's no consolation. Just as the word doesn't exist. The transformation through nothing into otherness: "Catastrophe is not completion. It is the culmination of the confrontation and struggle between points of view (of equally correct consciousnesses with their respective worlds). Catastrophe does not reduce situations, but the opposite, it unfolds their irresolvability in earthly conditions, casts them aside unsolved" (Bakhtin). Pushkin's *Mozart and Salieri* is an idiom, the imprint of a cyclone, accumulated oneness, returning the idea of sacrifice, division, distinction, finding meaning in its very slipping away. "Does speech exist?" (Chuang Tzu).

The transformation of a question into questioning, about the boundary, border, outline of meaning, about the liberation of the senseless by the senseless exists only in the promise, in language, in poetry. History is not a wafer of space melting on the tongue. Courage consists in an unending affirmation of thought which overcomes "the order of actual truth" itself.

Poetry is an expenditure of language "without goal," in fact a redundancy; a constant sacrifice to a sacrifice. It is possible that one should speak here about love, in other words about reality, or the probability of answering the sourceless echo—about responsibility.

Nasturtium as Reality

Clad in sweat
you drink cold water from the pitchers.
                                        —*V. Khlebnikov*

1.

An attempt
at describing an isolated object
determined by the anticipation of the resulting whole—
    by a glance over someone else's shoulder.

A nasturtium composed
of holes in the rain-spotted window—to itself
it's "in front,"

to me, "behind." Whose property is the gleaming
tremor
of compressed disclosure
    in the opening of double-edged prepositions
                                        in
a folded plane
of transparency which strikes the window pane?

2.

Attacked by white, dessicated and exact
(so precise it's as irreducible as ellipsis)

                                                a wall
in the turquoise blue distortion.

                                    To the nasturtiums
the storm left a legacy of limestone and heat
in a purple semi-circle
and steam gleaming in the cloverleaf courtyard.
A sign, inverted—not mirror, not childhood.

(A version: this night shattered apart
by the rays of the dragonflies' concise deep blue
drawing noon into a knot of blinding
                                    foam . . .

A version: tonight the rays of the dragonflies
crumbled, by day they sewed together cattails and sedge
in the marshes, where the steam is dazzling, like a cobweb
                                        in summer, and—

the total renunciation
of any possible embodiment in reading: neither
a dragonfly, nor that which forms and is
                                    formed
or is washed away
by this awareness—but the clearest forms
need mud. A version.)

As a living fretwork in blown grass
the slanting wind carries silence.
                                    A sound
from without
                    approaching
that which
the eye has blurred, an unconforming form,
it bares, rushes out 100 times into angles
where the obsessive attempt to outrun silence
persistently encounters the arrogant silence.

3.

The vibrating nasturtium
                    (immersion
of a bumblebee in the still unconsumed confusion of wings)
                                                    on
the thread of intentions strengthens the edge
(something is happening to the eyes—
                    they don't communicate with the brain)
of matter
in the nominative, near verbal fiber
                    of the flower—
it opens its leaves
                    mournfully rounded
(the shrieks of gutteral bushes as they fade
                    transform them into clusters
                                        of autumn tarnish)
in the dusk.
(the knowledge, which belongs to me,
  absorbs it cautiously, tying it
      to innumerable capillary nets:
  the nasturtium—it is a section of the neuron
  string . . .)

Some are eaten through by caterpillars, sun rays, aphids.
A sign sweats over the doorway:
"Voltaire has been killed. Call me immediately."

Damp words chalk.

4.

Do you remember
how the nasturtium
first separates from the plane leaf?

Where the will takes on the meaning of the desire
to rush a hairbreadth from death forward

until the vertebrae crackle in the pentatonic scale
and ants are at one's temples—
　　　　　　　　　　like thin-fleeced
salt—
　　　　with the dry enlivened ringing
of air fingering every hair

of what
is already a pitcher, water and sweat and plane leaves,
waterlily, necklace of dust
　　　　　　　　and blade, showing through
a gap
and all the rest that might continue

but only memory, opening slightly, jumps
to meet it, untangled by the eyes,
trying so ludicrously to seduce

what

henceforth is only a continuation
within the ends' immense proximity,
hurried persistent speech. The dialogue
　　　　　　　is common enough:

You'll say, "Where were you?"
She'll stammer, "I...　..." And right away
　　　　　　you prompt her:
"You were wandering around in the passage between order
　　　　　　　　　　and chaos..."

"Yes, if you want ... Yes."
"So?
      What did you bring with you out of the past?
And do you need what you brought now?"
"When? ...
                  Where? ... For myself?"
"Yes. You! For yourself!"
"O, everything that you tell me I'll remember ..."
(And the boring dialogue goes on, gradually
                              becoming noise)
So

the tree I read (what?) went behind a shadow.
And if I could instill my consciousness into its population
of leaves, into the register of sparks and twigs,
in the rumble of its branches, an unrolled papyrus
                                    will,
One would say: The shadow is ready to leave behind
its sources in the branches' tips,
                        having set for "dying"
the terms of an absurd confession of love.
                        Impenetrable.

5.

Blades pocked with repetition
(forty seconds spent searching for an analogy
                              to the upward branching
at the throat of the stem—instead
of this: "the emotions are
a component of composition, and expression,
          itself branching out into exclamation,
means as much as
the comma which precedes its appearance")

in radiating veins, like holes inscribed
in living epidermis,
                    flowing toward a precipice,
not calming the disordered fluctuations,
lie close,

dividing between itself and me
the space that preserves reason,
where questions about value ought to flicker. Arkadii
Trofimovitch Dragomoshchenko describes
a nasturtium, inserts it in his head. The chlorophyll

aligns galaxies of oxygen. The friction of light
against the green mass widens the path of the thing in the net
                              filtering the heavy rainfall,
another hovers
lazily, signifying at the shivering threshold
knowledge of wide losses, a gap that runs
                              into the cracks
whose bivalved power, like a melted pattern,
a grapevine . . .

having passed with strange mumbling
into a new space begetting something else
                              from the immutable.

A.T.D., proclaim the rhetoric of accumulation
and affirmation: are they the same swifts (of three years
ago)
     like molecules of darkness, which will weave the theme
               of evening for the stars again,
dropping a muscular line into the crowning bay?
That nightly subsidence into the green and lore
                    in silt
the mercy of soils . . .

The nasturtium
and anticipation rainy as the window and wind-
ow behind wind-
ow
(he in it, it in him)
like meanings smashing each other
(I don't say, metaphor . . .)
                drawn
by emptiness,
one of the distinct details—
straight,
thin,
line pulled across the tree,
mouth,

the shadow its weathervane, sorting the horizontals
                   of decision,
thought,

6.

) without time to be born, dressed briefly
                              in speech)
forming rows of luminescence in aggravated
                              matter (
into its opposite
spattering number, genus
on the different sides like narrow glass beads from ecstatically
                                        torn thread,

Just as, without time to evaporate,
a water drop is thrown off the scalding stove.
The turn of the head is dictated by the necessity
                    of comprehending the trajectory
of a feathered body whose mass is squeezed
into the corridors of vision's gravity,
                                        cutting
its inverse perspective
into the thicknesses of prolix equilibriums. The mechanism
of the keys, extracting sound, hovering over
                              its description
in the ear,

protracted with reverberation into the now. When? Where?
Me? Vertigo conceives
                                        "things."
And its outlines are unalterable, in order to cut off
the decrees, the frame, its verticals serve as examples
of how the palpable enters reason—
zaum returns with the conclusion that it has absorbed
and dissolved into pure plasma each day:

the nasturtium, unusually simple (empty)
at the first line (from either end)
of equilibrium's position.
A parenthesis, which one doesn't want to close.

7.

On the yellowish blue the white is violet. The pores drink
                              the limestone's heat
and semi-circles of sun rust in the grass.
                                   Only
through another
(multiplication tables, game boards, needles, a logarithmic
bird, cabbage butterflies wandering in the gardens, the valence
of days, nature . . . little word figures through the formulae
                                        of dragonflies
and attics,
where Saint-John's-wort dozes, and slightly honeyed wood dust
                    pours from the sweltering ceiling beams,
where sun-filled wasps are wakeful, and where, tossing her skirt
                              on the broken bureau
with wood dust in her hair,
a neighbor girl, spreading her legs,
puts your hand where it is hottest
and the hand learns all that it always saw
                                   through
multiplication tables, logarithmic bird, through
                         the stars of her mouth . . .)

—and the point isn't which kind . . .

there's another kind of modeling made by the tongue's saliva
                         under the dark lamp of the throat
As if going backward in intentional ignorance it should happen
that a time occurs, worthless even for nonexistence,

and bends the bones into an arc
simultaneously carving
                    the lips into a strange smirk,
                                        a wave.
And the air

chases your gaze along the curvature of the earth,

which from the window is scattered with grass, hieroglyph
                                                          flowing
in the rapids
of a finished spring on the brink of an over-full moon
the one that for us "having reached fullness"
stopped the blood in the solar cycle
having almost touched with its fingertips
                                        (not having quite reached)
summer's zones,
like a water drop reflected by heat . . .

and as if fear was reluctant to evaporate . . . .

8.

> *Where the will takes on the meaning of the desire*
> *to lean on the hair of the breeze.*

There were eight of you at her bed.
She had to begin counting: the first or ninth

in the stench of disintegrating cells (childhood terror!—
pushing fangs of vomit at the sight of the waxy gloss
approaching the sweet mask whose mouth flows out of the ears
and the candle scent in the fumes of memories of one
who like a log stripped of bark is spread out
                              in the lush loam!)

and
in the rotting of sweet connections—young lunar uterus—
                    are accustomed to the divisions of time.
And only the others' glance
blindly holds the plasma . . .

But you write that "waiting," "discontinuity,"
losing sense and substance, like a third color
wove her
          into its own pattern, a work accomplished free
of knots,
and all the more unbearable the meaning of "her" ripened in you
while the quiet work went on revealing
                              thoughts
(you, her) from the sheath of feminine pain
the silent symmetry crumbling in the immense proximity
                              of the end.
And the tree grew dark in front of you, and the guiding wind
led the white grass, confusing its names . . .

And here, in the forty-first year of life,
a pampered fool of the cold clouds
leads his brain with his eyes around the circle of moths, and obsessed
    with who knows what fantasies
                            testing the fingers'
craft
I contemplated the truth behind events listening to the vividness
                                of the erased words
ready to expound on the defects of precision, as
"all that you see over another's shoulder

                          already—you are
and another's shoulder again;
powerless to continue anything
into knowledge, dividing into a single . . ."
"Grammar book—landscape" through the X of comparison
                      a substitute nasturtium
flickers. It creeps behind the windowsill.
Somewhat cold.

Shimmering slightly.

Sunset.

9.

Lightning (on the craftiness of touch)—ring
                                    of nature—
will split open some prior ocean,
the mollusc of the brain and water, outstretched
                              on both sides,
the latter left
finished for a long time

so that in the future it might creep with linked twinkling
                                    static
or spawning squeak diagonally across the room
which by heart the fire grooves.
                              Don't ever let yourself
smoke in bed.
                  On the water
where surviving the cells' mutation
in dividing mirrors, in the play of this and that
in the rustling reverse side of amino acids (it seems, in fact,
this is where the division into male and female occurs
in the mollusc of the brain and on the ripple—wind's manuscript)

a figure will be glimpsed
as a consequence (a few fluctuations of its contours
                        miss the membrane of the throat!)
in flapping folds
stepping barefoot on the ripple's indifferent letter
                            which tickles the sole. This fish
can expect to be divided into five,

the bread—into starvation, one. The grapes—to grow

in gaping possiblities of the metaphor of blood.

10.

> *And here in the 41st year of life*
> *A pampered fool, whose speech continually*
> *misses the point,*

Obsessed

by the thought of putting my fingers to crafts of transgression
      which from various sides have occupied the horizons'
ends
pecking through the window shell

I follow from burst to burst, from explosion to explosion,
      faces, like magnesium petals floating by,
which permit those who remain a misprint in memory
to be recognized.

The bed of coal
—countless imprints compressed to the possibility
of ash.

Torn by someone's hand the microwreath of sweet-scented stock
              descends and clings
like a magnetic-green moth to the bend of the elbow.
The door is banging on the whitewashed balcony: where are you now?
The grimace of time. The chalky scowl's carcass
           in the cold furnace where the nasturtium
distills

existing like leaves that appear just at evening
and in the goblet's shape (edges flared)
              which speeds
                the spiral
of the flower.
Azure slightly clatters from an airplane
crawling behind the clockface.
           An unidentified object is raised
to the rank of enemy.

Iconology.
We hurry with the word's identification, before rumor
                                        can destroy it.

The poem is a late arival on time. A change of prognosis.
Even the dullest town extends beyond the borders
of the pedestrian who crosses it
                            to set out the substance of memory—
I intend to say . . . I in . . . that
what is said and emptiness, drawing in a selection
                        of the elements of utterance,
correlating,
discover desire's inexhaustible source—
what is said cannot be said again. The mailman explains:
                                false sense of shame . . .
Remnants of winter—a scarecrow stuffed with rags and straw
burns, enchanted in the round dance's rays. Gnosis
                                        of weather.
The ecstasy of unthinkable closeness (death knots
the slits in the shore—a plastic operation)
                                    leaving behind
the remnants of reason—through to the bone
from the first touch (reflection) on the skin.
thanks to the verb, meaning more often senseless
                                        walking
along the sand or a swimmer, peeled by the imagination
from a point, trickling down the edge of the eye,
like a pea from a peapod

or intimacy with cold, bitten through by the cotton
                                        whiteness,
rippling canvas, fading between current
and
weight, heaven knows where from and where
to against the deafened silver's wool,
                                clinging
to the intangible object of discord. Conjecture is simple—
the nasturtium is not

II.

necessary. It is composed from the exceptional exactness
                                        of language
commanding the thing—"to be"
and the rejection of understanding. We say sometimes. Sometimes
        we speak: of another time. Right into the snare
of the mustard seed

signs, reminiscent and leading to reminiscence
in the disintegration of the poem to the last coil of the cocoon
                                        of exhausting breath.

12.

The nasturtium—it is the undiminished procession
          of forms, the geological chorus of voices crawling,
                    shouting, disclosing each other
when
day transforms evening into a hill of drifted insomnia
and a chirp
               creeps into the mouth of an old man on a bench
but also a shriek, through the birch slides of fetid air
                              from the neighboring house,
by which you could check your watch, for the third year
                              the same swifts,

paper, taking root in the table tops' rough wood

a gas tank behind the crossing, near the gas pump,
collecting heat in the lines, and a face in the intrigue
                    of the anti-corrosive layer,
the center's different architecture. A particle is not related
to prayer. But see. Threading the seen through the needle
                              whose greed
fits the impeccability of its choice—the narrowest

opening of form.

The nasturtium bearing fire.

Nina Iskrenko

NINA ISKRENKO was born in 1951 and lives in Moscow. Since the early 1980s she has been active and influential in Moscow's literary and performance circles. During its brief but vital existence, she was a leading member of Moscow's "Poetry Club." She was a participant in the "Crossing Boundaries: The Soviet New Wave" festival in San Francisco in 1991.

Address to an Assumed Interlocutor

I
/from conversations with a confrere, 1986/

They often ask me. Rather, not often, but sometimes. Rather, in general, they don't ask. Simply no one ever comes up and asks: What is it, frankly speaking, that you write about?
Really—what is it?

About the passing.
About the relative, instantaneous, nonuniversal,
about the self-denying and self-sufficing in their own denial,
about the respect of the world for its own blood brother–antiworld,
about the desire to know someone who does not desire, does not try
to and does not know you.
From the viewpoint of a saucepan
i read too much
i read too little
from the viewpoint of a feather-pen
About what all people are—one person, uniting within male and
female impulses, about what art is—a bridge, and life—movement on

this bridge. On these bridges. Foot bridges. Footlights.
BRIDGEOSAURUSES. A bridge is a link, established at a point where
before there was not one. A poetic bridge is a metaphor, a
confrontation, like the ultimate essence of art, its primary
artistic thought. It unites, draws closer the ever more
"distancing," seeks out the commonality and kinship, hidden in the
nature of things. Each new commonality is a step toward knowing
the world and the person in this world. People have it good
together, when they know one another. Then they say: we have a lot
in common. Then they are kindred. About the thirst for kinship.
And its difficulty.
About the fact that when it is stale bread we pick
we give an indistinct sniff
and feel ourselves like blood and tick
in interaction
and perfectly understand one another
like rain
and cigarette paper
whispering together in the back row

About movement.
About the physics of spiritual processes and about the expenditures
of energy associated with them, about the habitual, naturally
paradoxical, about beauty, as a nonapparent symmetry, about the
tearing away of nuclear simplicity, like heresy, about complexity,
connected with attempts to go beyond the limits of this somewhat
sickening space, which can barely stand up on its own four feet.
A poetic work is an equalization
where x equals any not-x
because and only because
for every unopening parachute
there is somewhere a spare skydiver

About the acceleration of perception.
About the highly organized, yet mortal.
About the *so-not-called*.

II
/a biography from the opposed, 1989/

The author belongs to the generation born in the 1950s and realizing its creative strivings in that period of our history that proved to be an epoch of sharply developed absurdism and carefully preserved principles of highly artistic stagnation. Being accustomed since childhood to the paradoxical phenomena of everyday life with their unforeseeable consequences, knowing how to get by in the majority of situations without common sense or psychological ease, with a strict immunity to all that can be had without a struggle, that which is passed out one apiece—all of this sooner or later creates a corresponding supply of firmness, or, if you wish, a natural conservatism, protecting its bearer from simple decisions and direct paths to even the most obvious truths. This healthy conservatism lays a noticeable imprint on the stylistics and character of the depicted, and it also explains—metaphorically, at least—a cluster of phenomena that defy more reasoned means of interpretation. Specifically, these are certain facts of the "biography from the opposed." Having obvious inclinations toward the humanities—toward literature, music, drawing, etc.—the author nonetheless spends six years studying at Moscow University in order to, having obtained a diploma in physics, never again return to the natural sciences, those ex-personal forms of interacting with the surrounding reality; having selected, as primary orientation, the word, and as shelter of necessity—the trivial pursuit of work as a translator of scientific and technical literature from English to Russian. A family and two children convincingly fill out the picture of a normal existence for a Russian woman in the contemporary literary process, an existence that was secret for many years and even almost shameful in the eyes of others, to reveal itself only in the past year or two with a few publications. Thus, it is not surprising that the author accepts any signs of attention paid to her humble persona with a certain dubiousness and perplexity; for this she offers excuses in the form of gratitude, and gratitude in the form of a text whose rehearsal coincides with its final result.

Translated by Anesa Miller-Pogacar.

To Beat or Not to Beat

An egg so round on the outside
An egg so round on the inside

An egg so wintery outside
An egg so summery inside

An egg so primal on the outside
And such a hen inside

And three of its slanting verticals
like three linings in an old handbag
are like three nymphets at the fountain
                              San Michele
like bowling pins   here today
and still here
tomorrow
                    Dusia, Hey Dusia
                    Get lost
            I told you don't try to wear somebody else's shoes
            Don't roll out from somebody else's egg

An egg is like a sarcophagus
or a piggy bank
beautiful like an absolute army tank
Such an egg   in a checkered pattern
like a squirrel
And such a cosmic instinct within it

An egg so smart on the outside
An egg so delicate on the inside

An egg so cracked outside
and so peropolyurethane on the inside

An egg so glum when seen in profile
It keeps thinking till the wee morning hours

Such an egg coughs when it's only half awake
roams about in the darkness and grumbles at the hen

If you touch such an egg you feel
it comes from a *Co-Op*
It keeps rustling and computing something

An egg that saved its friend more than once
An egg that matured   became strong   and fired shots
woke us up at dawn

And I got so sick and tired of it
that I thought it over and ate it
And so now once again I don't understand whether

I'm on the outside or inside
in nature . . . or the firmament . . . or in a street light
or in the subway
at the Kursk railroad station

> Translated by John High and Katya Olmsted.

Still-Life

Saturated with agile flames
the carafe's color
flows down
the table's curved plane

In contrast—the pale and asymmetrical
wine glass is pinned
to the fulcrum

And movement's sucked itself
into the armchair's woolen cavity
after leaving beyond its limits
a tiny bouquet of chopped-off fingers
looming over the night's smoking shadow
in a mirroring ashtray

that's cold and estranged
in the electronic clock's
moonlight

  Translated by John High and Katya Olmsted.

To talk with you is like burning in the marsh
like climbing head and all into a roll your own smoke
like looking at the sky through a black cat
and peeing in the meat grinder

  Translated by John High and Katya Olmsted.

Polystylistics

Polystylistics   is when a knight from the Middle Ages
                 wearing shorts
                 storms into the wine section of store #13
                 located on Decembrists street
                 & cursing like one of the Court's nobles
                 he drops his copy of Landau & Lifshitz's "Quantum
                 Mechanics" where it falls on the marble floor

Polystylistics   is when one part of a dress
                 made of Dutch cotton
                 is combined with two parts
                 of plastic & glue
                 and in general the remaining parts are missing altogether
                 or dragging themselves along somewhere near
                 the rear end while the clock strikes & snores
                 & a few guys look on

Polystylistics   is when all the girls are as cute
                 as letters
                 from the Armenian alphabet composed by Mesrop Mashtoz
                 & the cracked apple's

no greater than any one of the planets
& the children's notes are turned inside out
as if in the air it would be easier to breathe like this
& something is always humming
                              & buzzing
just under the ear

Polystylistics is a kind of celestial aerobics
observed upon the torn backpack's
back flap
it's a law
of cosmic instability
& one of those simple-minded idiots who always
begins his talk with the "F" word

Polystylistics is when I want to sing
& you want to go to bed with me
& we both want to live
forever

After all how was everything constructed
if this is how it's all conceived
How was everything conceived
if it's still waiting to be constructed
And if you don't care for it
well then it's not a button
And if it's not turning
don't dare turn it

No on earth no unearthliness exists
no pedestrian blushed as a piece of lath
Many sleep in leather & even less
            than a thousand maps are talking about war

Only your love
like a curious grandmother
running bare-legged & Fyodor Mikhailovich Dostoevsky
could not hold back from shooting a glass of Kinzmarauly wine
to the health of Tolstoy the fat boy riding through his home town

Semipalatinsk on a screeching bicycle

In Leningrad & Samara   it's 17–19 degrees

In Babylon   it's midnight

On the Western Front   there are no changes
      Translated by John High.

Talking to my crested hen
who all the length of Pirogov Street
wore that blue kerchief bought with my pay

Telling her Rita let's move away from here
I'll earn enough for a hut
you'll have plenty of shoes

You'll eat oranges
we'll buy a striped rug
it's pretty there   it's the North

Brushing away her locks
pressing myself to her like a potato bear
saying Let's move away

Telling her Not a drop more—it's over
Rita I got involved
May the damn woman rot

Saying This is the last time
while a cigarette fell to the mouth
The store closed

Savagely and forcefully touching
crushing the cookies in the little bag
spitting unprintably

And so we went in lawful matrimony
toward all the past misfortunes and sour pants
Floating side by side

Oh those Russian brown cows
The blue footstools of
Maslovka-Taganka

> Translated by John High and Katya Olmsted.

Fugue

BECAUSE WHEN YOU look at a simple
                                        object
eyeglasses or scissors for example and think of something
not so simple or objective then later
after seeing these scissors or glasses at their earlier place
you experience a vague anxiety
as if traveling in
time hearing the echo or guessing the smell
of something familiar
something that never existed
BECAUSE WHEN SOMEONE'S outlived a husband and three
                                                        sons
quickly and quietly the unknown old woman dies
in the room there's no extra chair to sit in
and death ticks on the wall
the stove is not lit
and remaining is only the darkness and a small inheritance
a down pillow
two hundred rubles in the nightstand
the family savings for the handsome and tall grandsons
and two books on the shelf
the textbook on bee-keeping and a dictionary of foreign words
BECAUSE WHEN IT rains all night
and rains in the morning
and toward evening the rain doesn't stop
and at dawn it still rains then the carrot
and the other vegetables grow healthy
and the mud sticks sure to the boots

so that the head stays light
like the toy Roly-Poly
BECAUSE you're an angry and cruel boy and there's
no getting you to go to sleep and you force your mom
to sit for hours bent over you in a child's chair
which gives her a backache
BECAUSE WHEN all the windows
of the huge apartment building
face out to one side and all the clouds are gray
and all the shop lines are already long and it doesn't seem strange
that people can't talk
that they accuse you of not knowing how to listen
BECAUSE even when you peel potatoes
or work out a plan
it's difficult to hold on and not scratch open a little
deep black dot very black and very
deep
BECAUSE when she says to him
I do see you
And you don't see yourself
And he answers her What's wrong with your
Seeing me
But she having faltered speaks more slowly
No it's not wrong
But it would be better if I saw
what I want to see
And instead of becoming angry
he says to her very softly Don't leave
The bus suddenly brakes
Please don't put in your 5 kopecks

                Translated by John High and Katya Olmsted.

You're hungry

Here's an island of fireflies
Cool wells of grass   Here's the
peanut track of footsteps   Here's the wine
of hunting in the crane-shaped stalks
and on the sand the turtle's shadows
Here's her breast on the ocean's leaves
The tarragon blossoming
Go   Be pitiless
You're hungry
You're mortal
It's blossoming

You're mortal

Here's the evening's brown puddles
The star in the glass that cracked from salt
        You're hungry
And forget that face and
        You're mortal
Here's her belly
in a jug of whispers   And a silvery call
Break the jug and empty it
You're mortal
You're hungry
The blossoming
Go
follow the call

Translated by John High and Katya Olmsted.

Dmitri Prigov

DMITRI PRIGOV was born in Moscow in 1940. He has been a leading figure in Soviet experimental poetry and visual art for the past two decades, having been a founder of the Moscow conceptualist movement. He has read and exhibited his work widely in the West. He is currently an artist-in-residence in Berlin. His first book was published in the Soviet Union in 1990.

What more is there to say?

In order to comprehend any creative act it's important to understand the context out of which it's projected—the context of cultural tradition and environment as much as the context of the author's personal creativity.

This is especially true as the significance of focusing on procedures is increasing in our times, and also with regard to those authors whose art's larger significance comes from gesture in cultural space and from work with images rather than from individual masterpieces, i.e., for authors who work in conceptual, postconceptual, and postmodern stylistics.

My investigations in avant-garde poetry began at the moment I turned to conceptualism in the fine arts area of my creativity (at the end of the 1960s).

Just as conceptualism in the fine arts was marked by a strong verbalization of visual space, a similar process occurred in literature: texts were often transformed into three-dimensional, manipulable objects, so that many of them could be defined as a particular type of art only by virtue of the author's directly designating them so. (This pertains to my cycle of visual, three-dimensional, manipulable texts: the Poemograph, Mini-books, Whirligigs, Windows, Cans, Little Coffins for Rejected Verse, New Books, Addresses.) Paralleling this in my graphic work, words and texts intruded, and thanks to the characteristics of graphic space and its interdependence with words, they were like "names," the "logos" (in the Platonic sense) of this space.

Within the limits of strictly language compositions such genres as Alphabet Texts appeared, whose problem was the mastery and utilization of languages unusual in literature—the languages of lists, newspaper articles, public addresses and propaganda, of quasi-scientific reports, and lowly kitsch forms from the literary tradition.

The whole complex of these issues is reflected also in a normal, regular versification, which, because of its direct imitation of familiar poetry, in refracted form, often confuses readers who react to my works in such terms as "good" or "bad," as "successful" or "unsuccessful" poems. The heroes of my poems have become the different linguistic layers (quotidian, state, high cultural, low cultural, religiophilosophical), representing within the limits of the poetic text corresponding mentalities and ideologies which reveal in this space mutual ambitions and pretensions. Such a confluence from different language mentalities entering into a confined space permits not only the authenticity of each of them to be revealed within the limits of the axiomatics postulated by them, but also the absurdity of the total ambitions inherent in the desire of each of them to capture and describe the entire world in their terminologies. Another manifestation of the same tendency is the appearance in the poems (and the clash among them) of certain kinds of heraldic heroes: the Fed'ral Agent, Reagan, the Fireman, the Jew, Mary, each one representing certain ideas of sociocultural phenomena—the State, the Enemy, the Elements, History, Love.

In our times postmodernist consciousness is superseded by a strictly conceptual virtual distance of the author from the text (when inside the text there is no language for resolving the author's personal pretensions, ambitions, or his own personal ideology, but he, the author, detaches himself and is formed on the metatextual level). Taking the place of the conceptual, a shimmering relationship between the author and the text has developed, in which it is very hard to define (not only for the reader but for the author, too) the degree of sincerity in the immersion into the text and the purity and distance of the withdrawal from it. I.e., the fundamental content becomes the drama between the author and the text, his flickering between the text and a position outside of it. I.e., the result is some kind of quasi-lyrical poems written by me under a feminine name, when I am of course not concerned with mystification but only show the sign of the lyrical poem's position, which is mainly associated with feminine poetry. (For many, by the way, who didn't go through the school of a conceptual and naturally postmodern consciousness, these poems appear to be authentic examples of pure lyrics.)

The transformation from strict conceptual to flickering postmodern stylistics became for me the cycle of "Screaming Cantatas," which in themselves represent a type of performance, an action with singing, screams, and ecstatics, which is often performed with jazz and rock musicians. In these "Cantatas" the image of the rhapsode, i.e., that ancient beginning period of literature's existence when it was not yet separated from music, theater, and every possible element of ritual and shamanism, was being developed. (One should note that the flowering of rock culture provided an occasion as if to project these "Cantatas" on it, facilitating the possibility of perception but increasing the danger of identifying and confusing my activity with various kinds of rock performances, with songs and actions of social and other protests—again, in order to understand this the experience of conceptual consciousness and the recognition of gestures in cultural space are crucial.)

Finally one should note that the numerous cycles in my work were never for me the sole "confessional" method of self-expression, but they were always immediately formed into genres, images that lasted and existed in parallels, the totality of which, as a result, on a metatextual level (as the utmost life's mission for the duration of my existence) generates some kind of phantom image of the author.

Translated by Lyn Hejinian and Elena Balashova.

From Reagan's Image in Soviet Literature

Preparatory Conversation

Reagan: Why do you agitate my soul
Policeman: 'Cuz we want to appraise it.
Reagan: That is God's affair not man's.
Policeman: But that's what God went and put us here for.
Reagan: Don't destroy my poor spirit!
Policeman: You destroyed it yourself.
Reagan: Help me! Teach me!
Policeman: No. You were planned this way from the ages.
All we do are appraisals.

So they've picked a brand-new president
Of the United States
And they've dishonored the former president
Of the United States

But what's it to us, like, a president
Like, the Unifed States
But even so it's interesting—a Prezdent
Of the United States

I got used to Carter, though he is our foe
And there's even a rhyme already—provocarter
Now Reagan showed up yesterday from somewhere—
It's out the window with all my Carter

If only the wonderful merican people
Would just think this over:
It's all the same to them—this one or that
But four years of serious labor
Are being wasted here

Reagan doesn't want to feed us
Well, OK, it's really his mistake

It's only over there that they believe
You've got to eat to live

But we don't need his bread
We'll live on our idea
It'll come to him quite suddenly: Hey where are they?—
But we've already gotten to his heart

It's tough for us to live with Reagan—
He always wants to beat us
Beat yourself, you crazy man!
If not then things will come to such a pass
That you will have to beat yourself
With help from us

Like, it's clear—Reagan's a crazy beast
But even he's not completely outside
The truth—Quiet and holy, there is a
Small shoot of our objective idea
In him. And when that shoot grows to consciousness
Then his heart will bloom like a rose
And that beast will lay down like a lamb
And won't bite

O, Reagan, there's nothing more to say
Just so they don't reelect you
Otherwise during the next term
I'll hardly have enough strength
To abuse you here—but I must
Give me some other snake
To celebrate

So Reagan's been given another term
Fear not, O brothers, fear not
Arrange yourselves in large columns
He's no scarier than a little chipmunk
Singing in the cooling expanse

About what does he sing?—ekh, always the same, about peace
About the unique
Blowing
And fluttering with its light wings, the all laved, all illuminated
with light joyful radiationness, from time to time all across the
surface his visage will be distorted by an incursion of dark infra-
red bands, his teeth will click, heavy eyelids will rise with a crash,
mountains and trees will fall, floods will surge, fissures of the
field and life's spaces will run ahead breaking and again, again he
alone, alone, unique, uniquely being sung, being sung uniquely,
being sung, uniquely, uniquely, being sung uniquely, uniquely,
uniquely being sung!

   Translated by Andrew Wachtel.

Forty-ninth Alphabet Poem

(tsa-tsa)
(Moscow, 1985)

Opening Statement

So here we've gathered together again. Here sits Tarasov, I'm standing
here, over there I see Kabakov sitting, there is Rubinshtein, there
Chuikov, and where? where is he? a-a-ah there he is to the right of
Monastyrsky, over there is someone else, they're all sitting, they are
heroes, they are the heroes of Pushkin, Lermontov, Tchaikovsky (Petr
Ilich), of his First Concerto, of his Second Concerto for Piano and
Orchestra, of his Third Concerto, Fourth, Fifth, Sixth, Seventh, of his
Tenth finally! They are sitting! they are heroes! They are my heroes!

A-tsa-tsa
Ba-tsa-tsa
Va-tsa-tsa
Ga-tsa-tsa
Da-tsa-tsa-tsa-tsa-tsa-tsa-aaaa
Ye-tse-tse
Zhe-tse-tse
Ze-tse-tse-tse-tse-tse-tse-eee
It's the wrinkles of a dear face-ce-ce-ce

Concealing the wicked will of a fath-th-th-ther
Let them fly into embraces of the end-d-d-d-d-ddd
Ma-tza-tza-tza-tza-tza!
Not-tsa-tsa! ne-tse-tse! ve-tse-tse! er-tsr-tsrrrr!
Oh! Oh! Oh!
Pom-pom-pom-paaam, pammm! (Concerto No. 1 for Piano and Orchestra
  by Petr Ilich, yes, Petr dear Ilich Tchaikovsky!) Pom-pom-
  pom-paaam, pammm! Pom-pom-pom-paaam, pamm! pamm!
  pammmmm!
Raaa, raaa, raaa! Rararareeeraaa, ra-reee, rararreerararareerararareerarararam
Strange is the tale of horror I'll tell
Tralah, tralah, tralah, tralel,
   traaam, tam-taam, teetateetateeta
     (it's there again, again
     the concerto, Tchaikovsky)
So it was about a young girl, but then he came from some unknown
  capital in the north. She fell madly, tenderly in love
  with him, but he breathed unbearable cold on her
    And killed a close friend in a duel
    So to a distant land he went
    While she, accepting her fate cruel
    From home to capital was sent
     (tatattatatatat-taaa, taaaa!)
And married a general. He, returning from his foreign
  travels, meets her, now mature and wise, and his cold
  heart grows warm, but her heart is now like a piece of
  marble, impassive. He races around and around, throws
  himself into an ice-filled bathtub, but too late! too
  late! his heart is all surrounded by hellfire, all! and
  it burns the ice and his own flesh to ashes! if only he
  had the power to ignite her cold heart! DEATH! DEATH!
  All that remains to him is DEATH!
    (tararareerararareerararareerararara-aaa!)
  DEATH! DEATH! burdensome and painful! Death, death
  irredeemable, unavoidable, unremitting . . .
Uoo! (frightening?)
Foo! (frightening! frightening!)
Hoo-oo-oo-oo-oo-oo-oo-ey! (very frightening!)
Tsa-tsa-tsa-tsa-tsa

Cha-cha-cha-cha-choo-choo-choo, oom-tsa-tsa, oom-tsa-tsa,
        choom-tsa-tsa, choom-tsa-tsa
Sham-tsa-tsa, sham-tsa-tsa
Shcham-tsa-tsa, Shcham-tsa-tsa
Y-tsy-tsy, y-tsy-tsy
Eh-tse-tse, Eh-tse-tse
You-tsu-tsu-tsu-tsu-tsu-tsu-tsu-tsu-ooooo

Ai! I! Iamvlich! Iamblichus! Yangel! Yankel! Yageila! Yaveila!
    Yabeilaim! I am Goya,—I fly down to a naked body! I am
    Heine, I fly down to a naked genius! I am Goethe,—I fly
    down to a body without pressure! I'm Goya! I'm Heine! I'm
    goy-yayaya, I'm goy-yayaaaa, yaaa goy, I'm a goy, a goy,
    a goy-yayaya, a goy-yaya, yage-heh-hehi-ne-ne-ne (you
    hear? you hear?—there it is again, again, the concerto!)
    I'm goethe, goethe, gooooethe. I'm Pushkin! I'm
    Lermontov! I'm Derzhavin! I'm Nekrasov! I'm Dostoyevski!
    I'm Fet! I'm Blok! I'm pu-pu-puuu-shkiiin, I'm pu, I'm
    pupupu, I'm pupupu, I'm pu-pu-pu-pu-pu-pu-shkin! I'm
    Mayakovsky! I'm Esenin! I'm Sholokhov! I'm Dante! I'm
    Homer! I'm Shakespeare! I'm Diderot! I'm Robespierre! I'm
    Napoleon! I'm Hegel! I'm he-he-he-eee-geeeel, I'm he! I'm
    he-he-he, I'm he-he-he-he-hehehegel! I'm Aristotle! I'm
    Catullus! I'm Nebuchadnezzar!! I'm Tamerlane! I'm
    Tutankhamen! I'm Tchaikovsky! I'm Tchaikovsky (Petr
    Ilich)! And you all, all, all, all, all, all-all-
    aaaaaall, you all, all-all you all, my dears, beloveds,
    inseparable from my unencompassable heart, you are all my
    golden heroes!

Translated by Gerald J. Janecek.

Screaming Cantata
(Who Killed Stalin)

Introduction
The point is not who killed him—just, killed and
killed! The point now is how we're going to agree. Let's
sing. O.k., so let's all do it together: Yes! Yes! Yes!

Yes-yes! Yes!—you answer me, but somehow discordantly
and without confidence

What, you don't believe me? you really don't believe me?
but what's there to believe! although I didn't kill him!
O.k., once more, only all together:

You killed!

Yooou kiiilled! you say, but again somehow without
confidence, and you're right, you're right—I didn't
kill him! but if some kind of unit-unity, some kind of
collectivity demands it, then do it one more
time:

You killed!

Yooou kiiled!—great! great! if you only knew how
great! if only I knew myself that I'm not guilty, then
I'd believe!

O.k., great!

Who killed Pushkin?

You killed!

No, really!—no!

You killed!

No really, it's my joke!

You killed!

You killed!

No, no, no! not I!

You killed!

Not I! not I! D'Anthes! He . . . such . . .

You killed!

He took out a dueling pistol . . . and I . . .

You killed!

You killed!

I was simply next to . . .

You killed!

You killed!

(listen, listen! how horrible! like stone against stone it hammers out
    history and our guilt—You killed!—the insides—You killed!—the view
    of our universe from the belly—You killed!—on the surface in front of
    our eyes and in front of the whole world—You killed!—they take you
    by your pale and sweaty hand—You killed! You killed! You killed!)

Who killed Lermontov?

You killed!

Me again?

You killed!

No, really, no!

You killed!

You killed!

No, in 1940 I only . . .

You killed!

but already in the beginning of the 19th century he . . .

You killed!

You killed!

he was standing on Mashuk Hill[1] . . .

You killed!

He loved freedom!

You killed!

You killed!

You killed!

But Martynov hated him!

You killed! you killed! you killed! you killed!

You killed!

(quiet! quiet! let's rest! There are so we rested, dear God! what are we
   here for? life is all around! and they are all around! the killed that is,
   but like the living they flutter between us, they brush us with invisible
   eternal wings, giving us scarcely felt kisses! yes!)

Who killed Dmitrii?[2]

You killed!

No, no, not I!

You killed!

1. Mashuk Hill is where Lermontov was killed by Martynov in a duel.
2. Prince Dmitrii, the son of Ivan the Terrible, was reportedly killed by Boris Godunov.

You killed!

Not I! Not I!

You killed!

You killed!

No! no! nooooo!

You killed!

You killed!

You killed!

Nooo-i! Not I! Boriiiis!

You killed!

Nooo! Boriska! Boriska!

You killed! you killed! youk illlled! you killed!

Not Iiiiiii!

You killed!

No really! no! The will of the peeeeeeople!

You killed!

(what are they shrieking about? what are they about?
they themselves are miserable killers)

You killed!

You killed!

(there, there, as if their bloody footprints dragged on
through the vast hall to the ends of the city!)

You killed!

You killed!

You killed!

(but what are we here for? we're weak, we're poor creatures! we don't
have any strength!—You killed!—now this is my proper voice; No, no,
no! my other voice answers back; but you were killing! Look how many
poor innocent cockroaches you've killed!)

You killed!

You killed!

You killed!

(pure and innocent! says my first voice; Yes, yes! my second voice
replies—you did the killing! but he deserved to be killed, it's as if they
realized their highest destiny by means of innocent me!)

You killed!

You killed!

(there they are, shrieking! so o.k., now I'll ask them an insidious
question!)

Who—who killed Stalin?

You killed!

No, no, I wasn't doing any killing!

You killed!

You killed!

But he was a killer himself!

You killed!

But he deserved it!

You killed!

You killed!

Yes! yes! I killed! There, here I am on my knees before you! judge me!
sentence me! I killed!

You killed!

But I wanted things to be better! I wanted it for the better! I suffered so
much! I'm practically a hero!

You killed!

You killed!

Yes, yes, I killed! I'm a scurrilous killer! Oo-o-o-o! a killer! a killer!

You killed!

Yes, yes! but you too are great! all of you!

You killed!

I killed!

You killed!

I I I I killed!

You killed!

Yes, yes, I killed!

You killed!

You killed!

I killed!

You killed!

I killed!

You killed!

You killedyoukilledyoukilled!

Ikilledikilledikilledikilled!

Youkilledikilledyoukilledikilledyoukilledikilledyoukilledikilledyoukilled-
ikilledyoukilledyoukilledikilledyoukilledikilledyoukilledikilledyoukilled-
ikilledyoukilledikilledyoukilledikilledyoukilledikilled

I killed him!

Translated by Lyn Hejinian and Elena Balashova.

Sergei Gandlevsky

SERGEI GANDLEVSKY was born in 1952 in Moscow. He is a graduate of Moscow State University, department of philology, and has worked as a high school teacher of literature, museum guide, theater stagehand, and night watchman. He is a member of the Professional Union of Writers and a founding member of the literary group Moscow Time. Translations are all by Andrew Wachtel.

An Attempt at a Manifesto

The initial impulse for lyric poetry is a secret.

The poet's task is not to unveil this secret but to reproduce it in all its inviolability, so that someone who is privy to that same secret will recognize it in your words, in just the same way that an interlocutor, having interrupted you partway through, can finish telling your dream.

There is this kind of secret: spring, washed windows, sparrows chirping in the courtyard. "Knives-scissors sharpened!" cries the last (perhaps) knife grinder. A holiday. Sardines and cheese on the table. A whole beautiful day ahead. A beret, short pants, and white socks with pompoms are ready to go out. Housemates squabbling off to the sides, and neighbors greeting each other. May 1st, happiness.

Time passes, and we realize that the best years of our lives, the flowering of our five senses, unmotivated elation, are not completely—how should I put it—competent. They are just a fraud of childlike perception; that, more so than anyone else in the world, we were fooled. There was no holiday, instead there were blood, lies, general brutishness. Different things for different people. For some bicycles and linden alleys recall the bittersweet pre-revolutionary way of life, while for others they evoke the orphan holiday of May 1st (and even that turned out to be a fraud).

There's knowledge and knowledge, hatred and hatred, but what are we to do with love if it exists? What is a lyric poet to do with his central possession—the secret, if that secret has been disgraced?

A disgraced secret can become a source for lyric creation.

Various poets react variously to the shamed secrets of their generation.

The reaction can be tough-minded: yes, we've been deceived, everything is a lie, but we will grow, we'll get up on our tiptoes and drink the clean air of genuine culture. We'll shake off today's dust from our legs, and, in the end, we'll stand up freely. Authors in the grip of this kind of emotion write verses in which the words themselves, the syntactic structure, and the intonational cadences are all the fruit of a proud and enviable desire to discover freedom, to find the internal strength that will allow them to live, despite the disgraced secret, loss, and illegitimacy.

A second way to reinterpret a desecrated secret is through humor.

Deceived trust takes its revenge: pompous ideals, dead linguistic material, official authorities are all subjected to mockery. The sphere of mockery is broad, and it continues to broaden. Humor strengthens, inflames, heats things up. Its fire spreads to ideals in general, to language in general, to authority in general. The border separating the comic and the not-comic disappears, because it turns out that everything is comic. The world turns out not to be worth taking literally. This is how disappointed people take revenge on life for having disappointed them. But life does not take this lying down. Humor that does not allow for the possibility of seriousness, which has completely lost it, stops being humor. Laughter turns into work, and the joker becomes importunate, the carnival becomes boring.

And then, finally, there is a third way to experience the general secret of one's generation. We'll call it—for lack of anything better—critical sentimentalism. Its outline is nebulous. It occupies an intermediate position somewhere between the two described above. But an attraction to odic style, a yearning for a lost, elevated past cannot be realized here with a conception of total rectitude. The past has too great a power over the soul of this kind of poet. The power of the past makes a condescending discussion with the present impossible (because insincere).

Here, it would seem, we're going to come close to the ironists. But this isn't it either. Our emotions are not free, and poets like this have invested too much of their soul in this ill-fated secret from which there's no escape. A struggle with this damaging love would reek of self-destruction.

Beautiful butterflies and the crackling of ice on the Neva in March at the beginning of the century, and even so the heart believes that, at the end of life, the end of time, in the chaos of sounds of the world the elect will hear the ringing words "knives-scissors sharpened" like a password and a farewell.

So there's one secret and three poetic methods of preserving it, three ways to live with it. It's as if they flowed into an answer: Lomonosov's three styles. Does this coincidence tell us anything? It doesn't. Because the world has changed and its high, low, and middle have been mixed up in the craziest way.

If the high style is stubborn and refuses to take the movement of life into account, it falls into bombast, and, without the poet's desiring this, it heads into the territory of parody. The ground has shifted under the feet of the high style. And the Poets (with a capital P) themselves, can they really live or even simply survive in accord with the laws of this genre? Discord is inevitable, and with it hypocrisy.

The low style, caught up in the inertia of destruction, long ago forgot its initial impulse: trampled purity and common sense. Laughter from loss, spilling out over the edges of the genre, rushes into real life, becomes the norm, good form, duty. Born out of a call for freedom, laughter becomes its enemy, a declaration.

And it's only the middle style that retains its right to choice: if something's bitter, I'll cry—funny, I'll laugh. Finding itself between polar stylistic opposites, it borrows from each of its resolute neighbors when necessary, remaking their excesses after its own manner: cutting down the arrogance of self-righteous poetry, taming the riot of ironic poetry. This kind of poetic worldview is more dramatic than the other two, because its aesthetic is less regulated. It has nothing to prop itself up with other than feeling, intelligence, and taste.

Of course, we're talking here not about living poets but only about tendencies. One can easily guess that a poet whose orientation is completely odic or ironic is not a poet. But a poet who has managed to absorb the traits of the style that I value is indeed a poet, and not a minor one in these times. However, it's not good enough to fit into some kind of schema (no matter how exact or all-encompassing). You need talent. For speaking honestly, any conversation about poetry is a conversation about talent, a conversation in which, either through thoughtlessness or on purpose, the fraction has not been reduced to its lowest common denominator.

A poet is, by character, a quarrelsome kind of person. A battle with himself, people, society, nature, God is the main occupation (a rather joyless one, it must be admitted) of his soul. Writing is his way of concluding a truce with the world. This truce not only makes life easier but brings you closer to truth. That's what I think.

There's still some time before I'll be a patriarch.
There's still some time before I'll scare the kids,
By saying in a put-on bass when I arrive to visit:
"I carried you when you were just a tot."
However, the trajectory of motion
That started from the exit of the
Maternity department of a local hospital,
Continued through the halls of countless chambers
Through which in darkness I have passed
While groping all the while for the secret switch
That might shed light upon my life,
Is now becoming clear.
                              Behold my childhood,
It's waving sheets of music all about
My boyhood's playing ping-pong. Adolescence
Orating, while the years of youth,
Are precious just like those of childhood. But youth's
Lost track of airy, wonderful, and wandering miles.
Behold the years I spent within
The four walls of a Moscow alcoholic haze.
We drank, and sat, and sang together—
Of streams, and separation, dust to dust.
But you are bored: "You know, this song has got
A dull refrain somehow . . ."—But why?
It isn't dull at all, it's just traditional.

Round rows of railroad sheds
An idiotic puppy on a leash
Under umbrellas, wearing summer threads
The Moscow River, eventually we reached.
And here we live today. An empty
Professor's cottage with just six windows.
Capricious crabgrass where it isn't meant to be,
A balcony that hangs across the alcoves.
Tomorrow in the pail out by the well
The petrified water will
Come crashing round your feet and then remain
An icy wondrous cylinder.

And then, in just two days, a fence, some kindling,
A terrace streaked by frequent rain.
Beneath the ancient washstand
The grass like toothpaste's dirtied.
And then, perhaps, you'll see an azure strand.
The song just doesn't end.
                              In the refrain
We move to crossings stern
It darkens. It's slick like on a village square.
The seagulls soar above the naked earth,
And living speech becomes the scrape
Of voices on a record. Puppy's ears perk up—
His Master's Voice. It's no big deal.
We'll speak, and smile, and drink some tea.
It's time for bed. I guarantee
That I in my dreams again I'll see
A sullen, big, and probably majestic stream.

A lynch law of unexpected maturity
Is a mediocre sight
It lacks the generally accepted pleasure
Of walking out along a quiet river bank
Reflecting in rhyme. My utterance
Has long been watched by silence.
Have all those grammarians
Really been handed down from above!

In Russian poetry there's a tradition
Of breaking mirrors with revulsion
Or hiding kitchen knives
In the drawers of writing desks.
Uncle in a hat bespattered by a pigeon
Was reflected in a captured pier-glass
So don't tire me with creative hunger
It came out like that by itself.

It was once a little ship, a yawl
Or a sparrow on an empty hammock.

Is that a cloud? No, it's clown.
It's a crown in a woman's hand
It's habits of crowned tenderness
The scrape of oarlocks on summer ponds:
He licks a scratch and asks to be picked up
I'll never give you up to anyone!

Now it's serfdom, torture, jealousy.
The themes have been spilled out in droplets.
Bread and water. I meeow and I moo,
Having grabbed my noggin with open hands.
Why did I inherit
Someone's mask with an ambiguous mouth,
The tragedy of one-act life,
the conversation of a jester and a raissoneur?

Why oh why, my light-winged music,
Explain to me when I die,
Were you sitting with a nasty smile
At some endless feast
And bugging a sleepy youth
While picking at the tablecloth?
Is that a clown? No, it's a cloud.
And I don't count on mercy from you!

To Dmitri Prigov

Fidelity and fatherland, and heroism . . .
It used to be that the express train hurtled forward—
The tracks had been dismantled through an oversight.
It seemed that a catastrophe was unavoidable.
And there were people there! A boy scout came along.
He climbed atop the danger spot
Took off a crimson tie from round his neck
And waved the brightly colored fabric. The engineer
Looked out the locomotive.
He understood: there's something fishy here.
Adroitly he maneuvered all the levers
And the catastrophe was thus averted.

Or another case. Express was flying by.
The tracks had been dismantled through an oversight.
It seemed that a catastrophe was unavoidable.
And there were people there! An aged switchman
Stepped out onto the danger spot,
with pen-knife opened up a vein.
He stained a rag with boiling blood,
and waved the brightly colored fabric. The engineer
Looked out the locomotive,
He understood: there's something fishy here.
Adroitly he maneuvered all the levers
And the catastrophe was thus averted.

But now, if it happens that the train is going,
There's good track stretching out to the horizon.
Conditions great, so know or study
Or work, combine your job with
A correspondence course.
All has changed. The boy scout's now a grownup.
He's gone a bit to fat and really mellowed.
Become a railway supervisor.
He bawls the aged switchman out
And threatens to pack him off to the AA.

To Aleksey Magarik

Something on prison and painting.
With foam in the mouth and a tear.
Kostroma or Velikie Luki—
But at table in honor of Gulag.
This song is about how a son, now gray-haired,
With official permission returned to his home.
He drank some at Nina's and cried some at Kari's—
Oh my Lord, O my God!

Our station stands out in the open
A gutter is lisping in personal tongues.
They sing separation on platforms
Take hooligans off the east.

All day long there are people and bread,
And cargoes strategic which travel the homeland.
Something about ruined life—
My taste's undemanding.

In fall go on out to the wide-open field
Cool your brow with the wind of your homeland.
A swallow of alcohol is like a boiling rose,
It twists and it turns in your chest.
A night of the ravenous family twists
While distances whistle through fingers.
The fatherland hasn't got aliens,
And anyway everything's here—and the air feels

As if you awoke on an overcast day
Banged around and then carried the slops out,
And brushed your ridiculous hopes right away,
And they take you away, underground, in the distance
A pond, covered with goose bumps,
A semaphore's burning with all of its might,
Rain drips and an unshaven passerby
Speaks to himself as he walks.

To Aleksander Soprovsky

> *"In vain in the days of great council*
> *Where places are given great passion*
> *The post of poet's left vacant:*
> *It's dangerous if not empty.*
>
> *But do I really not count in five-year plans . . ."*
> etc.
>
>   *B. Pasternak*

When, having moved aside the logs with cutting edge,
The blade of flame comes into view,
And the hallucination of versification
Comes rushing on me from afar;
When Elbrus, like a flaming double-headed

Snowdrift—and I was there— is heading skyward
And when you vainly fight the chill
And tell yourself "snap out of it";
When my calling is beyond the law
And in the mirror guilt and graying hair,
And right at hand, how timely,
Are novels of Dumas and Stevenson;
When, at the established moment, through
The singing of parolees, through the smash and bang they
Announce by radio that someone got
Seven years and five extra breaking rocks,—
Pasternak's prattle comes to mind.
Where have you led us, o chatter?
And cursing, fearing darkness
"Away from me" I stubbornly say.
"You are a king,"—I quote. It is the poet's choice
To sweat at his beloved fantasy,
And, wandering the whole wide world, to revere,
To sing the praises of Vladimir Bukovsky.

Ah yes, the lilac this May. Bulging clusters
Topple fences in the villages. And in the darkness
They touch your face on the surrounding boulevards. A soul-stirring smell.
Crush your heart with your hands. Head for home like a blind man
Here on the boulevards I met a naked pre-schooler for the first time.
An archer with an artful face; the kid shoots real well!
A lot of water's gone under the bridge. Only an old splinter
Miraculously survived in the flesh. That'll pass too I think.
In the morning I sat here, proudly, legs crossed, near the entrance
To the gloomy abyss of the subway, a lilac branch in hand.
Blew smoke rings through my nose, drank seltzer at rush hour
Smiled and, in my heart, spake unto my fellows:
"Fools, where are you crowding? Oafs, I'm nineteen.
Never worked since the day I was born, and don't intend to start
Do you know my secret? You won't find it out.
I spent the night with Laisa. Viktor Zoilich's got horns.

To carry on a learned conversation
With dead poets, year after year;
To pace the room in darkness
In nether regions and to nod upon a book.
And with nasty grin recall
Natalya, Lidia, and Anna as you doze;
To gulp down pills; eat sloppily
And greedily at friends', and miserly at home;
Not to recognize yourself before the mirror
In that mangy monkey with the wettish mouth,
Like a proper gypsy from some show,
Somehow stuck with a railway-station relative;
And to let yourself down, as if lowering yourself
Into the green abyss, and splaying out your arms . . .

The dawn came late. The blanket slid
Down to the floor. A grayish light
Came peeping through the blinds and bit by bit
On one thing and another did alight.
And as it skipped inconstantly
And separated light and dark
A ray fell crosswise onto "Bagging
Deer." The shivering stag
Flew headlong. An ardent hunter
Was leaning on his rifle stock.
The light now touches lilac-
colored grapes and the smoky bottles
Of last night's feast. A pack
Of playing cards, a pomegranate
Peel. Now it traced a pellmell
Pattern on the dresser. A drunken smell
Came wafting from outside—making moonshine.
A turkey wallowed in the grime.
They went out somewhere on a whim
Wherever feet would go they went.
You clamber up the neighboring slope
And you could see from up on top

That overnight the first autumnal snow
Had cloaked the distant peaks.
You open up a pack of cigarettes
Upon the gloomy cobbled beach.
There is a kind of painful secret
Contained within this junk-filled scene.
A rusted-out old anchor,
A broken rake, a magazine.
October's oblique waves
Are cold and green.
I'm sure that far from shore
On the horizon of gray water
A tourist boat will sail right by
At just precisely half past five.
Batum-Sukhumi via Poti.
It's gone that way for years
And seagulls in their circling flight
Above it soar and squawk and jeer.
I've been aboard that boat.
It's always packed. The hold as well
Is filled with tourist dolts—
And drinking, hubbub, noise.
Bad beer's consumed in quantities immense
And Bonny M tapes, noisome scents.
A lazy local barman is
The ruler of the upper deck.
He's always singing pop tunes
And crossing ogling eyes.
He pours and plays betimes.
Above his head hangs
Uncle Joe, beside him
In an oval foil frame
Quite carefully controlled
Some kind of German dame
Is baring both her rosy legs.
They drink and sing on every side,
While bubbling out behind the boat
There shines a living liquid frost.
Walk down twelve steps and you'll retrieve
Your bags inside the drunken hold.

There's little money—lots of grief.
Batum is in the searchlight's aureole.
While out upon the pier, an iron-toothed
Old lady, breathing bathtub gin
(my angel of death will be akin
To her), can help you find a roof.
Get up, go on now aimlessly
Through blackberry blankness.
October's oblique waves
Are cold and green.
The light goes on in early dusk.
My arrow dozed unluckily
Above the sofa back.
And feeling feather-light the stag leapt.
This is the life. A pull of seltzer water.
Ignore the calendar.
Take all into account, except . . .
But that, they said in bygone days,
Is something for another tale.
I dream of tranquil hamlets
Quite near the Georgian summits.
For now my memory's still hale.

Olga Sedakova

OLGA SEDAKOVA was born in 1949 in Moscow, where she received her degree in philology from the Slavic and Balkan Languages Institute. Her first book was published in Paris. She is one of the most prominent poets of the younger generation. Translations are by Andrew Wachtel.

Statement

A gigantic portion of the meaning of poems consists of their being directed to an addressee who understands them completely. The person who finds him/herself to be the one to whom all these things, with their words, rhythms, vowels, etc., are directed is unlikely to desire outside explanations—including those provided by the author. It seems to me that this point of direction cannot be empty: *Someone* is looking at a painting that is locked in a storeroom, someone who appeared together with that painting. Words that have been heard and understood by another, a rhythm that has satisfied someone enter the poet's head. Mysticism? And why not, after all? Why not use this discredited word? In verse form, which somehow makes everything acceptable, such an idea doesn't bother anyone, and it doesn't seem "mystical":

> And the unseen eyebeams crossed, for the roses
> Had the look of flowers that are looked at.
>
> —T. S. Eliot

As soon as things get truly serious and important, it turns out that we lack acceptable formulae or comprehensible expressions. We only have words that grate on the civilized ear, like *mystical* or *the soul,* or metaphors that cannot be explicated any further. It's no accident that the important things elude our grasp and cluster around nebulous and unconcretizable words that serve to register flickering reality (here for someone, absent for another; a name now full of meaning, now empty). They, that is, the important things do this, I believe, out of love of freedom (their own freedom), which perhaps more than anything else differentiates them from things of a different order—not so important or serious things—and out of love for our freedom, without which we are useless to them. I'd prefer not to speak of these things using words like *invisible, otherworldly,* or *transcendental* . . . For they are also free of their own invisibility, otherworldliness, and transcendentalism, the realms into which quotidian thinking likes to herd them, and of the images in which it likes to lock them up so as not to be disturbed by them further . . . Capturing these free actors—or, rather, having been captured by them—art shares with them their doubts in the world, their unconfirmability, their flickering and selective existence, all comprehending and taking all on faith.

For anyone who would like a guaranteed and perfect organization of everything on earth, or for anyone who hopes that this will come someday, the eternal freedom of the most important things in the world (which extends even to their names) cannot but be experienced as misfortune. But any attempt to get around this quality or to tame it resembles the strategy of the Grand Inquisitor and his famous conclusion: "You have overrated humankind."

As strange as it may sound, the main problem for me is poetry and truth, or, more simply, poetic truth. Reduced to questions of "poetry and prose" or, even more narrowly, to "poetic speech and prosaics" or "conventional poetry and free verse," it seems to me that this problem has been resolved completely unjustly in our contemporary poetry. We associate "truth" with low style, everyday detail, ordinary emotions, and ordinary (or eccentric, which is generally the same thing) "ideas." What amazes me is the span of this leveling evolution. Perhaps "lowering" was innovative and truthful in Wordsworth's time and in general in any period when the lyric soars overmuch. But today where is the overblown high style of thought and expression, the sublime? Who is "brought back down to earth" by prosaic elements? No one, I think . . . Maybe we have already reached the limit of where "lowering" can go to get closer to "truth." Perhaps the limit is that social nobody described by Rubinshtein's verses on cardboard or Kabakov's blank pieces of paper. The conceptualists are more correct than the others in the sense that they are logical: They don't try to say too much. But it's possible not to try to say too much in other ways.

To make this all clear, let's recall an old but still useful literary hero—Tolstoy's Ivan Ilich. In the course of his literary life one can see two "truths," or moments of lucidity. The subject of the nihilist avant-garde is the "normal" world of Ivan Ilich. The subject I like is what Ivan Ilich sees when he is finally torn away from his normalcy by his impending death—that which he *really* sees at the end. (Leo Tolstoy doesn't tell us all that much about this.) The point is not death, but there's no other way to crack such a difficult person as Ivan Ilich. What could he possibly see, or what do other Tolstoyan heroes see in their dreams, or partial ravings? "Life after life"? "Another world"? It seems to me that he simply sees the *real,* the real that is perfectly at home in our world. If we say that this is all behind his back we're not correct—we're just attributing to things the tendency of our own eyes not to see what they don't want to see. There's nothing to see in those things, we say, except perhaps behind their backs. It's that *real, what is in fact that* I, speaking in the first person, would call the truth of poetry. Its discourse strikes me as reassuring and comforting, but that comfort and assurance are such that it is easier to put up with the repulsive unhappiness of meaningless "reality." Which is, in fact, what we do.

But from the technical point of view: How can we express this discourse in the first person? I imagine that we paint a portrait of a speaker in human form. We paint what is subjective in a person, intentions, as opposed to those "objective" features that a person doesn't choose (this is how love views another being). It may well turn out that the portrait does not even reproduce the features of the person's face. Perhaps only something like the pupil remains, like Malevich's Black Square or some other kind of shape . . .

But despite what one might conclude from all this, the ideal exact replication of this discourse in the first person appears to me not as a configuration far distant from any recognizable form, nor as a word that in its multivalence has lost all connection with the dictionary. Quite the opposite. The goal (is it reachable?) seems to me to be a new union of this "discourse" with the form of the "speaker," a newfound recognition of the thing incarnate. As if the thing and the word in the dictionary are one and the same but opened from both ends, like a present, like news, like endless meaning . . .

From the Cycle Stellae and Inscriptions

broken hexameter

To Nina Braginskaya
who has studied antique epitaphs, and much else, insightfully

A Boy, an Old Man, and a Dog

A boy, an old man, and a dog. Perhaps its the grave of
a crone or a woman. How can we know
what a person's reflection will be
                        when looking into the watery deep
that's alabaster smooth?
                              It could be like this:
A boy, a dog, an old man.
                       The boy is especially sad.
—I've done wrong, dad, but I'll never be able to right it.
—Well—the old man says,—I forgive you but you
                            will not hear,
it's nice here.
—It's nice here?
—It's nice here?—
An echo is heard
in the hallways.
                    —So you called and I came.
Hi, dad. They redid the bedrooms at home,
Mama is pining
               —My son, my late, my only, listen to me,
I'm speaking in parting: to nobility always adhere,
It's the best that the living can do . . .
                 —Mama told me to say . . .
—You'll be happy.
             —When?
             —Always.
         —That's hard to take.
         —What can you do
that's how it is with us

                    In silence the dog is observing
the talk: the eyes of that white water,
of that picture—
A boy, a dog, an old man.

The Figure of a Woman

                    Having turned away,
She stands in a large
                    and voluminous shawl. It seems there's a poplar
next to her. It seems that way. There's no poplar.
But she would be willing to turn into one
Just like in the legend—
If only not to hear:
—What do you see there?
—What do I see, you lunatic people?
I see the wide open sea—That's easy to guess . . .
The sea and that's all.
                                    Or is that too little,
for me to eternally grieve, while your curiosity's piqued?

Two Figures

Brother and sister?
husband and wife?
daughter and father?
all that and more?
Which of them died, who is alive to order this slab,
a monument to meeting?
Who wanted whom to remember
at parting? not meekly, not greedily.
                                    One doesn't
have to remember much: we can't take a lot.
Native earth, just a bit, in an alien land—that is enough.
The rest will remain where it feels right at home.
An attentive glance, death, you won't take away the legitimate
handful
from the one who is leaving, still grieving for us.

                                        Who is that leaving?
who, having pined during long separation, just barely
will finally touch the dear hand?—
                              shadow to shadow, past to past,
pale to pale. What do they say there?
They are saying:
                         —It's like that.
                    —I swear that it's like that.
                    —It was and it will be,
even if it won't be. Like that.
                         O, passerby,
love life. Offer thanks for it.
Spirits don't need much:
a monument to meeting.

Mistress and Servant

A woman looks into a mirror: what she sees can't be seen;
It's unlikely that anything's there.
                              On the other hand, why then is she
admiring one thing and figuring out how to fix something else
with one trick or another? why study herself?
It's clear something's there. Something that needs an affectionate
balm,
pendants and beads.
                         The servant stands silent
awaiting a wish that she'll never fulfill.
Yes, we never understood each other. That's understandable.
It wasn't hard. Something else was harder. We knew
all about everyone. All, to the end, to its
final and tender infinity.
Not wishing, not thinking—we knew.
Not listening—knew
and considered their wish in our minds, the wish that they
never had time to make known or to think about even. Of course.
For we've all got but one single wish. And there's nothing besides
that wish.

Pitcher. Tombstone of a Friend

You want—a pitcher, you want—a spear, you want—a distaff.
And if they lied when they spoke of the ringlet, about how it was
found in the sky,
they lied for a reason.
In the most trivial thing, saddened minds will discover
the stuff that makes up constellations,
the sounds of inaudible names,—
it will burst into flame and curl upwards,
like a garland in garlands which soothe mortal hearts:
Every evening Perseus rescues Andromeda—everyone knows
which star it's that saves him, having snapped up
the one who is no longer with us.
So give him whatever you want.
You want a pitcher, you want a spear, you want a distaff,
whatever comes up, as he won't ask for more. And then that will
be able
to become like everything. All one must do is to not clutch at
everything.
Put copper coins in their places. He'll figure it out by himself
He'll lift up a hand of a kind that we never saw here,
the hand of a constellation:
Take it, o boatman, you see,
how we live here on earth:
Distaff, Plough. Spear. Pitcher.

Child Playing

In anticipation we live through
that which will never be. Great glory.
The wedding night, sage energetic old age.
Grandchildren—the children of a nonexistent son.
No, empty dreams do not play with men's hearts.
The child knows what soothes him.
What he plays with.
We don't see the face. We look upon it, like a mother
did, through the door, and we peacefully go away:
he is playing.

A white ray on the floor.
—He'll play some more,
I'll have time to do all that I must.
Time doesn't wait, he is playing.
Before the disaster our anticipation deserts us:
Now it's not external, it's we ourselves. Sublimely
in this inaudible music, in the white room.
That's how he plays at the heart,
a child, who's playing checkers.

Inscription

Nina, in a dream, or my mind—we were walking
one time on some old-fashioned road,
Alongside, as it seemed to me, various
white and smoothed-out flagstones.
—Not the Appian, some other one,—
you said to me,—it's not that important, the number of roads
in their cities that crossed from one grave to another
was legion.
—Hello!—we heard—
hello! (that, as we know, is the favorite word upon parting)
Hello! How clearly you look at the earth that's so dear.
Stop: I look with the eyes of the gigantic earth.
Only the emptiness looks. Only the unseen can see.
So go ahead faster or I'll leave you behind.

Lev Rubinshtein

LEV RUBINSHTEIN was born in 1947. Since the 1960s he has been a central figure in the Moscow conceptualist movement. He studied philology at Moscow State University and now works as a librarian. In 1991 he was a participant in "Crossing Boundaries: The Soviet New Wave" in San Francisco. Translations are by Gerald J. Janecek.

Statement

1.

The artistic system which I profess—it is customarily designated "Moscow conceptualism"—deals not so much with language as with consciousness. More accurately—with complex interrelationships between individual artistic consciousness and general cultural consciousness.

As far as the problem of language is concerned, this then is rather a problem of *languages,* i.e., the interrelationship of different spheres of language, different *genres* of language, in specific cases—genres of literature.

Characteristic for this system are genre dislocations and even formal-typological dislocations: colloquial speech in the role of poetic speech and vice-versa, a fragment of prose in the role of a line of verse and vice-versa, etc.

The problem of *newness* is resolved not on the level of style but on the level of *relationship with style.* It is generally a system of relationships and the elucidation of relationships—between the presence and absence of an author in the text, between "one's own" and "others'" speech, between direct and metaphoric meaning...

2.

Each fragment of my text (in the original) is placed on a separate sheet of paper or card. This is the format in which the majority of my things exist, beginning with the 1970s.

What is the purpose of this "card system" for me? First of all it is a material metaphor for my understanding of the text as an object, as a three-dimensional unit, and of reading as a movement into the depths, a sequential removal and overcoming of layers, a metaphor for my understanding of reading as a labor, a spectacle, and a game.

Each card is a universal unit of rhythm which is equal to any speech gesture—be it a line of verse, a developed theoretical remark, a fragment of descriptive prose, an excerpt from a telephone conversation, a stage direction, or an expletive. Cards that are blank serve to articulate the realm of silence, but the rhythmic and semantic role of this in my poetics is another subject.

A Little Nighttime Serenade

1.

Nightingale, my nightingale
He appeared here in the dale!

2.

Like a phantom in the dale
There appears a nightingale!

3.

Nightingale, my nightingale,
Where are you, where in the dale?

4.

In the leafy hills and dale
Sang his song the nightingale!

5.

Look, he's there, the nightingale!
Flying all around the dale!

6.

See amid the hills and dale,
Joyful herald, nightingale!

7.

Tell us now, O nightingale,
What you see throughout the dale!

8.

Foo! Right here in nearby dale
Heartthrobs at the nightingale!

9.

Mischievous small nightingale
Singing always in the dale!

10.

From the hidden, secret dale
He attends us, nightingale!

11.

Night angel—the nightingale
Flitters-twitters from the dale!

12.

In the moonlit dwelling dale
He has settled, nightingale!

13.
Muse's captive, nightingale
In the hidden, secret dale!
14.
That is he here in the dale—
Muses' favorite—nightingale!
15.
You and I, O nightingale—
We're alone amid the dale!
16.
(Applause)
17.
-I wonder whether premonitions come true or not?
18.
-What premonitions do you mean?
19.
-Well, there are certain premonitions . . .
20.
-About what?
21.
-It doesn't matter. If they're right, you'll find out . . .
22.
-Oh, well . . .
23.
(Pause)
24.
People are not nightingales,
Even if they're in the dale!
25.
People are not drums to beat,
Even if they beat the heat!
26.
People are not flocks of clouds,
Even if they're strong and proud!
27.
People are not piles of cliffs,
Even if they pant and sniff!
28.
People are not god knows what,
Even if they wear a coat!

29.
People simply aren't like that,
Even if they're just old farts!
30.
People are so necessary,
Even if they're solitary!
31.
People are not solitary,
If they're really necessary!
32.
People surely get th' idea,
If they're just not idiots!
33.
People are not idiots,
Even if they miss th' idea!
34.
People are not human beings,
If they're not true human beings!
35.
People would not be against
Saying no to fighting fights!
36.
(Applause)
37.
-You already know?
38.
-You have what in mind?
39.
-The same thing as you.
40.
-But I don't understand...
41.
-Yes, you do. Yes, you do.
42.
-No, I don't understand...
43.
-So you don't understand, never mind.
44.
-Well, if I don't have to, I don't have to.

45.
(Pause)
46.
People go to many places
Where there's quiet contemplation!
47.
People go to many places
Where they feel they have to be!
48.
People go to many places
Where they've stopped expecting them!
49.
People go to many places
Where they're not expected now!
50.
People go to many places
Which they can no longer leave!
51.
People go to many places
Where they're now at home for good!
52.
People go to many places!
People go to many places!
53.
(Applause)
54.
-The air burst aloud . . .
55.
-What say? Allowed?
56.
-Not allowed, aloud.
57.
-But I heard "allowed." That sounds even better.
58.
-Maybe it's better, but I said: "The air burst aloud."
59.
-I already understood what you said, but "allowed" is still better.
60.
(Pause)

61.

-Yes . . . Levels of communication . . .

62.

-What about "levels of communication"?

63.

-Here's what I think: there is, no doubt, a means of attaining those levels
of communication which are unattainable by any other means . . .

64.

-Well, no doubt . . .

65.

-So there you have it. But you say . . .

66.

-I say?

67.

(Pause)

68.

People need to sing a song,
If the soul requires it!

69.

People have to have some love,
Or they're not true human beings!

70.

People have to suffer some—
Thus they purify themselves!

71.

People have to sleep a bit—
When they have a headache pain!

72.

People have to have just all
That they think is necessary!

73.

People have to live a bit
If they are true human beings!

74.

People have to live a bit!
People have to live a bit!

75.

(Applause)

76.

-It's important to find rhythm and order even in noise.

77.
-But are they there?
78.
-They are. You only have to listen carefully.
79.
-Then that's no longer noise . . .
80.
-Then that's no longer noise.
81.
-Then, of course . . .
82.
(Pause)
83.
People cannot live aright
Without being allowed to sing!
84.
People cannot live aright
Without being allowed to love!
85.
People cannot live aright
Without being allowed to suffer!
86.
People cannot live aright
If they do not have a thing!
87.
People cannot live aright
Without being allowed to die!
88.
People cannot live aright!
People cannot live aright!
89.
(Applause)
90.
-I don't understand . . .
91.
-What don't you understand?
92.
-I don't understand a thing!
93.
-What do you mean "a thing"?

94.
-Just what it means. I don't understand, that's all!
95.
-Strange...
96.
(Lengthy pause)

97.
(Applause)

From Thursday to Friday

1.
All night I dreamed of the borderline regions of being. When I woke up, I could remember only something between water and land, silence and speech, sleep and waking, and managed to think: "Here it is, the aesthetics of indeterminacy. And here it is again..."

2.
I dreamed as if he whose tracks, it seemed, had grown cold suddenly appeared and looked at me so well, so attentively, that I woke up with a pounding heart...

3.
I dreamed that it would be necessary to get up and look to see whether he was asleep or not. When I woke up, for a long time I couldn't remember who I had in mind. Then I remembered...

4.
I dreamed that it would be necessary to be closed inside myself until a certain time, and there, as they say, it would be obvious. When I woke up, I thought: "Well, I don't know, I don't know..."

5.
I dreamed as if joy indeed knew no bounds. When I woke up, I thought: "Yes, of course..."

6.
I had a dream that only four times in life is a genuine opportunity presented. When I woke up, I thought there was definitely something to that...

7.
I had a dream as though the main thing was to find the most adequate form of sympathy for one another. Then I woke up...

8.

I had a dream that the idea of a clean piece of paper was the short circuit to any consistent aesthetic experience. Then I woke up . . .

9.

I had a dream that one could take as a point of departure that our sense of self is the sense of self of characters which have created themselves and which figure in their appropriate time and space. And that the point of departure for such a sense of self in fact also brings us closer together. Then I woke up . . .

10.

I dreamed of two whole arguments in my favor, but of course I couldn't remember them . . .

11.

I dreamed also of a third argument. But it, too, remained there, in the dream . . .

12.

I dreamed of the long-awaited appearance of a hero. He often had a gloomy look, but there was also no doubt of his readiness to make merry. What was quite impressive was his open and intense relationship with reality.

When I woke up, I thought there was nothing to add to that . . .

13.

I dreamed of rare flitterings of dying hopes. They didn't shine, didn't warm, but only quietly decomposed in the breezeless depths of consciousness.

I managed to get used to them; my tired brain hardly ever focused on them; when they appeared, my head no longer tossed upward as before, my nostrils didn't dilate, my pulse didn't increase. Nothing, it seemed, could disrupt my despondent calmness. Nothing, it seemed, portended change.

14.

I dreamed of trees plunged into deep meditation in an old park. Down its shaded lane toward me moved a solitary figure. I noticed it already from afar and almost immediately guessed who it was. And you, too, no doubt have guessed . . .

15.

I dreamed that they were obviously not alone there. Someone was sneaking about noiselessly in the night like a thief. "Quiet," Henrich said with just his lips, "don't you hear something?" Both listened intently. Again quiet returned. And suddenly as though lightning had cut the darkness . . .

16.

I dreamed of creaking floorboards and threadbare rugs in a little board-inghouse on the shore of the lake at Baden. The weather during these days was rainy and unpleasant. The landlady of the boardinghouse was a kind, frail woman of fifty. At the table there were usually about ten or twelve guests. They were all of various nationalities, had different customs and interests. There was absolutely nothing to talk about; the dinner was bland. Boredom and despondency reigned at the table.

Meanwhile one of the guests drew my attention. He was a young Italian of sickly appearance who was silent all the time and only rarely threw strange, somehow indeterminate glances as if something no one but himself noticed was drawing him out of his usual stupor for a moment...

17.

I dreamed of the massive gray building of a steamship company. It was located two paces from my apartment of the time. And my windows looked out on the same dismal square. And past my windows every morning and evening marched a faceless line of office workers. Could I have predicted at the time...

18.

I dreamed of little Kolya's groundlessly happy face and the concentrated faces of his relatives and the impatient face of the driver and all the other faces—of relatives, acquaintances, people hardly known or completely unknown. They were all becoming diffuse in Konstantin's foggy consciousness, were coalescing into one rapidly rotating spot, and he, like someone cut down, was falling to the damp asphalt on an empty morning train platform...

19.

I dreamed of his sharp, unpleasant voice monotonously repeating one and the same phrase (unfortunately I don't remember it—something about our not living properly). Nadezhda Ivanovna was meanwhile becoming covered with raspberry-colored spots, Anatoly was mechanically tittering, and hard-of-hearing Semyon Lazarevich was smiling at each and every one with uniform affection. Strukov was trying not to look at anyone: He felt ashamed and nauseous.

Meanwhile it had been raining nonstop for the third day now and god only knew how it all would have ended if...

20.

I dreamed as if the situation were such that, if a pure and trembling voice had arisen suddenly amid the inarticulate roar of the crowd, then it too would have become aghast at the gnashing. And those who would have heard it, would have only looked around, nodded their intelligent heads and perhaps with this it would all have ended if...

21.

I dreamed that we all had to live by touch: Here's a hole to crawl into, here a fence, there a solid stone wall...And our life was passing from decision to doubt, from nods to expletives, from daydreams to drudgery...

22.

I had a dream as if the light went out somewhere there in the middle. And the voice crying in the desert was no longer audible. And the warmth had been disbursed—never to return. Only glass looking at glass—fleeting and inarticulate...

23.

I dreamed of acrid smoke and my own death mask...What will we give as a souvenir of ourselves? What will we hold on to in the final analysis? Grace is not received—and we now walk not in pairs. This is so elementary that it isn't worth explaining...

24.

I dreamed that at night the heart is taken from its scabbard. What do we know? What can we do? Let him who knows be silent...

25.

I dreamed of the emptiness of the sky. In it you, my girl, and I were both lost. You said: "That swallow sitting over there will remember you and me to the grave..."

26.

I dreamed as if we were saying farewell on a bridge...We're tired—we'll rest...nature is not without purpose after all...We are hardly guaranteed an ecstatic reception...And you and I together cannot assume what will happen a day from now, no less two days from now...A final meeting... We say farewell on the bridge...

27.

I had a dream that he lay in the damp earth deranged. And the long flame of a candle burned heatedly.

28.

I dreamed as if he had lain down in the sand forever. Who, if not he, could understand the earth's turmoil? And that all is not the way it is... And that the message is unclear...

And now our dear friend is weaving around above the earth...

Let's go there, too, where water does not want to flow. Where brains crumble, where there are screeches and total darkness...Let's go, too—it's time, time for us to leave this clime. We assumed we would have our own lives, but that's what you get...

29.

I dreamed toward morning of a snow-swept balcony, my colt's withers splashed with red and killed by fangs, the extinguishing of lustrous fishes instead of the avenging glances of wolves dashing into the forest.

I heard over my shoulder the fleeting outcry of a gun, an insane chuckle instead of the screech of a falling animal...

A stallion expiring, white steam from a gaping doorway, a continuing blizzard, a ski trail overgrown with snow...

30.

I had a dream that my ship was going to the bottom scarcely breathing. And I was creating a wonderful prayer in the stormy expanse...

31.

I dreamed of a couple of trivia—stupor and patience. Meanwhile we would hide our beaks in our feathers at the intersection of draughts. We know the value of the one and the other. But who to leave in charge of the stage when we take up the staff and the knapsack? And how to walk into such a mist not for just an hour, not for just a day, but for a thousand years—with a huge finger in the pocket, tête-à-tête with the cold wind?

32.

I dreamed as if they—my remaining days—were running, looming ahead of me, having left me behind.

A tremor of six transparent wings uncovered much for me in me, and I woke up...

33.

I dreamed as if he were here, sitting on the edge of the bed. But it is clear that indeed he is here and at the same time is not here.

Who would know, if not he, that all is not as it was before, that there is no haven for hope and the unbiased mind.

A tremor of six transparent wings uncovered much for me in me, and I woke up...

34.

I had a dream in the morning of a semi-demon in a gilded frame, a semi-corpse with many eyes. He said: "It's not worth waiting—a miracle won't happen. If you have somewhere to run, then get out of here." He said: "Why don't you go with me and I'll show you the way."

And with a heavy head I woke up...

35.

I dreamed of a balance of paper and memory moving off toward sleep. To the accompaniment of flowing moisture I slept through yet another spring.

A definition of the meaning of existence twisted on my tongue and pinched. But a long ray fell on the blanket, and I woke up . . .

36.

I dreamed as if sleep brought relief, but also took something away forever. And I woke up . . .

37.

I dreamed of the expression "a blocked muse." Waking up, I lay for a long time with open eyes . . .

38.

I dreamed that retelling dreams which you don't remember—was also something to do. Waking up, I thought: "So what?"

39.

In a dream the question was asked whether it mattered who cried from what onions. Waking up, I wondered whether it really did matter . . .

40.

I had a dream that if they said "Today is Thursday" on Thursday, then that meant that today was Thursday. If they said "Today is Thursday" on Friday, then this was either a lie or a mistake or something else . . .

Waking up, I thought that really what was important after all was not only what was said, but also when . . .

41.

I had a dream that it was as if we were sitting here and doing the same as right now. Waking up, I thought that there was nothing all that unusual in that . . .

42.

I dreamed of an innumerable multitude of other possibilities and variations.

Waking up, I tried for a long time to remember something, anything at all . . .

43.

Already on the edge of sleep and waking I dreamed that what was really was.

Waking up, I thought: "Well, that's right . . ."

Nadezhda Kondakova

NADEZHDA KONDAKOVA, born in 1944, lives in Moscow. Her first book, *Miraculous Day,* was published in 1975, and her most recent collection, *I Love—and Therefore I'm Right,* was published in 1989. She is a member of the Writer's Union. She visited the United States as a participant in "Crossing Boundaries: The Soviet New Wave," a poetry and arts festival in San Francisco in 1991.

I'll go there, I don't know where

> *No great artist ever sees things*
> *as they really are. If he did,*
> *he would cease to be an artist.*
> —*Oscar Wilde*

To tell the truth, I don't as yet know what poetry is, for whom, nor why it's necessary. Or rather, my new *knowledge,* primitive in its unexpectedness, leads me aside each time, away from the intuitively felt proximity of the main road. It's like mushroom hunting or being lost a-wandering in a forest entirely of birches: you return following your own footprints but come out on the far side. Moreover, you remember the message of the Russian folktale: go there, I don't know where; bring that, I don't know what.

   Probably it's true that the fear of forgetting a word gave birth to poetry. In this precataclysmic (or euphoric?) experiencing of life or language (the word *yazik* [language] confounds the words *I, speak,* and *shriek*) combinations of words appear, as if torn out of a forgotten context that has lost its original meaning. Unquestionably throughout its existence poetry has rejected the prose of human language, just as practical language rejects the sound equivalence in poetry. Poetry is bound to sounds and essences, like lightning from

the Prophet Elijah's chariot and an oak sundered by it. And in this sense
poetry is a highly selective phenomenon.

An orientation toward the masses, as cultivated in Soviet poetry from
the 1930s through the 1970s, is nothing but an attempt to cross artistic
creativity with the office monster—socialist realism. Here, in passing, I would
note that for the best poets of the so-called new wave, this monster either
didn't exist at all or it lived in the realm of ironic consciousness and awareness
of our surrealistic reality.

The greatest influence on me, I think, was Salvador Dali, sprouting
from the soil, during the thawing-stagnant time of my growing up, through
the barbed wire of the regime, fearlessly breaking through the terror that
was in our genes and through our distrust of the Word. Or, rather, in different
years different teachers came along, and their overcoming of their experiences
in their work marked out my own personal path "from the Varangians to
the Greeks," through the poetry of Nekrasov, "A Knight for an Hour," great
but beyond language, through a fatal struggle with the age of Akhmatova
and Mandelstam—closer to a velimirkhlebnikovian soaring in language and
bathing in sounds that long to be speech, free from the "quotidian intellect."

Magically flowering sound rows in the space of live speech excite my
mind more than all the philosophical books in the world taken together,
since "lubomudre," *love of wisdom* (thus Russians from the beginning literally
translated *philo sophia*) only explains the world, but the word creates the
world anew. In the word itself the highest sense of being is hidden, and
therefore its parsing, like a new collection of morphologs, results not in the
simple mental game called punning but in the drilling of essence-bearing
(essence, real) chinks that make our life unsenseless, but sense is unfeelingless.

Now for the main thing: Inner freedom, that "caesura between inhaling
and exhaling snow," which I (all of us = all, less all who are not us) didn't
receive but endured and nurtured within myself despite the conditions of
aesthetic and ethical totalitarianism. I should say that my literary destiny
began in August, 1968. Exactly at that time, a few days before "the march
of the tanks," I passed my exams and was accepted into the Literary Institute.
Thus, the end of "Prague spring" automatically introduced my generation
to the regime of "least propitiousness." Further "events" followed one after
another: the crushing of *Novy Mir,* the firing of the main editor, the trials
of dissidents, the expulsion of Solzhenitsyn. In contrast with the generation
of the 1960s, which had time to taste the fruit of its own unrestrained social
criticism (although nowadays for the most part it looks quite innocuous), we
chose in literature (and partially also in life) something else. Some (Sasha
Sokolov, Yurii Kublanovsky, etc.), semianonymous (compared to the famous

Aksyenov and Gladilin), became émigrés, while others emigrated to strict scientific libraries and the secret libraries of their friends—to Berdyayev, Rozanov, Shchestov, Shpengler, Danilevsky, to early Slavophiles, late Westerners, to Sartre, Camus, Nabokov, and once again Nabokov. Thus, the best of my generation today have a lot of free time, while our literature, exhausted by vivisection and confiscations, appears before our readers more or less complete.

Personally I use this time only in order to nurture in myself a bird with double vision, revealed to me suddenly during the days of the Chernobyl catastrophe, in the summer of the year nineteen-hundred-and-fatal:

seeing "The Danaë" my vision doubled
in detail I saw another cell
not a woman and not paranoia
but the nest a swallow makes with saliva

Translated by Lyn Hejinian and Elena Balashova (extract from poem translated by Jean Day and Elena Balashova).

Double Vision

what can one say of détente between empires
the bolt is rusty and the computer's jammed
the pound-keepers are happy
outlaughing us panthers of the zoo
                    hell is superfluous

what can one say of dissonance
when its depth is reduced to a framework, like a well
and like blame a tide at its mouth holds back
or like rain coursing behind walls
                    one will have to invent hell

what can one say of empires guilty only once
of retinal reverse, singling shoes
swelling the echo of the miracle's scribe
shoved through the slit between Freud and dream
                    hell is doubling

what can one say of sexed competitions
two regimes, two kids in detention
logarithms of a lie looking for sweetness in détente
as hate turns to fear
                    hell or ashes

there is in the materiality of prophetic ideas
a false advantage a euphoria in knowledge
a joy in superiority—Prometheus himself falls
for them—*jedem seine,*[1] final sign
                    in not-hell
              Translated by Jean Day and Elena Balashova.

Tick

against its own foul rinse
the sea rises in defense

---

1. *jedem seine*—German, "to each what he deserves."

ominous
and so the forest might survive its human swill
the tick appears
bouncer of the forest (he lives on the outskirts)
one false move and you're history
as he drops on your neck
kamikaze of the woods
like a burglar (don't look back)
you wear the obstetrician's rubber gloves
and on sterile grass open your pack
splash gas near the crooked birch
and cut the paw-branch fir down with an axe
then you'll see aspen grow
aspen grow lean like Koshchei[2]
stretching long arms to your throat
and as you retreat
you see him, now many
a tactical unit, winding in a heap
like a snake

the war is civil
when nature turns its own to blood

every species' days are numbered
tarpan and heron continue to fall
the ruins of the steppe carry this cross
and the infected Pripyat[3] flows on

       Translated by Jean Day and Elena Balashova.

The Way

from insults bad luck what's left of pain
from the struggle of the street
you appear as if from *Underground*
bullets staring you in the brain

---

2. Koshchei—in Russian fairy tales, a greedy old man.
3. Pripyat—name of both the river and the town where the Chernobyl nuclear reactor accident occurred.

miserable queen at the funeral feast
at the dregs of life's banquet
who recognized or acknowledged you
wretched stand-in for a nightingale

the deaf's hearing is more acute
than the fear of erasure in a bout with acids
knowing the final shirt
only god can take away

from the night-cherries in the school square
from the soft giggling of muses at their party
the way is long from disbelief to faith
and both doors are bloody

Translated by Jean Day and Elena Balashova.

Hobbled Light

the apples have a different, an invisible essence
and teeth bite its nakedness
through a negative just forming its skin of light
the void in its fullness appears

the sum of vacuums then is different
beside the green yoke of zero
beside trajectories of a moving glance
to the filament of a lover's gaze

in space, ach, dust sticks in the throat
its sound almost paper, particulate
and the transparent apple hurries to fall
tearing itself from homeless hands

your eye marks the spot
your lasso draws itself a song
and the river makes its bed
like a bent piston through the Valley of Valdai

but in these valleys and hills you wandered
learning the alphabet of subtraction
the willow's lament, its babble, its shame
the throat's frightened dereliction and pain

and in the grudging sweet of grim commerce
answers echo in the play of tongs
in these ordinary things an unseen essence
but all this material evidence sickens

outside the apple seeds ripen
and the hobbled light rests, an impossible horse
as murder and creation echoing answer
miracles like plague just out of sight

Translated by Jean Day and Elena Balashova.

Pompeii's Binoculars

how do you know the catastrophic
is light—pure, lyrical, and angelic
who in search of your square root missed it
called Matthew a mediocre poet

an unbearable delirium exhausts the soul
irradiated and poisoned
piously imagining the first sinner
and the beautiful child at her feet

feathery rains on goose-grass rustle like foil
independent of eternal themes
and wrapped in thunderheads by blind engineers
lightning bolts sleep like angels over the earth

over Pripyat's reddened clay
over the memory of families fed
to huge iron throats
blind as nightingales from the beginning

like faked marriages these words are useless
to salve decay the scabs the rust
why repeat them over the oozing sore
immeasurable boundary between them and us
          Translated by Jean Day and Elena Balashova.

Rembrandt

seeing "The Danaë" my vision doubled
in detail I saw another cell
not a woman and not paranoia
but the nest a swallow makes with saliva

having molded a little corner for my infirmary
all my trials I worked into a ball
like a ball of stolen wool or bast
celebrating our native landscapes

in the metro a triangle of knees
I covered with feathery plaid, a shadow
and to the cell whose afterimage I saw
I returned the dead vision after dying

so the capillary fills with good blood
and the sick lantern shows the light of day
the cyclops' universal eyeball broods
as before the Evangelist and before the flood
          Translated by Jean Day and Elena Balashova.

Et Alia

etcetera
that is, those who failed to pass through the needle's eye
weren't listed were not inscribed
leaving a hole in the text
who fell instead backward through earth's vagina

etcetera
that is, those and others
dear strangers like a trace
from the unconscious to nostalgia
chewed to authentic delirium

etcetera
that is, those who at one time
or other, dates erased,
names unrecorded, times mixed up,
deck stacked to the limit . . .

and now the devil take you high and low
among these equally incredible fates
from extreme prejudice to the last mile
etcetera   and so on   et alia

let the verdict be enforced
in the rigged play of a counterfeit game
only dreams and doubts can then remain
of Russia's triangular hole

Bermudian, a memory it can't recall
(inappropriate *and* anathema)

how painful for them to lapse and fall
et alia   et alia   et alia
      Translated by Jean Day and Elena Balashova.

Humus

cut the hot earth
by machine
and an abyss appears abstract and possible
a different measure
as in an hourglass the receding pain
thins before eyes
and the world where you live on the rights of a bird
sprouts like a bean
flourishes in the heavens of empty nights

the tin carts will rumble
through the poor ubiquitous whitewash of stars
and from the veins of birches flow
the immaculate stain of black holes
burnt-out ozones
under the bulldozer worlds open
repulsive and moaning
and in the green twining of shadows without roots
is an overgrown boulevard
where no Stradivarius can match the scraping key
horses play

> Translated by Jean Day and Elena Balashova.

Pseudonym

I cry in the dative and vocative, stay silent in the accusative, guilty only in
your glorious, luminous, magnanimous, circuitous name (I'm afraid to name),
though I hide neither eye's inner rhyme nor the mirror's, where the seer is
sovereign, where in the cauldron of centuries' sinful lilac and tender honey-
suckle madness, dark against dark appears, and they fill with tears—not
from the withering preview of night's heavenly bodies, but because your angel
visited me—not in a woman's disguise—all hips and hair, not in the terrifying
fits of the *oprichnik*[1] (as they were called then) striking crazed heads from
shoulders left and right, brandishing their power, reveling in the moods of
the executioner, whose mutability is endless and finds its kind in anything—
from the single eternal cell to the panopticon, like Pilate (they'll accuse me
here twice). I'm not afraid to be known as Russian or stranger—and I laugh
in the face of my family name (all three hundred years of it) when grief
makes me cry and get all confused—and bitterly I drink to misfortune, paying
real tears to forget . . .

> Translated by Jean Day and Elena Balashova.

---

1. member of a special administrative elite under Tsar Ivan the Terrible.

Honey

like a blue fly in amber
not in vain were you caught in transparent days
and these lucid thoughts
your living tongue can never outgrow

there at the market stand thick-lipped pitchers
and a young woman in a cheap foreign scarf
pours transparent honey into clear jars
pouring and licking from her little finger

there in the gauzy light of collapsing dust
like shadows the transparent cars
there the pale girl in organdy bows
there for your heart the state clock stands

where, if you look at the sun
death, time, and the second are one

      Translated by Jean Day and Elena Balashova.

Butterfly Effect

    To Dr. Vadim Anishchenko, who introduced me to the law of synergetics
    called the "butterfly effect" by American physicists

between two dragonflies a lyre
and in flowers' sex a homeopath dreams
prototype of an extinct world
not in the mind but in numbers lost

pinned at the solar plexus
is his delicate confusion
and the mediastinum tears
as wings discover motion

surpassing light
dividing vision in flight
from equilibrium the lyre like a stranger
suddenly floats beyond sound

and the light of hidden ravings will blaze
as if from nowhere an iceberg rises
into the light of your last sense
of what was once a butterfly

Translated by Jean Day and Elena Balashova.

Ivan Zhdanov

IVAN ZHDANOV was born in Siberia in 1948 and now lives in Moscow. His work has appeared extensively in translation in Europe and the United States. He is an elevator repairman by trade. Two of his books have been published in the Soviet Union: *Portrait* in 1982, and *Unchangeable Sky* in 1990. His work is represented in the Penguin Books anthology *Child of Europe*.

The Personage

For him, you're a newcomer, a deep secret behind the seven seals, another personage among his many visions. He looks into & beyond you & sees something more than the basic fabric. A fool's cap has been placed over his figure, like some glass jar over a fly. As long as it's alive, the fly will flitter back & forth—but for him the enslavement presents a completely different scenario: he doesn't notice the pointed cap, though it follows him like his own shadow & the pursuit's not in the least a dream—he's ready to stretch his hands toward you, as if you too were only a segment of his own apparition. Turn toward his glance & there you'll find the World's Edge, take a step back—& you'll be swallowed by Nothing; yet even then you won't recognize the overturned glass, won't see that for him it's only a panoramic screen these countless personages of his own "I" move through—this disorderly composition of tiny pictures, reproductions of blurred reflections, scraps of film, letters scattered from a case of polygraphs, the torn pieces of what before was a book. The World's Edge begins immediately behind the screen, at that point where the mind's capacity for resolve ends. He can't see himself from a side view: a shroud like the mourning mirror covers his self-consciousness. His "I" surrounded & locked him into the perimeters of this pointed cap. The doors to the outside world were closed long ago, & if not all, then some were confused with others: if you open one door with the sign "director" printed above it—you'll see the vertebrae of the Ural's Ridge diving into the steppes.

What are we, how do we know ourselves? How & what do we know about the line? By intersecting the planes? How do we know about a color? By mixing colors? What do you see looking from within the color's hue, from the inside perspective of the line? And that within my soul, should it also exist beyond its own borders?

He's tarnished, his body's tarnished, but he has no doubts about himself because he speaks on behalf of authority. And here he's a personage from that "tale told by a fool." And that makes him crazy. Keeps him aloof. Isn't it because he understands the system he's become a part of—recognizes that it's immutable, crucial, as if sacred with a sure purpose. And so it goes when identification with something leads to a war—not a war with the system, but with one's own self. Could he really identify himself with it to begin with, make himself an equal partner in this pretense for principles, or a Universal Principle? He castigates himself before he's able to experience the demise of identification. He goes beyond the World's Edge.

But sin—it's not a border freely crossed here & there. It's a panoramic screen, an inscrutable pointed cap, & to enter within this dead zone requires giving up one's sense of sight & sound. And then it means you'll never suspect that others have what you do not.

And yet, no matter how odd, everyone has their personal screen, perhaps they're all collated with one another, maybe even organized within the All-Pervasive Screen, and so, to some extent, they're ghostlike. But to see beyond it beforehand—if nothing else, is one way to abandon it. And so, its light begins to vanish!

Translated by John High and Ivan Burkin.

Hills

This hill in the steppe—naked, not by its own choice—
a tangle of space, a stockade to the light.
The heart's alarmed & swept away by
its heavy rhythm. And yet there's no wind.
The sagebrush skulls like some moaning of the wilderness
stun the senses with their smell of decay, obliterating the path.
And the path sifts the crushed stones into nothing but rubble
until at last it becomes dust, the sought-after goal.
The parching heat sways in a monolithic dream,
hell's semi-precious stones radiating in the spectacular glow,
and as the path goes higher, the dust grows more weightless,
breaking away in the air, in the putrid light.
And that same hill in the steppe, steep & naked—
& that same path becomes faintly visible in the thicket of brush,
ascending along the precipice in a joyous yearning,
dissolving the crushed stones in the dry fog.
Falling among the sand like vertical dust
the path shatters in the air, which is equally shredded
in bits of monolithic rot, a parching heat, the decay—
only the light is somehow different & strange.
Or maybe it simply appeared as such: after all, this hill's still
the same one—then how can they both part here in the emptiness?
Yet one & the same—like blood under the skin—
their ore swells with its own nerve fibers.
Will I remove the stone from the hill, so that
somewhere on another hill, this place will become deserted too,
or if I tear away the flower of an unseen color,
as if separating someone's palm from its gesture,
or if I simply put my foot in the sand
so that there, where the stone disappeared and was forgotten,
and the flower, unfavorable to God, vanished as well—
then will my footprint appear?
But on these cliffs only the contagious sand
frays into a blinded heap.
So why does a different light reveal
the hill, situated nowhere & everywhere?
In yourself you see that here
the celebration & the crime take place in every moment—

and someone's being dragged to his execution along the desolate path,
as the exploit begins & the suffering lingers.
He stands, face in his hands—
a deathly solitude, alone, squalid,
surrounded by Judas & other enemies,
agitated by this frenzied blood of grief.
Or is he—a singular one here, & they
knew this all along, in spite of their rage,
in spite of the light's deadened mask—
their callous will, diseased mind?
The act could have been an offering: this & the other one—
an exploit—if he feels his solitude & it provokes terror,
or the celebration itself—if under his hand
this crowd & the plowed land come alive as one.
The sacrifice—this one & the other—
find their token & debt of continuance in his execution.
Only this different light radiates over everything:
the reproaching light & a celebratory light of redemption.
Or is it that indulgence's sorcery threatens with love,
or that the lightning tosses these martial banners,
or that the hills are decorated & stained by the scalding blood
like a letter soaked in ink from front to back?
You, standing there with your face covered,
lower your hands & let it all awaken
from your own confinement, which was imposed by the centuries!
Your bread's bitter & the sacrifice can't be touched.

> Translated by John High and Julie Gesin.

Table

Domestic animal, which the rustling became
and a forest trail—here is this comfortable table.
He confused the wild life in its depth
with roots' commotion, secret and turbid.
And from its surface sometimes
under the noise of branches, tangled in a squeak,
like a tablecloth of hands, the triumph
of bears' eyes descends, stopping the lindens,
their soft honey, sliding down the trunks,

through bees' paws, through frozen smells.
On all tables at that moment live
mute faces on bears' paws.
Translated by Lyn Hejinian and Elena Balashova.

Home

All that I was, became really—my past
everything deciding a me that you
weren't a part of—I want to obliterate
and forget, even if it's saved me, yes
and may still release the emptiness &
despair (over & over).
Will a house continue, if what remains
is only bulk, smoke's taste, an undying smell
of *place?* Snow looks after it all
stopping above the roof
though the roof is already gone &
the snow is parting itself in a perfect point above
where the walls once stood,
preserving all that space
once contained within.
No windows are left either,
but the red & green maple branches
sway toward the markings,
and these bare, frozen trees
restore the window's image, helping these streetwalkers
to capture their passing reflections in
vanished glass.
Will a house survive, when we abandon the house,
when the house we've departed, forgets us?
A kiss lightens it. You said,
God bless the day that joined us
& what follows.
And what was next is protected by snow now
creating parallel lines of the window's refracted light
like a tomtit's heart tossed headlong into the wind
bending under the light.
The kiss's light (which the snow welcomes)

did it suit you too
lifting your eyes toward the window?
The one you awaited, the man you later met in this house
invented himself for you
                              not even knowing he had done so.
Rather it seems I was simply there, a witness to
                                                luck.
So I want to forget it.
A dying man reveals more of himself than the living.
As for the past, there isn't one for those
who consider it in the hour of
the jubilant opening doors.
No sky over a sky either
                    no earth over earth, no love over love.
        Translated by John High.

I'm not the branch, only the prebranchness.
Nor a bird, simply the bird's name.
Not even a raven, though somewhere in the prewind
the horde of ravens is discussing my fate.
        Translated by John High.

But already sensing terror—
the angel in a child's boots,
winter's gone through his body.
Child, learn to move in their circles.
Spirit, learn to breathe in the snow's
ice. But as for that strawberry-scented
soap—leave it under the sky's wing.
        Translated by John High.

Portrait

You might well be blond and immortal
until that day before the mirror
when you'll suddenly cry out, a pain in
the heart, dropping a comb like someone
staring hard into the twilight branches,
into their obscure witchcraft, so as to touch
the wind's cool skin
against your own skin,
just as the bare trees watch their own fallen
leaves in the pond,
the foliage probably drawn there
by the leaves' legends
of a past.
Both the mirror and comb beside you
like the trees and pond,
and your eyes exist because of your secret
hiding something behind their glance.
You're falling into the mirror,
its immeasurable gloss,
its depth covered with silvery silt,
like melting ice, like wax.
A sparkling fan altered forever
into a temple.
And Aphrodite's eternal calmness
invisible here but present—
her smile and coy shyness illuminate your face,
and in the distance,
there's a ring that shines from your trembling finger.
You'll remember you're engaged to someone
in a land that's so unreal.
And the red mirage of a gesture
will envelop your own hand.

Translated by John High and Katya Olmsted.

I'll always take stock in
my guilt & mistakes.
The cloth reverts back to its thread,
so that grief can evolve into a smile.
No more hope remains
only this faith in the miraculous—
but a light hangs over my head,
and no one knows where it comes from.

      Translated by John High.

Andrei Turkin

ANDREI TURKIN was born in 1962. He studied for one year at the Moscow Aviation Institute and, after spending two years in the Soviet army, studied for two years at Moscow State University.

Statement

First and foremost: nonobjectiveness. Objects (including words) form the arrow of a vector speeding toward self-destruction. I greet entropy gladly in every way and rise to its defense, as I endeavor to deprive words of sense.

Such is my creative method:

As I repeat the words "to slip," thirty times over their sense becomes lost, and there remains a vacant object. I try to fill such objects with a vacuum and solder them shut, so that no sense can crawl back in. Then, lined up in a verse, the words suddenly explode, absorbing in a flash all the world, that is so very dear to my heart. From this is created the impression that the world is a kind of package for which no packaging exists.

Here is one of many riddles, those most paradoxical figs: It is death that most often becomes my muse. I often imagine myself in the hospital. There are people around my bed, looking at me with an attentive, medical eye. They look long and very quietly. Then one of them says sharply, almost in a whisper: "It's over . . . He's dead . . ." When I imagine such a scene, there is neither sorrow nor fear, but only a primary feeling, filling my heart, that I am perfectly flat and endlessly extended. It is this feeling that I call inspiration. My inspiration.

I have a great love of the Old Bulgarian language. It is soft, deep, and impoverished to the point of idiocy. (The latter two words formerly had a different meaning than they do today. *Impoverished* [ubogii] meant "close to God," while *idiocy* meant "an existence outside of civil and social laws." Thus, Socrates, to all appearances, was an impoverished idiot.) Old Bulgarian words, or words used in the Old Bulgarian manner, are often found in my poems.

I have a great love of banality and kowtowing, for these two characteristics serve exceptionally well to distinguish man from animal, which is at once sad and gladdening, as in tragicomedy. In my opinion, a man must change his views every five minutes, must submit, be a conformist, behave as unobtrusively as possible. Only in this way can he deceive matter and the materialists, which, of course, is absolutely necessary.

Translated by Anesa Miller-Pogacar.

In the Woods

I finish my cigarette in silence,
and a pleasant feeling of release
makes me pee on the fern fronds,
take a dump in the skunk cabbage.
I melt more and more into nature,
pissing with the force of the beasts.
I'm a jackal! A boar! I bite!
I'm a wolf! I'm the wolf's wild wife!

Translated by Paul Schmidt.

I bought Lenin's *Works* (Selected)
and the more I read, the more I
stopped being a thorny delinquent
and became an uncluttered young man.

No longer a misfit, a paranoid freak,
I was calm as your pet mouse.
When I save up enough for his *Works* (Complete)
what kind of man will that make me?

Translated by Paul Schmidt.

I moved a book to the table's edge
and brushed against it without thinking.
My lover was sleeping next to the table.
She didn't notice me.

In her bed, an abundance of leg
between two blankets.
Between the soles of her small
feet, a bunched sheet.

She had bunched it while she slept.
There was a bicycle in her dream.
She was a letter carrier
in the country, only seventeen.

She was delivering a letter to a man
she was in love with
because he had a hairy chest.

Later that morning
I knocked the book off the edge.
It was almost noon.

        Translated by Paul Schmidt.

You have inquired—this blood—
Where is it from? Come here!
I have gulped down a Hero Star
To have it in my chest.

So that it could amalgamate
With me, and drink up all my blood.
And, by illuminating people's faces,
I'd glitter like a symbol!

I'd rise to heaven like a star
And trembling like the savior's tear,
There I would glitter, burn, whenever
Your eyes would light upon me.

        Translated by Michael Makin.

Long ago we left the earth.
See the crosses side by side?
You and I—we are these graves.
I'm the left one, you're the right.

On a little bench of green
Our children are drinking Cahors.
And my cross, my cross is casting
An enamored shadow on your mound,

While it reaches toward your cross.
Only sometimes in the crossings
Are our faces similar,
Just on pleasant summer days.
Translated by Michael Makin.

O, how I value the town center!
Where Prince Dolgoruky's arm
Seems to seek Karl Marx's beard,
But will not ever find it while
Dzerzhinsky's eyes keep watch on him,
And pierce the buildings just like enemies.
And all in vain his foot
Seeks to dispatch the giant horse.
Translated by Michael Makin.

I met a woman with a jackhammer.
She squatted by some broken asphalt,
And suddenly began to sing. I knew the tune.
And I was captivated by her penetrating contralto.

She sang selections from *La Traviata* and *Carmen*
And drew out the melody so clearly and so boldly
that I concluded—wouldn't it be great
If any proletarian instead,

Instead of cheap vulgarities,
Instead of drinking bouts,

Could master singing as an art and even
Tune his voice just like a string,

Then how much confidence there'd be
in their performance of the *Internationale*.
Translated by Michael Makin.

Spring

Your little fingers drew
Upon the sheet of paper
Two double things
With paws and tail.

Did you not realize
In your pure simplicity
What your little fingers drew
Upon the sheet of paper?!

But suddenly you grasped
The sketch's own simplicity,
How rapidly you made
A ball out of the sheet.

And out the window flew
The sheet into the bushes.
And once again you closed
And locked your heart.
Translated by Michael Makin.

After scratching your cheek with a nail
I'm disturbed to have discovered
From the cluster of blood on your cheek
That inside you're entirely alive.

That beneath your chilly skin
Fermentation is concealed.
And by pressure, by blood's quivers,
You are brought to motion.

I move differently though,
I'm all levers and veins.
Hiding thus their own mechanics
Machines thresh out grain.

So accept the proposition
To unite in matrimony,
For the different movements
Have one goal—to merge!

Translated by Michael Makin.

You bent over the river with laundry bowls,
I was digging a trench facing you,
You and I exchanged glances,
A suggestion fell down between us.

You said, "Private, I bent over,
You kept looking so straight and sharp
That I dropped a nightdress and it sank,
Just as if I'd been pricked by a needle."

But between the two banks the suggestion
Went on sinking and serving suggestions.
I, attracted by your legs,
Placed a log on the suggestion.

And you have a deep stream inside you.
I will make you a suggestion for it,
And then carry you back to the porch.
A bit later you'll sit by the window,

Though I'm not to be seen beneath it.
I'll lie down for a sleep at that time.
Oh, what joy and what distress it is
That I've got to dig the other trenches!
    Translated by Michael Makin.

I'm afraid of your penetrating glances!
They are so much like knives.
On my body you carve out some patterns,
But, tell me, what patterns are they?

Now you've grazed my heart and neck,
And you're raising your eyes to meet mine.
On my body you're carving—a lily?
But refuse to utter one word!

Or you're carving a bush of
Unappealing bare twigs of willow?
This is why I'm transparent as air,
And afraid of your sharpened knives,

For deliberately, without hurry
Now the blade will slice in two
Not a lily, and not willow twigs,
But my heart, in love with you.
    Translated by Michael Makin.

Vladimir Aristov

VLADIMIR ARISTOV was born in 1950 in Moscow and graduated from the Physics and Technical Institute. His poetry has recently appeared in various publications in the Soviet Union and has been translated in France, Romania, and Yugoslavia.

Statement

Nowadays, one-sided attempts to clarify the relation of human beings to the world of things, to reintegrate fact and value, actually place limits on persons and on things. This leads to imitative intensity, strain, the exhaustion of individuality. However, this doesn't mean the obliteration of the self: rather its opening out into the ambiguous expanse of the collectivity. Trying to designate this indistinct and incomplete thought, I would employ the prefix *meta:* metarealism, meta-metaphor, metabolic, and so on, as terms that divide whatever's general from a professional poet's specific figures to show forth innovative forms of representation. Such words indicate like ostensive signs, markers pointing toward what's not yet in existence, but what's around us and known well enough to be represented as having a kind of reality.

Some kinds of things, from the start, are perceived and represented as immersed in nameless multiplicity; with other things, from their birth as it were, we know the names of the newborn infants. Reversing this process, we can decipher the connection of the object with the world; this appears in writing through the conversion of forms, through a profusion of metaphors that take us on paths within a language that's mute. For me, this process does show that a common life can exist; and because it can, the lyrical "I," indestructible, dynamically unified, can tolerate within poetry historical personages and other, unknown people. Accordingly the plot of the poem can move with dramatic fluctuation among these all-but-undifferentiated oppositions.

Also, this interchanging, reciprocal act comes into being through an internal expansion. Possibly we can call the summing up of all such random movements an internal plastic theater. As a general methodology, then, for use and not for show: perception and creation of the spreading internal expanse.

Now in this expanse, with its own hugging outline, there are also created new elements of poetic expression. This isn't on the level of tongue or linguistics but on the level of logos or creative knowledge. Here, our approach to the physical, mythological language takes the pulsion, the before-word, as the gist of expression, bound up with the word-as-symbol but not restricted to that. In this way of thinking about things, feelings and sensitivities play a role; the whole person moves at once. The analogue of plays and films comes to mind: because of the need there, too, for transferring to the audience a layered, dramatically organized structure of consciousness. Even now, the possibilities of and for the artistic word remain latent. You can not and should not convey directly onto film the strictly visual forms that come before the lens. In films we know and admire, the director always brings forth the double of the material external world, namely, his or her internal world as an analogue. Now poetry can share with these other arts the means of creation, secret tension, the moment of elusive transformation and conversion: bringing out in writing a partly connected chain of expressive devices. Of course, it can be shown that in poetic texts there exist breaks in the emotional logic or in the mode of representation. But the primary moving impulse in this kind of poetry comes from pulsions of fluctuating consciousness and the breaks are explained by transfer to other levels of the passage of dramatic action. Very likely, when contemporary poetry is considered boring this is because of the absence of internal dramatic tension.

A new unification of external and internal: our search demands inquiry into poetic forms, from which we've been prevented by excessive rule mongering. Absolutely we need to reckon in the international prominence of free verse, but we also need to reintegrate inner and outer by listening in at the linguistic depths of the nation. That is, we must reckon in the powerfully drawn-out rhythms of ancient Russian poetry, the magic of charms, the beautiful long lines in songs of lamentation and praise. For now we must look to another world of unification, flowing together, in the attempt to express a contemporary relation of mind and world. The real task in our search for integration is in the striving itself, so that out of this poetry the reader takes away not a Taoist emptiness as of a computational cipher but, rather, a dynamic, actualized figure of fullness.

Translated by Donald Wesling.

Music

How did you choose this sacred sheetmusic
Wrapped up in veins of notes?
There are right sounds in this world,
You took them out of the world
And the place is grown over with weeds, as if nothing were ever on it . . .

What remains is the wasteground and this crazy talk of the stonepits,
The dry blueness of the sky buttons
On the cheap jackets in brick slagheaps,
Only the waxed thread of mouths, bushes, crossings
Of faraway hilly skies,
Everything healed over with weeds, so weedcovered you might cry.

How can we dismiss this killercold century,
Hurtling down the mountain in an icy traincarriage,
From the steep bank of the lost lawn
To darkness of earth and silence of embraces.

The silence murmurs about what's forgotten,
Don't, neolithic epoch, leave us,
With a rifle pointed across the width of the river,
With a disappearance of the turning point of life,
Behind the sparkling small wheel of water
Where the swollen wing of a glass bird
Has risen up through cynical power of thought.

The age of meteorites hasn't yet arrived,
They're still similar to trees or people,
From the tenderness of the earth they're not ready to fall,
Flatlands still belong to us,
And the trace the wolf leaves is a melting impression of fullness.

Through an open window the deserted backyard of earth
Brings voices under a full moon,
But we didn't manage to harness this steady chaos
Neither into the starry barber's emptiness,
Nor into the cities of deep granite.

Don't take our sound through to music.
Because the sea is already speechless before us,
Will it be more empty without sound?
No need for music, no need for stars
Near our ancient sea without names.
  Translated by Donald Wesling.

She Speaks

Triangular pack of milk.
If you cut off the corner
White melancholy will pour out. Like
An unread letter
That disappears in the night.
Hush. Be quiet.

Diluted with dew, sunrise
Becomes cloudy, grows around the corner, where waits
The job that you hate.
I've forgotten him,
Meaning: in memory he'll never die.

On the night windowsill these colored pyramids
Of milk are piling up on one another with floury sides.
Feeling this unsteady stream, this thread
Of milk—this memory I can neither stretch out, nor stop dead.
  Translated by Donald Wesling.

For Bach's Visit to Berlin, Capital of Prussia, 1747

Inseparable body from wig,
Indistinguishable mirror-smoothness of river
From curls of greenish grass.

Why do I need a tailormade suit,
Which anyway lies dusty

Like an old envelope on the bottom of a lightcolored river
In the year one thousand nineteen forty-seven.

You shouldn't with the door of a mirror-carriage
Catch someone else's sunbeam
To send light into yourself,
For in the forgotten room of shadows
Everyone is lying in a heap of ridiculous poses,
And the blood of the nineteenth century
Now looks like shaving gel.

Who can give me a hint what to do
If the body's just a temple,
Who can whisper into my ears
Along with the noises of a greenedged street
The royal theme and the sixvoiced canon.

It is as if pale copper were spilled all over
And turquoise rash is on the wrists of the birchtrees,
Did you really think that you'll take me
With a castiron hum from the horse's nostrils,
Like saving a parcel for the century that will not be,
Burning it in the air like a chemical signature,
You'll send off your bow of greeting.

The muteness of a wall is flashed off the mirror-lenses of a turquoise river.
        Translated by Donald Wesling.

Baltic Reflections

Like daytime walks,
The islands are far away.
And your footsteps are cautious:
Not to leave a print on the world.

There: expanse of seascape over houses,
Of seagulls the resonant bobbling,
And sunset doesn't quiet down the dawn,
Like Altdorfev's battle
That pulled itself tight, bunched toward the horizon.

Here: nature of light is pure.
The light coordinates
Have found a home in your face.
But always over your silence and the sea's
Is the beauty of your face.
And the loose little tail of rainbow
That died, beyond the forest.

Only the water retreats
Passing across the salty spikes of grain,
Next to the monuments
Where the children are playing,
Hitting the ball into their reflection on the pedestal.

Still grinding salt, flour, or money
Are mills above the expanse of sea,
And radars like windmills
Turn on a clearing behind the hut.

Only wind circles
Through delicate wings,
Only the children smack their ball
And hide it in the hollow of the hand.
Translated by Donald Wesling.

From The Dolphinarium

(A Poem in Fourteen Statements)

Dedicated to the Armory Baths

Dolphin—a sea mammal from the
subclass of toothed whales,
serves as an object of trade;
its fat is used to produce lard,
its skin provides durable leather,
its fins and tail provide glue.
—Dictionary of
Foreign Words, 1954

Let us go then, you and I . . .
—T. S. Eliot, The Love Song of
J. Alfred Prufrock

I

Well, let's go then,
You and I . . .

And in the sidestreet
Beyond the watery smoothness of the air
We will part
Here beside a wrought-iron fence,
Around a graveyard of autumn airplanes—
Of maple tinplate disfigured accidentally.

You concealed yourself in the last archway,
And I circled the inside of my lips with my tongue,
And my tongue lay motionless,
Its tip come to rest on my teeth.

You flitted by like a dolphin with a raging face,
The fire of a cigarette
Going off into the Moscow night.
And my tongue sparkled
And sank into my depths,

Making its way through my blood
Holding the lantern of speech.

Come up to the surface, dolphin;
This body of yours has emerged in the dark
Of still early damp sidestreets,
And from your and my
Moist depths
Came a marine voice.

A dolphin chattered in the fountain
With a splashing brass mouthpiece in its beak,
Bestilled before the entrance
Near curtained portholes of eyes.

II

Who heard the cry of the dolphin?

Not I . . .

Who deciphered their voices at night
From the moist prescientific dark
In a home sidestreet,
Who spoke with them in an esperanto of interjections?

And burying your head
In falsified oscillograms,
Raised their voice in your arms?

But is it there we're really looking for it?

III

O bashful charms of the Armory,
It seems I will see your walls no more—
The construction dust has blown away
Above the dusty mirror living in each puddle.

Dolphins lived in the Armory Bath
But their faucets have no doubt been covered up,
And gathering for a meeting here's in vain;
As can be seen, it's not been opened.

Only the wooden grating remains
Of that splendid staircase
Toward which a reveille summoned to sacred steam
From the snoring sidestreet.

I've drunk beer with you, though time was short,
And I've whispered through the communal foam
That we are surrounded by water and blood,
But water no longer runs down the tiled steps,
And the dolphinarium is dry.

                              V

He who with a waterless mouth bellowed
In a submarine tremolo of consonances,
Who, with the jingle bell of a transistor radio
Shaking a hungover head,
Wandered toward the watering hole—
He will understand you.

He, the young dolphin
Lost in the sidestreets.
I saw—you secretly eavesdropping on yourself
By a wire going to your ears,
Where the subgastric tape recorder sang
Through its steel cassettes.

This is he, your guitar idol,
Whispering with you at the very water's edge,
Summoning you from the sea.

For at one time he, too,
A guitar athlete
In the disorderly worldwide barrage,
Ever more clearly emerging as a sculpture in water,

Threw off the transparent channels,
And became still over the world.

There, reflected in the water,
The city lights were flickering across
And little red dolphin eyes
Were hiding in the subway of the sea.

But in the shimmering sparks of dry clothing
Not a sound from the gutted bathhouse,
And your summer night dolphinarium is dry,
Your night dolphinarium is empty.

XIII

If the water enters at night,
The deserted souls will pour out in boiling rain.

And you, bestilled by bathhouse legions,
Turned sullen by tiled ledges,
Soaped up to the eyebrows,
Will paddle the rainbow of foam away with your hands
Toward the steps at the entrance.

You will slide by a tile reflection
In expendable sadness,
And the steam released will descend
Upon the opened, spotless sea.

Translated by Gerald J. Janecek.

Pavel Pepperstein

PAVEL VITALIEVICH PEPPERSTEIN was born in Moscow in 1966. A visual artist as well as poet, he is a leading member of the Medical Hermeneutics group. He currently works as an illustrator for a children's magazine. All translations are by Gary Kern.

Statement

It is almost fifteen years since I first took up literature. For a long time my favorite genre was the novel. From 1979 to 1983 I wrote four "secret novels." These massive tomes were created within the confines of the exotic literary principle CNT (confidential-nature tactic), which I practiced for nearly seven years. These texts are kept under a veil of secrecy; parts have been destroyed. The decision to write secretly was engendered by my enthusiasm for spiritualism at the time and also by my desire to work out a complex system of relationships between several so-called private religions. Included among these was the practice of symbolic suicide, which I performed upon the completion of each text. In 1983 I developed the genre of "mediumistic prose" and in this genre wrote a novel entitled *The Yellow Leniniana,* ascribing the work to a number of dead writers (Dostoyevski, in particular). From that time to this I have retained an unabated interest in the image of Lenin.

In 1984 I gave up the further development of "personal religions" and "literary spiritualism," having decided that the literary process should strive to realize the hidden demands of the current linguistic field of culture. I rejected the principles of confidential-nature tactic and secrecy. The first characteristics of postmodernism were beginning to appear, and these more closely corresponded to my aesthetic positions at the time. I worked out a technique of producing "slogans" (that is, transferable linguistic orientations) and used these slogans as guidelines for my literary activity. Thus, I took for

myself the slogan "Literature should be literary." This is a calque from the
official Brezhnev slogan of the time: "Economics should be economical." The
latter, in my opinion, constituted an ideal slogan, for it locked "the crystal
heavens of ideology" into a self-sufficient sphere that immediately stood
"separate from earth." In other words, it existed without any link to real
life and posed no threat to it whatsoever.

Operating under the slogan "Literature should be literary," I wrote the
novella *Temple of the Corpse* and, likewise, the cycle of verses *The New
Decadence*, or *Farewell Gestures*.

The problem of self-expression through poetry never particularly con-
cerned me; I was more interested in exposing certain "poses" of culture and
the methods of its self-reading. Thus, in the cycle *The New Decadence* I
tried not only to make the characteristically postmodern "gesture of rela-
tionship" toward a definite tradition (in the present instance, Russian sym-
bolism) but also to identify this gesture as the expression of a definite and
sufficiently clear aesthetic model. Eventually this line found its most adequate
expression in the work of composing the almanac *Star of Love*, where all the
avant-garde Muscovite literary figures are represented on the whole by excep-
tionally traditional and ostensibly decadent texts. In the introduction to this
edition I attempted to describe the situation in the following manner:

> The traditional conception of the avant-garde is rigid and ascetic: it
> sees the avant-garde as a forward detachment sent ahead or thrown
> into the desert to break the path, and it presupposes charisma in the
> positive act.
>
> Decadence always rests on the topography of spires, of spirals (the
> curliques of Borocco and Jugend-Stil), and therefore, passing through
> a period of decadence (i.e., postmodernism) as through a country of
> mirrors, the forward detachment appears, as it were, behind everyone
> else. From its position "on the edge," it abruptly transfers to an "empty
> center" saturated with tradition, from which it can calmly make "ges-
> tures of relationship" (having the character of "farewell gestures")
> toward any tradition which in the final instance represents the same
> "saturated" or total tradition.

Now, however, the aesthetic and mental-ideological space of postmod-
ernism has already been sufficiently mined and seems already to have man-
ifested its chief characteristics. At the same time the most interesting task
for me personally has become not the attempt to represent or perfect post-
modern devices but, rather, to model the next level of culture's self-
understanding.

This in fact is the task of the group called "Medical Hermeneutics," consisting of three people: Sergei Anufriev, Yuri Leiderman, and myself, each of us combining in one person theoretician, artist, and writer. In the process of creating a large field of theoretical texts and discussions, we set ourselves the task of composing the Empty Canon of "The Orthodox Hut," in relation to which we then established a definite aesthetic and mental-ideological space, conditionally called "the orthodox." This work presupposes a gradual crystallization of certain new literary principles and positions—in particular, a new image of the literary man, namely, the "literary lector." (As an old Chinese novel puts it, "One experienced literary lector has two hundred unrestrained magicians and three hundred werewolves up his sleeve.")

Yet the preceding aesthetic space of postmodernism is not subject to abolition and annihilation but, rather, to inclusion and "disintegration on the shelves," and likewise to a certain filtration in the more expanded and at the same time more elite space of the orthodox. In [the Russian version of Lewis Carroll's] *Through the Looking-Glass* there is a dialogue between Alice and Humpty Dumpty in which the latter says that *glory* means "I explained myself, how to disintegrate on the shelf." [In English he says that *glory* means "there's a nice knock-down argument for you."] If this inter-pretation of the word *glory* be accepted, then our goal is precisely "glory"—that is, "canonization" and "disintegration on the shelves." Thus, it can be said that in the space of our intentions to replace decadence there comes a kind of classicism, but such a conjunction, of course, is far too approximate.

Concerning the poems at hand, one can, if he likes, regard them as a certain field of emotional and aesthetic relaxation (small remissions) from the flat and dry spaces of theoretical disquisitions. But then these little pits should not turn into caverns, to which is dedicated the cycle *Caverns of Love,* saturated with a strange, ambivalent, and self-destructive emotionality. In general, experiences that annul one another are often used in my "lyrical work." On the other hand, in the "layered" space of orthodox interpretation all these verses possess a sufficient quantity of "constructed" meanings. In the final analysis they all constitute a sort of "verbal excrement," which by their combination permit every reader to guess the condition of his own "vocal" fate.

From the Cycle **The New Decadence**

The concert grand stood open wide . . .
—A. Fet

The children at play killed a monkey.
Oh, look at the dead reproach
In its glistening eyes. And on a dickey
Orange juice went splash.

Slender fingers accidentally
Scrunched up a paper cup—a sudden alarm.
A little kid on a little white stickie
Gallops around.

Specked by the sun is the pavilion flag.
See there, over the bush, that little blaze?
Aren't you surprised? Why don't you ask:
"Oh, where is my poor little beast?"

In strings of lighted lamps, in garlands of witticisms,
The evening garden galloped like a specter from the ball,
And an effete dandy, twisting his mouth awry,
Let fly whole sheaves of lunar aphorisms.

All this took place in August, and putrid
Were the swamps beyond the ballustrades.
Beneath the stonework arches, a nocturnal fountain
Erected columns of silver haze.

The bushes dropped an ashen madness,
The sleepy stench admixed with sweet perfume.
And drunken orchestras in colonnaded apses
Like witches bleated beneath the full moon.

Spreading wide his wings in a disheveled fan,
He flies and capers like a monkey.
And beneath him, in an endless wrinkled bald spot,
The surface of the ocean rolls and murmurs.

But hardly does he see the cypresses afar
Than he lands, giggles, weeps, laughs,
And sits on the yard, where the ships sail,
And above the deck his cloak ruffles.

Solitary, nasty, his leathery face
He digs with a claw sometimes.
He is accustomed on dark and windy days
On hotel cornices his food to find.

The hotel boots, a sick Englishman, a marquis,
Two old women and several servants . . .
With a light rustle he flies to the cornice
And takes food from the hand.

Then off he flies with a piercing laugh,
Disappearing behind flocks of smokestacks.
And under the glove of the sick Englishman
The imprint of his wrinkled lips is kept.

From the Cycle **The Astral Whisper**

Dedicated to D. A. Prigov

I confessed that I killed the old woman.
They came and led me away.
But the lathe of the earth up on high
Produced a shining shaving.

It shined and twinkled in the sky,
And spun in the field spiralwise,
For so long, so long I've not been here
That now I only squinch and laugh.

She softly went on her way,
Turning down her wrinkled mien.
I thought: This life has grown cold,
And now is consuming its end.

And now the memories of death
Have drawn me into the depths of time.
You don't believe my moans and groans,
I'm drunk with a distant heaven.

Only life—it went away somewhere.
I seek it, seek it, but it is gone.
I found only her little brother
In the fading black garden.

We sit side by side on a bench.
I asked: You died—it was when?
He answered: In this watercan
The putrid water stinks.

When the sun found itself in the window,
Having played on the transparent glass,
I remembered my very first murder
In the merry and fresh light of dawn.

At that time I'd reached three years of age.
Childhood, the dacha, walks to the pond . . .
A little monster is how I see myself,
In the beloved net of minutes wound.

In the evenings above mother-of-pearl waters
Columns of fog hung in the air,
And flies in transparent clusters
In the warm twilights swarmed.

Ah, how those creations made me suffer,
Winging all over my skin!

While buildings arose in the distance:
Pumphouses and dirty churches.

There he is, there—revolting, thin.
He stopped his vampirish buzz
And landed on my elbow, so as to begin
With his nose to search for blood.

Well, I didn't wait—with the flat of my hand
I slapped once and he was murdered.
Only a dark little spot remained,
And a most delicate little foot quivered.

And then in this soft and easy evening,
Where the reservoir gently glowed,
Suddenly I recalled my snowy homeland,
Suddenly I thought about my God.

I confessed that I killed the paper,
And more than once ice gripped my soul.
With the paper I wiped off a bit of kaka
And dropped it down the toilet bowl.

And suddenly, while I stood and stared,
I was struck by both wonder and terror:
Only the water flowed down undisturbed.
And sparkled like a thousand arrows.

So I too shall perish—just a little clump
Amid the sound and stream of existence,
But I shall leave you to these lines,
This golden secret of mine.

Now I lie on the floor in the bathroom,
And the electric light flickers,
But I hear how in the obedient chasm
Float constellations of planets.

And on each, amid craters of pain,
Amid high ridges of despond,
Only transparent moth pupas
Softly slumber, dug deep in the sands.

My dear reader, it's you that I love.
To my tremulous lines you attend.
But still it's you, it's you I will kill.
What for? Well, you yourself comprehend.

Because there's nothing else I can do,
And you too can do nothing else.
To get out of life I'll help you,
And you'll take me into your heart.

You'll lay me on the bottom of your immortal soul,
And there I shall sleep without worry,
And together we shall live from this moment forth
Peacefully, pleasantly and forever.

From the Cycle **Poems from the Front**

The blue eyes of Eva the adored
Are like the sky above our realm,
In brown clothing she stepped forward,
Wrapped in the dim light of morn.

And on the marble loudly fell a little slipper,
And amidst the columns a soft laugh . . .
The Aryan body—athletic, slender,
And the lips with which I'm in love.

In the bronze lamps little wreaths of flame,
Come to me, dear one, come to me,
We shall intertwine naked
On the banner spread out between.

The battle of muscular bodies in loving gymnastics.
A goddess are you, a god am I,
On the background of a huge pagan swastika
The pattern of tormented thighs.

The tender vagina squeezed tight,
And like snow juice, streamed a column of seeds.
He burned up his Aryan insides,
Germany's insides he burned, and spewed, and beat.

Caught the lips the moist tremble of lips
And the taste of saliva, the blow, the flexible tongue,
You were so tender, so stern and so rough,
As you leaned with power toward your morose spouse.

A masterful coming together was created and lived
Like a battle slowed down by sweet oppression.
The youthful giants gave hearty laughs
As they watched you from the stretches of heaven.

But it was late. The ring made a clink.
Some kind of rustle, as if from wings.
"Adolf, that's enough!" Lowering his face,
He sat down quietly, suddenly losing strength.

And we pounded them. The voices of ack-acks
Above the desolate farms burst so noisily.
Potapov shouted: "Burn 'em!" And the woods
Picked up the shout merrily and terribly.

"Fuck the Fascist bastards! Fuck 'em in the mouth!
For the homeland! For happiness! For Stalin!"
And in an avalanche, forward we moved.
Like terrible weather raining down from heaven.

The snow swirled up in a fountain of smoke,
Like a paper roll a Fascist tank ignites.
How easy for me, a real joke,
To advance to the voices of ack-acks!

From the Cycle Caverns of Love

"The glass coffin seemed as if to shake..."
—The Man Who Saw Lenin

Your brown eyes shine me the way
And your vest I dream about at night,
You crowned naked children,
Leaning toward the candlelight.

You slurred your *r*'s and made a crafty eye,
O my Lenin, my sign and my emblem,
You live in my quiet soul as a little spider,
On your back the hammer and sickle.

Ah, my soul is a dark, deserted house,
How much rubbish on the high shelves!
Beneath the round table I have lost my touch
And look at you, as at dust.

Nadya, Stalin has come! Put on the pot.
Nadya, Stalin has come! Rub your dear eyes.
How long, how long he's not come to see us,
In our charming Gorki not stopped for tea.

Nadya, Stalin has come! He's walking down the lane.
How heavy his tread, his smile is the same.
This is life looking at us with a stunning gaze—
In a plain field jacket it's coming our way.

Take a look at it, take a look at him.
They're a two-sexed hero, a youth androgyne!
In those sultry eyes a young wine
Gives off a dark and misty shine.

Nadya, Stalin has come! We two have become children,
With our furniture in covers, two decrepit children.
The end of my painful life has arrived.
We'll pray a long time with tears in our eyes.

The daring dreams of willful admissions:
Know you, know you of what they are speaking?
Know I, know I, for I am a clergyman
A connoisseur of glass cats in succession.

The thoughts of today's sad excavations:
The places of strikes and the factories of misers.
Know you, know you the events of October,
The sharp secrets and the hunger of our fathers?

Know I, know I, for I am an artist,
With the water of gall having washed my lips.
Yes, all of us together have shaken the tripod,
Marvelously empty was heaven's chalise.

Remember you, remember you the red flags,
Of proud sailors the desperate look?
Remember I, remember I the fiery moisture,
Drunk my fill of the lads' oblivion.

Horror then, horror is what you must cherish,
Or the dry bliss of losses could it be?
Lenin I once was named by the people,
Now Pepperstein is what they call me.

Mikhail Aizenberg

MIKHAIL AIZENBERG is an architect and poet who was born in Moscow in 1948. He has been writing poetry since the mid-1960s. His poems have been published in various émigré and samizdat journals. All translations are by J. Kates.

Something Like This

Manifesto-ness is inherent in those literary movements that see themselves from the outset as innovative, avant-garde, tending toward change. I myself belong among those authors who were formed in a period (the mid- to late 1960s) when it seemed as if there were no poems to speak of (we didn't know the few that there were)—and so, accordingly, there was nothing to sweep away or change. It was up to us to reinvent poetry from scratch. In search of some kind of foundation we looked reluctantly back to that time in the 1920s when poetry was in its "Silver Age." Apparently, something from this frame of reference has become established and permanently ensconced. At the very least it all began with a sense that poetic language is somehow different, special, a blend of birdsong with what had become obsolete. A very strong tensile strength of material bred a distortion of speech, a strained babble, nearly *zaum*. Words, out of phase with their customary contexts, began to seek out new places and new connections, no longer submitting to the old ways of shades of meaning but to the internal attraction of self-composition, the development of their own form.

It came to be understood that the chief thing was to learn to set words free; they do the rest themselves. Poems in any case are more of a dance than a narrative, a dance of words on paper, a dance of meanings. The dance can also tell a story, but in its own true language with its own necessary key. And, on the other hand, poetic language is individual without being artificial.

It has to intersect with the ordinary, with the everyday, with speech. Everything happens precisely at this point of intersection. The possibility of an absolute absence of style—straightforward speech—is illusory but always exists specifically as a Grand Illusion. Like hope. There is hope for a style arising from its own disappearance, by an instantaneous current expulsion across literary boundaries.

A system of poetics exists when there is a *definite* principle of the isolation of the word from speech, a uniformly functioning mechanism. But poetry lives in the break from a system of poetics. This, apparently, is precisely the satisfaction of poetry, that it should reserve for itself this ordeal—to be born all over again time after time.

It's understood that such a frame of reference dictates a special attitude toward innovations. Innovations are not valuable in and of themselves; they are still, as it were, forced. They are born out of attempts to avoid stylization, to create a living, vibrating poetic text, to create a continuous fluid poetic fabric—an organic chemistry of verse. It's bad luck (or good?) that this has to be understood purely in practice, feeling—it's impossible to clarify or describe. An organic chemistry of verse does not allow the word to be treated as known to be someone else's, alien—and this nonalienness, of course, is very vulnerable. I am sure that luck, happy accident, lies at the root of the renewal of writing. It is glossolalia, it's a random "dyr-bul-shchil" that by chance gets magically composed into an intelligible utterance.

What kind of sense is there in any of this? I don't know how it may be for others, but for me that's how it is: the generation in my personal life of a kind of ultrasound, which not every ear can detect. Here it's not a question of delicate hearing but of a particular construction, in which there can even be a defect, but a defect also particular, idiosyncratic. A structure comprehended like this has a single, definite, human character. Universal recognition is not only impossible for me but even unwelcome.

That is, there is a kind of signal, sent not to communicate something but to reveal somebody:

"Aha! Where are you? Are you out there, on Earth?"

It'd be good to escape into direct crazy speech.
It'd be good to break out into the straightaway.
For the word not to fade.
And not be swathed in cotton batting.
And not burn in the blue flame of cultural activity.

No, I be no great cultural prize.
I be no man of culture.
I am a man of profound yearning.

Ah, yearning . . .
My only weapon.

An everlasting vibration,
after long expectation cracking up
the brick of existence.

They terrorize us: we are not afraid
They swear at us: but we are not dismayed
They sting us: we experience no pain
They whip us: we continue unrestrained
What kind of human beings, quailing breed
of bird are we? Weeping and weak-kneed,
What do we do but grind our teeth, and creep
into futility, or burrow deep,
stay on the safe side any way we can

I live, live saving nothing for the future
As if time dragged itself backwards, topsy-turvy,
as if nothing but dusty stubble
blanketed our days.

We see the year off
and time grows a long beard,
like an annoying story
stranded somewhere in the memory.

There are these two nomads, brothers
creeping slowly toward a rendezvous—
see who will get there first:
stubborn Chukchi and stubborn Jew.

Here is Achilles, and there Ulysses.
One is Ilya, the other Mikula.
Jew and Chukchi traded kisses.
Over their heads, lightning flickered.

Come, mighty statesman!
Conqueror of our souls,
Ruling passion,
incomparable ringmaster!

Here's a fine to-do.
A flea hunt of an affair,
back pocket thunder.
                    A villainous view.
It all sinks without a trace.
A new idea never drifted
            into our harbor.

We rave in place. Who
the fuck needs Mahavishnu?

We go on living between Tiber and Sinai.

Which way is up? Which way down?
All of us country kids—
we know how good it is:
the seed in the ground now.

I was hoping that speech
would open up to me.

I was hoping that thoughts
skillfully depicted
would turn into a wind off the river.
like the top notes of the register—
easy and profound.

I was hoping for the wind,
enlisted for a holiday
of the extension of things,
would become cleaner and more dangerous
like a proverb—no one's.

All youth long this magic trick
turned out to be sweet:
a peace dove out of a cap,
or Logos from an ashtray.
And what came from where!
From a cloying tune,
from a thoughtful twin
and from the scent of hair.

I inhabit the century, hope for it all.
God, what am I doing now!
How to expect experience
will raise a forgotten war cry?
And, having called the Muse
to a nod, to a whistle, to a crust.
You say, "Darling, what drivel."

Somewhere special in the air
at times with a friendly bark,
at others with a dispatch call
we animate a panorama.

. . . .

A warm day. A swig of communion wine.
Soon, summer. Summer, soon.
Looking toward Easter.
Mudseason in the Summer Gardens
and on a clay pathway
the track of a baby carriage.

We made up a kind of Censorship Squad,
but hung out together at sixes and sevens.

He was always up to something.
                              And me?
Who wasn't always up to a little everything?

Deep in his eye a mirage glimmered like glass.
Young, but looking older than his age.

Sometimes he played around.
                    Dropped by the times into a rare courage,
and then into the country, he didn't look down on
                    playing politics.

He loved the guys at the Voke Tech,
he loved actors and didn't care for Jews.

And so?
        So what.
So he dawdled around, and it all unraveled too soon.
So he died a few years ago.

There are people here lucky to be alive,
all decked out in double array—
free, of course, in their servants' livery—
not exactly married.

Our hero, pure as refined sugar,
obeys with only a single fear.
Not a servant, of course, and not free—
and, when free, married.
And sometimes, life gets to him,
and sometimes fate is what he earns.
He is a distant cousin to the law,
a closer cousin to the east.
And insofar as anybody knows
he doesn't suffer from cruel deception.
He sees: the sun going down
shines golden in black oil
and this commands your admiration
something more than stand and spit.
Alongside, an old bolshevik
walks around with a pension book
awkwardly for him, accustomed as he is
to tuck all reality under his arm.
A bird no larger than a forage cap
drags out into the skies
the leitmotiv of the weather report.
And we hear these songs
set like a modest marigold.
Life is as homely as a blade of grass
or black as an oil stove,
quiet, until its term expires.
There's time enough before
a well-informed tomcat
peeks through a sooty peephole
and picks apart the little wick.

Who now remembers what kind of animal
a "cratic fox"[1] was? Those were the days, my friend.

Coded common pages kissing each other exchanged
vows not in words but in quotation marks.

Everything now—it's all removed from the books.
The poet ruined, the reader poisoned sick.

Grab the gift for yourself.
                    It burned where it touched—
it's not for handing around to just anyone.

No more quotes. You can't return to the past.
A blackened penny saved for a rainy day.

Only your linen hangs snapping on the line.
Everything's over—all that you counted on.

No room to spit, your stuff all over the place.
No courage left to go on. Not enough malice.

The survey stops where the road begins to turn.
Robinson explores to the edge of his land.

Life has its limits.
                    Then, how should we live?
A clenched fist shows you how.
Keep an eye on the trail.
                    Live on the lookout
for the first thing coming along. The random sign.

Live however you're prompted by the tale.

---

1. Author's note: "cratic fox" was a misprint in the first Russian edition of Nabokov's *Lolita:*
"cratic" instead of "arctic." The whole poem is an address to a small circle, a brotherhood of
readers of this first edition—only they can know what a "cratic" fox is, because there's no such
word.

Elena Shvarts

ELENA SHVARTS was born in Leningrad in 1948. She is one of the most prominent poets of that city and was active in Club 81, a highly influential group of younger writers and critics. Her first collection in the Soviet Union, *Cardinal Points,* was published in 1989. Her work is represented in the 1990 Penguin Books anthology *Child of Europe.*

Statement

I was born in Leningrad, in 1948, in the "Egyptian building" with pharaohs standing at the entrance and the god of writing on the gates. In the form of a bird. So there was nothing else for me to do but submit to his power and write, which I began to do around the age of seven, with poetry coming later, at thirteen. I was a poor student and constantly found myself in a state of war with the teachers. Then for a year I studied at the philological faculty of the university, but everything there was just like school, and I moved on to the Theatrical Institute as an external student. I graduated—why, I don't know—I'm an autodidact, so my knowledge is wide but superficial. The only things that have ever really interested me are poety and theology, separately and together. My first two published poems were in the newspaper of Tartu University in 1973, and until 1983 nothing else was published in my own country; but any time now my first little book will be coming out here. Starting in 1978, though, a lot has been published in émigré journals, and then three books came out: two collections of poetry, one with Russica in New York, and one in Paris, with Beseda; and a novel in verse (sort of) with Ardis Publishers in Ann Arbor about the mad nun Lavinia.

Translated by Barbara Heldt.

On the "Four Elegies to the Corners of the World"

Not everything in these elegies is comprehensible to me, let alone to the reader. However, a few points were cleared up by reading Florensky. He says that the world is a circle divided into corners by a cross, by which they are held together, through which they live.

The meaning of the elegies, it seems, is that the earth and the corners of the world and the parts of the body (a natural cross) have come apart and separated from that foundation, fulcrum and base. Each one is rushing in its own direction ("Eyes in formation are flying due south . . . ," "Backbones are flying due east in formation," etc.). The world is breaking apart and efforts to pull it together, to tie it up again into a whole made by man standing in the center (we are all in the center) are in vain. The fabric of the world has degenerated, become alienated has been pulled apart from its iron (golden) foundations. Such a world cannot exist and, shaking (but not just with horror, with relief as well), it sees through its final day.

At the base of the first elegy is a vision: three nebulous and clear figures—the Lion, the Eagle, and the Calf—appear in the sky. Only the angel, who should be there according to the prophecy of Ezekial, is missing.

II begins with a description of a marble statuette that depicts a couple embracing. They are without heads, with one arm and one leg, but when you look at them it seems they have everything and don't even need what they've got. Glancing at the statuette you see the invisible growing from the visible as if coming out of the fog.

III—Cyclamens under glass, the greenhouse in the Tauride garden, flowers at night under electric light and the nebulous thought of a glass coffin. In general, the theme of flowers, blooming in the frost amidst the snows, opening up in horror as if feeling the end of time, is important for the whole cycle. Their world, in frost and darkness, in the cracking of destruction and the scraping of someone's footsteps along the snow—and, even so, flowering and warm as never before.

At the base of the fourth is a dream about the Antichrist. He is described there in detail. Ksenya is St. Ksenya of Petersburg, walking barefoot in the frost in the uniform of her husband. At night, in the cold, she brought bricks for a church that was being built.

And that, schematically, is all.

Translated by Andrew Wachtel.

Four Elegies to the Corners of the World

I. (Northern)
M. Sh.

Through Moscow's twists and turns, along its hopeless windings
Someone's shadow flew, in tender desperation,
She pressed some hardened leaves to her eyes, and
Kissed an emerald duck in a pond,
And laughing, she slithered away, from a tram-car-steer.
Warming herself with the tram-car's spark.

"A Bergman flick" was announced at the theater that night,
But scenes from your own life were cranked into sight
One hundred times each. Who knew that hell rents the theaters by night?
That the dead are tied to chairs in there?
That tilted heads are looking back?
That they bring them there like soldiers to the baths?
A telegram for Charlotte: "Waiting, Love. Your Marat."

She sloughed seven skins off, eight souls and her clothing
And found a ninth soul in her breast,
She shook in my hand, like a meek mole,
Like a broad with a broom, blue beneath the snow.
I pierced through her eyes and she died.

Look, the heavens are covered, a fallout of feathers and wings,
Can't sweep them up in a week, you'll be buried forever in them.
Look, a lion, a calf and an eagle are flying right under the moon
And you sleep, you are lying 'midst bodies of serpentine rings.
Where's the angel? You ask me, so here's how I'll answer:
There where there's darkness, there's shining, where the whole world is
    maimed,
Grasping plant, thus an angel was twisting through darkness.

Steer for the blackness, for desolation's darkness.
Steer for the shadows, the shade, for the cliffs, for the roiled, the pit,
Is that angel playing tag? Yes, there he is, in the earth, under foot.
He's no worm. So don't dig, don't go looking in the field.
Do you see—toward winter bright birds fly on by to the pole?

She looked and she groaned
And she flew all night long, and she banged into prongs
Dripping blood on the hospitals, factories, boulevards . . .
It's OK! For your death is the birth of a luminous angel.

II. (Southern) A propos of a marble statuette

To I. Burikhin

Young lady! Did you drop something?
Akh, it's nothing. It's OK! My foot.
Like a narrow glove. And like dust,
Ringing, my shin is blowing away.

In glancing at you I was catching myself—
The old love is gone and the winter is too,
The future is naught but a flame on the mast
It's blueishly burning, and howls from the dark.
And over my head flocks of palms fly around,
Like seagulls, they peck, and they carry my memory away.
And darkness is petrifying, cliffs wheeze
And furiously, it seems as if someone is ripping up fabric close by.
And life is diffusing, an oily circle,
Though it once was a painful point. Broken-up pieces float by.
Pray tell, was I precious to anyone
On earth? Did I glide or float by in the dawn?
Did I pluck mother goose for her emerald grass, was I tearing it out
While we whispered la-la and la-la?
Eternity lay in a pond and I drank of that source.
That pond like an ocean expanded, for where there are knives in the waves
They tear and they cut, o long lines—life!
For God is who made us in fact—and like diamonds
He placed us in settings of bone.
For God is who made us in fact—
Like cyclamen planted in snow.
He quivered and burned and he shook in the act,
Thus everything shook and resounded and quivered,
And falling to pieces, like fire and like blood, everything flew into darkness
Where you are rapidly ripped into shreds
Where fathomless maws fasten onto your back

So pull out the honeycombs of memory—they're out of control.
Alone love is shining. Lot's wife, as it were,
It hangs like a lance in the mute abyss.
O, magnet of diamond, tell me where is the pole of the Universe!
That glimmering Thing, all in white and in ice
Whither Nansen and Peary and Scott from this day
Will be rushing while whipping a team made of famishing shades.
I'm going there too, where a bear colored lilac is sleeping
all covered in ice, where the magnet of diamond is pointing.
There burns in the sky an ethereal fire it seems
And eyes in formation are flying due south.
Little crosses of God, under-birds!
A multitude tears you to pieces and again you are legion,
You lead us right up to the threshold
Of darkening blue where they give us a team and a sled,
Ourselves we will not come together again,
Where the road through the tundra eternal is blazed.

III. (Eastern)

To E. Feoktistov

On your feet! Aren't you shamed to be sleeping in front of all eyes?
On your feet! Resurrection's time will be coming soon.
Crematorium—That's quite a place that you've chosen to sleep!
On your feet! And I'll set out a wee split of wine.
Oh my Lord! Is that me, a store window's reflection?
Is this poppy seed my incarnation?
Well OK! So I'll go take a look at the cyclamens under the crackling snow
Like a birdy, I'll slide under glass, run away.
Like a birdy, I'll slide under glass, run away.
For everyone is a birdy singing on a branch,
Though nobody wishes to listen we warble even louder.
I cover myself more thickly in golden plumage.
So prophesy, prophesy, on my thick coffee grounds,
For that drink, now deceased, I resemble,
And I feel strong enough for my future ordeals.
Oh my God, peck the seed out of me and the sooner the better,
I will be like the salt of your tears and on them I'll get drunk.

We're all of us warbling birds—just admire us all.
And through snow, breathing hard, grows a boiling flower,
Backbones are flying due east in formation.
The wind in the shape of an angel, it will enter unnoticed.
Death will eat round your contour, go round it exactly
It's powder corrosive, it's like aqua regis.
So fly to the firmament full speed ahead,
The wind in the shape of an angel, it blows at your head.

IV. (Western)
N. Guchinskaya

To the west, to the west by the shadowy path
All is howling, carried away to the place that is darker.
Like old clothing and faces and rings, or like bowling-alley spheres.
Through a chute for the garbage—and everything melts in the mist.
So then, what am I? I'm the everlasting vessel of the depths,
And within me the Mediterranean sparkles at low and high tide,
I'll stop up my ears, and I'll hear that there's noise in a shell,
And the seas and their hearts will dry up.
What traces remain on the fast drying sand?
I will count them for you on my fingers, despairing:
There's mollusks and verses and slugs and a ringlet,
Now the sand's started rising, it's already squishing.
Man's voice, swelling up, is approaching the cry of a bird, or a song,
Ah, Cry out like a gull and you too will acquire tranquility.
But already I'm horribly quiet.
(The flowers bloomed in horror although it was freezing.
In heaven strode the Antichrist midst clouds and stars.
He suddenly began descending and he grew before our eyes.
He strode within a thin blue beam,
While helicopters, faithful as pugs, were flying behind him.
And the people, on bended knee, were crossing themselves in the shadows.
He approached—eternal cold from his eyes streaming forth
He seemed never born, as if painted and wooden.
No, you weren't crucified for our sake!
But he surely and carefully touched all the bended heads)
All is howling, carried away, and only the holy return.

(Hey, do you see Ksenya? she's barefoot and wearing the clothes of the
    emperor's guard to her heels,
She's carrying bricks and floating above her's a halo of ice)
The wind carries all to the west by the shadowy path.
Space like a cross has ripped up all sides of the world.
How will you stand midst the shaking and breaking? On what?
We'd better float right on up to the sky.
There to the dusk where Persephone pale,
Looks in despair at a telephone dial.
Where shadows and pieces thereof are both boiling and suffering,
There you will shake both your hunger and thirst with a pomegranate seed.

    Translated by Andrew Wachtel.

Elegy on an X-ray Photo of My Skull

The flautist boasts but God's enraged—
He stripped the living skin from Marsyas—
Such is the destiny of earthly flautists:
Grown jealous, he will say to each in turn—
You've licked the honey of music but you're just muck,
You're still a lump of that same dirt
And lodged inside you is the stone of death.
Apollo was the god of light
But he grew dark
When round his hands, you Marsyas,
Twisted in pain.
And now he is a god of glimmer,
But eternal also are your groans.

And my God, growing dark,
Slipped me this photograph
In which my glowing skull
Etched from the invisible
Swam, blocking out the dusk
And the stripped naked park—
It was a mass of fog
Embraced in liquid dark.
In it shadow and cloud were blended
And my hand began to tremble.

This skull was my own
But it didn't know me,
Its intricate pattern
Like a damascene dagger
Is skillfully crafted,
How pure and how strong.
But the mouth is bared,
Still alive its grin.

Bone, you yellowed a long time,
Grew as heavy as sin,
Like a walnut you aged and you ripened,
A present for death.
Grown brazen inside me, this yellow bone
Has lapped itself in a sleigh-rug of skin
And taking my reins sped off headlong
But come to a halt at my brow.
In anguish here before my God I stand
Holding my skull in a trembling hand—
O Lord, what shall I do with it?
Spit in its eye sockets?
Fill it up with wine?
Or put it on my neck and wear it once again?
So I hurl it aside—this light-looking shell
And it flies off thundering among the stars like a pail.
But it returned and, landing on my neck, reminded me in consolation:
Way back at someone's house, its fellow stood as a table decoration
And led the deathlife of a dehydrated plant
As if it were a temple or a chalice.
There was a lot to drink but not enough—
And someone took this skull and began to pass it round
To collect the money for a vodka bottle.
Small change was scattered clinking on the dark occiput
But straightaway I confiscated it,
Put it back where it belonged—calm down—
And like a kitten it rubbed against my palm.
For this I shall be granted as reward
That nobody will desecrate my skull—
No worm will crawl inside it, no new Hamlet take it in his hands.
When my end comes—I shall walk up the aisle in flames.

But something else strikes me as weird,
That I can't sense my skeleton inside—
Neither skull nor flesh nor bones—
More like a crater after the explosion
Or a memory of missing news,
Mistiness or mist
Or a spirit drunk on its new life.

But you will be my lodgings when
They start to pipe the Resurrection.
You, my spirit's navel, fly
Sooner to the East. And I
All around you as a dusty cloud
Erupting, swirling, setting as the Word.
But what a shame you won't be filled again
With all that soft old curd.

Translated by Michael Molnar.

Voyage

Ignatius, Joseph, Chrissy, May, and I
Drifted in a warm heat-cracked boat through a dazzling fog.
If the Vistula were our Gulf, we were probably drifting across it.
We were naked—though hidden in cloudpuffs of rosypink motes,
Hardly visible one to another, like flies in a cut-glass jug,
Like a grape's pips under the skin of the grape.
Body had gone inside, but souls—like germinating crops
Were outside, blanketing us in transparent sleeping bags.
Where were we going so slowly—drifting as if we weren't drifting?
A long time all of us gazed at the shallow seabed's glide.
"Joseph, is that spot a birthmark on your forehead?"
He answered me and all went dark before my eyes.
"I was the warden in St. Florian's church
And on my forehead here, this is a fatal wound.
Somebody shot me, probably they were drunk.
Look, Chrissy's shimmering in lilac-bluish silk,
She was burnt up yesterday at her home near Czestochowa."

"Nie ma już ciala, a boli mnie glowa."[1]
Like an overroasted chestnut she is all dark and warm.
"Was hat man dir, du armes Kind, getan?"[2]
What he told me about myself—it wasn't that it was awful—
I just don't remember what—I tried in vain to grasp—
Not grazing consciousness—it had been somehow blinded,
Deoculated—what was happening to me there?
Whatever it was—no, it wasn't happening to me.
Hiding as usual in a cage's image
Three canary-cousins and coevals
Sported in the sheen of song. Shot clean
Next to me a one-eyed squirrel crouched.
The stream was shining and it was so languid and so shallow.
Oh, I'll take squirrel and canaries now
And wade across—what of you, Joseph, Chrissy?
The shore is over there—it's not yet hidden in mist.
"Only the water bright with static illumination
Seems awful, like high-tension—current will shock,
Will pull away in one direction
And don't even dream of getting back.
The squirrel's hide is being soaked in tannin,
Your ashes dry, delighting in their urn.
What's over there? But here, dear sunlight warms."
"Well then, what of those I've loved,
Will I never see them any more?"
"Don't worry! You'll be seeing them. With the tide
The water will carry them toward us here."
"And if forever"[3] then
"Muzyka brzmi"[4] extracts out of Strauss.
The water has thickened all over and turned to cream!
But no one drinks it. Oh, if only you could just
Give back our previous hot pomegranate juice,
Which swirled around so long, which—clacked and sobbed—
From the heart, in the heart—sacred, subcutaneous coal,
Scarlet thread stitched and sewed up Your creation!
O you, mere concept of blood circulation,

1. I no longer have a body, but my head aches (Polish).
2. What have they done to you, poor child? (Goethe).
3. Byron.
4. Music thunders (Polish).

Are beautiful like an avenging angel.
How many boats, how many fragile boats are circling round,
And I look to you alone, my old drowned friend,
And my killed kitten suddenly
Leapt up onto my shoulder
Stroking my cheek with his white paw.
Together we haven't got too far to float.
Like a creaking of doors
The wingbeat of rowlocks is glad,
To plumb the murky soul
An angel will drop like lead . . .

       Translated by Michael Molnar.

Animal-Flower

Presentiment of life abides till death.
A chilling fire burns along the bones—
When a bright shower passes over
On St. Peter's Day at break of summer.
Scarlet blooms are just about to flower
On collarbones, on ribs, upon the head.
The cluster will be tagged *Elena arborea*—
Its habitat is freezing Hyperborea
In gardens made of brick, in grass of stone.
Eyes sprout dark carnations. I'm at once
A bush of roses and forget-me-nots
As if a savage gardener'd grafted on me
A virulent florescing leprosy,
I will be violet and red,
Crimson, yellow, black and gold,
Inside a dangerous humming cloud
Of bees and wasps I'll be a sacred well.
And when my flowers fade, O Lord, O Lord,
What a bitten lump there'll be left over,
Grown cold and with its skin split wide,
A faded, half-dead Animal-Flower.

       Translated by Michael Molnar.

Timur Kibirov

TIMUR KIBIROV was born in 1955, studied to become a teacher of Russian language and literature, and graduated from the N. K. Krupskaya Moscow Regional Pedagogical Institute. From 1975 to 1977 he served in the Soviet army. He now works in an art institute as a junior research assistant. The selections here were translated by Paul Graves and Carol Ueland.

Banal Thoughts on the Purpose of Poetry and the Duty of the Poet

Poetry (especially Russian poetry) has served just about everything: religion, politics, philosophy, pedagogy, and linguistics. Even economics. Even the Ministry of Defense as well as various other ministries and departments. There's really nothing so horrible about this tendency. Sometimes it even ends up producing unexpected successes.

On the other hand, any thoughtful reader (not to mention the poet himself) knows that in practice the basic purpose of the poet's task and the core of poetry itself consist of something else. As it has in the past, this sense still tempts one to consider poetry generally devoid of any extrapoetic purpose and to declare poetry "aimless, like life itself." But the statement "Poetry's purpose is poetry itself" will today satisfy only well-read tenth-graders rebelling against the state pedagogical institutes. (By the way, the same is true of the statement "Life's purpose is in life itself.") This problem will probably never be definitively solved. I'd like to present my own wholly primitive and unfounded arguments on this perpetual topic.

It seems to me that poetry (and art in general) is given to man as a universal means of fighting entropy, necrosis, and banality: i.e., fighting what's generally called the devil. The poet's real, everlasting foe is the mob, who embody banality and celebrate it in their language, ideology, and daily life.

The classical way is as follows: the poet composes lofty, beautiful verses, distracting the souls of his sensitive fellow citizens from the prosaicism of life, from the vain bustle of the marketplace and the battlefield, so that, filled with the rarefied sounds of harmony, they accept God's world like a miracle. Then the poet has fulfilled his mission.

But it's become clear over time that banality is by no means defeated. And the poet notes, with repulsion, that the mob singing his songs is still a mob, that the creations of his exalted lyre have themselves been turned into the dullest of banalities by their contact with untransfigured life, and that his very name calls forth the yawns and curses of schoolboys.

Then the poet decides on a desperate step: In order to escape the dreadful and importunate company of the petty demon, he surrenders himself wholly to the crimson-winged Great Demon, "the Spirit of negation and doubt," does his best to frighten the Philistines with his arrogance and derision, to dumbfound them with pictures of a nature never seen before and of unheard-of passions, and flees everything ordinary. But here's banality again! The mob greets the raving romantic and individualist with applause and eats up his most exotic stew with relish.

And the poet runs further, to immorality, madness, and gloom; he mangles the language and glorifies the most abominable sins.

If only he could break off and walk away! Unfortunately, his path is hopeless.

It also constitutes desertion. Unable to defend Truth, Goodness, and Beauty from banality, and having surrendered the whole world to banality inch by inch, the poet finds himself at the end of his tragic journey face to face with laughing Ugliness, Lies, and Evil, with banality in its terrible, undisguised, primeval form.

But there's another way. It requires great strength and courage. And cunning. Don't run from banality; don't fight it face to face (that always produces the most tragicomic results). Attack from the rear; dig in where language, consciousness, and life have long been considered completely under the control of banality, where attack is least expected. Free the banal and the "all too human" from the rule of entropy; transform them with harmony and reanimate them. In this, it seems to me, is the purpose and duty of contemporary poetry. In this, poets as different as the classicist Gandlevsky and the avant-gardist Rubinshtein, the lyricist Aizenberg and the conceptualist Prigov, agree. And I too try to serve in this way with all of my strength.

When Lenin Was Young

I

Vladimir Ilyich's father, Ilya Nikolayevich, was at that time an inspector of
state schools in the province of Simbirsk. He came from a simple background,
lost his father at an early age, and only with the help of his older brother was
he able, with difficulty, to get an education....

Vladimir Ilyich's mother, Maria Alexandrovna, was the daughter of a doctor;
she spent most of her youth in the country, where the peasants loved her very
much. She was a good musician and knew music and languages well: French,
German, and English...

—A. I. Ulyanova

I often think how unimaginable
it is—and yet it really happened!
Otherwise, he couldn't have been born.
That means, however hard it is for the mind
to accept, that his appearance on earth,
his writing *What Is to Be Done?* as well as
The Three Sources of Marxism, that the *Aurora,*
the ElectriRuss state plan, the lunar module,
the nuclear-powered ship—it all depended
on one (and only one!) spermatazoon's
successful penetration of Maria
Alexandrovna's genitalia. How strange!

I imagine their little house out in Simbirsk.
The year is sixty-nine, the twilight deep blue.
The inspector's in his study. The table lamp
agreeably illuminates his forehead's
Socratic bulk. His pen scratches on paper...
but now from distant rooms a quiet melody
unexpectedly starts to play.
What infinite delicacy it shows,
what heavenly, timeless, feminine sadness!
A dreamy sweetness clogs his energetic mind,
and his hand freezes, not even finishing
the sentence. He extinguishes the lamp.

He stands and tiptoes to . . .

                              the living room,
where no light has yet been lit; at the piano:
Maria Alexandrovna . . . Unwittingly,
while lost in admiration of the shapely,
sad woman's silhouette against the windows,
Ilya lingers at the doorway. The minutes
are flying and the melody is swelling
with melancholy and unspoken love,
with promises of happiness, with sobbing . . .
And finally he coughs.
                              "O, my dearest!
O, how you frightened me!" "Maria!"
begins the inspector in his basso, hoarse
with tenderness. "It's late. It's time for bed,
Maria." And there is something in his voice
that makes Maria Alexandrovna turn red.
"But, dear, what are you . . ." "Mashenka, let's go!
Come on, it's late; come on, my little Masyusya!"

It seems to me that she was frigid,
or almost frigid; and the inspector's ardor
was something she yielded to against her will,
not right away, but later on, when she
had thrown her delicate arms and legs around
the mighty torso of the schools inspector:
"Ilya, Ilyushechka, Ilyushechka . . . Ilyusha!"

When Lenin Was Young

II

*He began to walk at the same time as his sister Olya, who was a year and a
half younger than he. She began to walk very early, and, somehow, people
around didn't notice. Volodya, just the opposite, learned to walk late, and if
his little sister inaudibly fell, or "plopped," in the expression of their nurse,
and then got up, leaning with both her dear little hands on the floor, all on
her own—well, then he absolutely had to flop his head down and raise a*

despairing howl to the whole house. Probably his head was weighing him
down. Everyone would run up to him, and his mother feared that he would
seriously fracture his head or become a little imbecile. And their acquaintances
who lived on the floor below said they could always hear Volodya banging his
head on the floor, "and we would say: he'll grow up to be either very smart
or very stupid."

—*A. I. Ulyanova*

Dear reader! I admit, I just don't know
what to say here. Of course, one can imagine . . .
but it's best not to try. A mind like Euclid's
would unsuccessfully endeavor to untangle
cause and effect's inexorable knot.
But we refuse to guess! We'll bow in silence
before great mysteries, before the strange game
that superhuman forces play . . .

When Lenin Was Young

III

He played very little with toys; he'd rather break them instead. Since we,
the older kids, tried to prevent him from doing this, he would sometimes
hide from us. I remember how, precisely on his birthday, when his nurse
had given him a troika of horses harnessed to a sleigh made out of papier-
mâché, he suspiciously hid himself somewhere with his new toy. We looked
for him and found him behind a door. He stood quietly, concentratedly
twisting the legs of a horse until they all fell off.

—*A. I. Ulyanova*

Hey, Godunov-Cherdyntsev, check this out:
the Muse of Russian History behaving
like some insistent merchant at the bazaar,
offering her inferior goods to
her undiscriminating little sister,
who's got a weakness for Calliope's junk.

Hey, troika, flying troika! Who made you
to be like this? Where were you rushing off to?
Your bell rang madly, first with laughter, then

with sobs; the wind was howling like a bandit;
and alien tongues recoiled and froze in fear
as the whistle of the knout played over them.

Meanwhile, the pepper-sausage German, slide rule
in hand, was staring bewilderedly into
the carriage window: "Hey, you, flying troika!
For God's sake, where d'you think you're going so fast?"
. . . No answer. And there never will be one.
The little boy with the curly hair and large
untroubled brow is twisting the last leg off.
"No, we're not going this way!" How strange. . . .

Shouldn't we have gone by paddlewheeler or
by steamship? . . . faster and faster, so the people
would rejoice and all would be made glad?

When Lenin Was Young

IV

*Little Volodya loved to catch birds; he and his friends would snare them.
Once, I remember, he had a linnet in a cage. I don't know if he had caught
it, purchased it or been given it. I only remember that the linnet didn't live
long; it became bored, curled up and died. I no longer know why; was
Volodya to blame for forgetting to feed it, or not? I only remember that
someone reproached him on the subject; and I remember the serious,
concentrated expression with which he looked at the dead linnet before he
said, decisively, "I will never keep birds in a cage anymore." And really, he
never did.*

—A. I. Ulyanova

Fly, little linnet, join the throng of shades
in that realm where the blind swallow has returned,
where Venus's turtledoves still hang around,
where Lesbia's sparrow plays, where the Falcon,
wounded, hails the flight of his little brother,
the Stormy Petrel, where the terrifying
slain albatross takes his drastic revenge

on the English mariner, where he's avenged
by some French sailors who get back at another
of the same kind of albatrosses, where
the dacha-renter sent the Seagull with a shot,
where nightingales sing over roses and
bullfinches pipe out army songs, where even
a lapwing serenades Young Naturalists,
where a baby starling clings to a twig,
where raven to raven flies, and to mad Edgar
upon the midnight dreary, where birdsong
pours out between the Russian earth and sky,
where chickens love to live, where you can hear
the beloved voice of robin redbreast,
where the singer gave the little bird
its freedom, thus preserving the olden custom,
where there's a speckled hen, where Halcyon
soars over Batiushkov's sail and Philomel
fills darkness nightly with her murmured plaints,
where the blind swallow has returned, still blind . . .
And you should fly there too, my little linnet!
You've earned your immortality. So fly!

When Lenin Was Young

V

*He would run off fishing on the Sylvaga, and one of his friends told me
the following story. One of the lads proposed that they go fishing in a
large, full ditch nearby; he said it was a good place for catching carp. So
off they went, but when Volodya leaned out over the edge, he fell into the
ditch. The silty bottom started to swallow him up. "I don't know what
would have happened," said this friend, "if one of the workers from the
factory hadn't heard our cries, run up to the edge and pulled Volodya out."*

                                              —A. I. Ulyanova

It was the Worker's arm that saved the Fatherland.
No matter what the S.D.'s say, without
this person's role in history, everything
would be different. Already Mother Russia

had started sliding down the bourgeois track.
And so, of course, that's how it would have been!
She was headed down what you might call
an inclined plane, along the iniquitous path
of least resistance. She probably would have
picked up easy ways and been corrupted.
O, how completely rotten she'd have been!

And they'd still be eating their pineapples
and munching grouse right now, and hardly could
have dug their way through the White Sea Canal.
They scarcely could have bested prostitution.
And Nicholas the Bloody Tsar would have lived
unpunished, together with his wife and children!
And mind, honor, and conscience would have languished
in exile in Shushenskoye! And then
our Serafimovich would suffer mockery
from cynical, degenerate modernists,
and God only knows, but Yevtushenko would
have to perform in bars around Odessa.
Now that's a terrifying thought!

And here's another terrifying thought,
although an interesting one: what if
instead of a Worker, some Muzhik had pulled him
out of the muck—Marey the Muzhik, or Platon?
Then would he, our Ilyich, fall suddenly
in love with the humble sagacity and barefoot
qualities of the people in coarse cloth,
and live the simple life, and wander Russia,
a beggar dispensing blessings? What a strange fate . . .

Or try imagining that a corpulent Merchant,
complete with beaver hat, was passing by? Or maybe
the Cornet of Horse, shapely in his uniform?
Or some Priest's Son in the double-breasted jacket
of a student? In short, what if it were anyone
from that whole gang of dogs and butchers? Then
Volodinka would have become a Constitutional
Democrat and not the blossoming of spring,

the call of victory . . . O, how strange!
It's all so strange, if you only stop to think . . .

Christological Diptych

Part I

> *"Roses are blooming. Beauty, beauty!*
> *Soon we'll behold the infant Christ."*
>   —*Andersen*

Dimly shines the Wormwood star.
In its light it seemed I beheld
the knife of Dzhugashvili bared
as the hoofs of his Pale Horse fell.

Forgive me, it may be I'm wrong.
Maybe it still isn't the truth.
They say that, with his shining wings,
heavenly Khrushchev will see us through.

Excuse me, this is nothing but rot.
Go ahead, look: your Khrushchev flies
with the angel-swarm from the pit
and his shiny dead bald spot terrifies.

How amazingly large they are!
And their name is Legion in the book.
In my head from day one they've roared
out their songs, their horses run amok.

This battle will be our only one.
And it's clear we've already lost.
You see, there is Stalin, quite young.
He's the man no one will stand against.

Forgive me and pay me no heed.
Many years now I've been obsessed.

I shudder still, because I see
the empty orbits of the horse's eyes.

The gates of hell are open wide.
And no longer can the infant Christ
find anyone who would keep Him hid
under a shirt, against a sweaty chest.

Laugh, laugh; don't listen, just laugh!
So I'm blind with fear; but in the dark
there appeared to me Satan himself.
Now I know what his face looks like.

This isn't politics, I swear!
Why be political here, anyway?
In my dream Baby Jesus appeared,
who, I know, will soon be betrayed.

This isn't politics, you clod!
When will you ever understand:
in the manger, defenseless, unclothed,
He'll be sold for loose change again.

Then, finally, you will understand,
and at last you'll bellow in rage,
as the fucking Apocalypse comes on
and you and I are snuffed for loose change!

Once again the Kremlin's chimes struck.
Once again, soccer on Channel One.
Once again, the daybreak cry of the cock.
In renunciation, he's picked up and gone.

Christological Diptych

Part II

You're in a new dress today,
the color of the ocean's waves.

Like the golden sands that line
the Riviera, your hair's ablaze.

All of you is like a carefree
cruise down European shores,
that patria we'll never see,
although it's forever ours.

No, we won't see it! Why should we?
No, we shouldn't. O, let's go!
—through the old neglected garden,
singing our songs as we stroll.

Yes, we'll sing and trail along
on the track of butterflies.
You and I: just like a picture,
singing about future times.

Nothing will divide us;
Mother Earth herself cannot
divide us, for the poplars have
let us in on her flying thought.

Sunburst, look what happiness
there is, despite death and fear.
A bird, as if at First Communion,
turns heavenward and soars.

Bird of God, o bird of God,
sing, don't be afraid, you're right!
And our skin is gently stroked
By the golden-azure sky.

It's all because we are a cell
in the Kingdom of Future Love!
In vain the villainess Fate
sneers, her lips stained with blood.

You and I together singing,
strolling in the blue, the green!

Because certainly we know
what the final answer will be:

Nonsense! Everything passes?
Nonsense! Don't believe it, friend!
Everything comes back to us
in its own time, already soon!

Everything will get even better,
like the water at the wedding feast,
under the lightness of fingers
that somehow blinded both of us.

So look, feast your eyes on summer,
on this garden, overgrown,
on this midday happiness,
as if many years ago.

Color of the cool sea wave,
gold of Russian waves of grain,
pure, pure merciless motifs,
childhood memories run again.

And our Europe is with us,
and Russia is a part of it,
and our holy banner is
the new dress I find you in!

Viktor Krivulin

VIKTOR KRIVULIN was born in Leningrad in 1944. He was editor during the 1970s of the *Northern Post,* the first samizdat journal inside the Soviet Union devoted exclusively to poetic theory. His poetry has been translated into a number of languages and published in Russian by émigré presses in Paris. A book of his work was published in the Soviet Union in 1990, and his work appears in the Penguin Books anthology *Child of Europe.*

Poetry in the Sunset of the Empire

Speaking of poetry is the same thing to me as speaking of poverty and sickness. The poetic word, in my view, starts its weaving once some lack of the most essential ingredients turns up, once the springs of pure drinking water dry up, once the reserves of foodstuffs catastrophically give out, and the words *blagodushie, dobrodushie* (*kalagatia—prekrasnodobrie*) and *miloserdie* [all high-class words indicating "magnanimity"—Trans.] take on irreversibly ironic overtones.

I began writing verses at the end of the 1950s because the world around me was impoverished, squalid, and ugly. I spent my childhood in a communal apartment, transformed from a huge suite of rooms in a nobleman's living quarters, typical of Petersburg, into an overpopulated Soviet dormitory. Outside the high windows of my misshapen, angular room lay postwar Leningrad—numbed, hushed, and depeopled. It had experienced a number of catastrophes which one after the other had snuffed out the slightest spark of intellectual or emotional freedom glowing in its pseudoempire walls. I belong to the first post-catastrophic generation, whose pathos may be defined as spiritually archaic, for precisely to us belongs the dubious, yet true, honor of first discovering under the layer of ashes of Leningrad that city that while already semi-transparent, nevertheless possesses to the present day a more magnetic and more real reality (forgive the involuntary redundancy). To designate this city as Petersburg would be wrong, insofar as we are speaking here not merely of some geographical point but of the two-hundred-year chunk of European history transcribed into Slavonic.

This city seemed to us in our youth all the more wonderful in that it existed in a different "time-place" from the reality guiding the majority of people who in recent decades had settled in it. For them it was foreign and remains so, an almost hostile city, just as the entire European period of Russian history is alien to them. They have no relationship to this beauty, this blood and guts, this supernatural design. Thus foreigners occupy the capital of a conquered nation. Thus the Aztecs and Mayans took over the ancient Toltec city giants, using for their blood rituals complexes of temples constructed for purposes unknown to them, for purposes perhaps more humane than their regularly scheduled human sacrifices.

Poetry became for me something akin to "Toltecness," a concept that in the Mayan language expressed the highest degree of nobility and perfection, albeit only in the past and in a foreign culture unattainable today, yet which enlivens the inhuman everyday order of things perceived as "bad," "false," and "damaged" in its reflection of the higher reality, the World-As-It-Ought-To-Be.

I do not deny the Platonic sources of my poetry, even the philosopher's idea that the "State" should mercilessly drive the poets out of the ideal society. This strikes me as the height of poetry.

In a way, the postwar Soviet empire was a private and imperfect attempt to realize the Platonic state, and poetry born in the dividing space, in the cranny between the world of ideas and the monstrously ugly everydayness of communal apartments, was literally torn apart in the foredoomed effort to justify one through the other. The functional superfluity of the poet in the Neoplatonic state had already been felt in the 1930s by Boris Pasternak.

And if in days of the Great Soviet,
Where places are set for the higher passion,
A vacancy is left, that of the poet—
It's very dangerous, if not yet empty.

I sensed this danger fully, and that is what made the writing of poetry an attractive pursuit for me—and not only for me, I dare to think. In an impoverished society the poet is always something of a millionaire, and if this society is strictly ordered on the verticle line, the poet who does not receive his title from the hands of power but usurps it by his "calling" is nothing less than an underground millionaire and finds in his underground business that bit of romanticism and adventurism which makes the boredom of "civilized existence" quite impossible.

The elements of pseudoempire present in most of the "self-proclaimed" poets of the Leningrad postwar school are destined to become the converse of their adventurous selection, to counterbalance the spontaneity of commonplace life with a rigid "forum of forms."

Every poetic text impresses me as an arena for a dramatic contest between two spaces—the space of speech and the space of silence. The intervals between the words are more important than the words themselves: Here in the gaps and pauses the specifically poetic, personal content of the text is realized, and the pause is the hierarchically organized structure of the logico-grammatical unity is the more significant the more rigid and imperative this unity itself. In the continuum of the imperial linguistic cosmos man himself is like a pause, a gap; his person comes forth as a magnitude added negatively, and the borders of his silence may be juxtaposed with the borders of a separate human life, which by its "emptiness' unites the compact "fullness" of a linguistically generic chain, the compact "fullness" of "history" unfolded in the time of a phrase.

Hence the principle, which I find valuable, of "the new historicism." Outside this principle the fundamental silence of a man speaking a language in space cannot be formulated. The new historicism regards any speech, including the speech of the poet himself ("the lyric voice"), as "another's word." "One's own" can only be silence.

I began to write verses not from a desire to say anything but in the attempt to overcome the insupportable silence of existence by designating it as part of the history of other people.

Having experienced the influence of Russian poetry from the "Silver Age," primarily Mandelstam, Khlebnikov, and the Oberiuty, an influence that was devastating for most of the Leningrad poets of my time, I preferred not to struggle with "other voices" in order to define myself in the process but to accept certain defeat as an imitator, an epigone, to assume the obedient pose of linguistic humility, which permitted me at long last to discover myself as a unique speech lacuna, almost palpably marking off the borders of my own poetic "I."

Translated by Gary Kern.

From the Cycle Poems on Maps

into the fluting of the spinal cord
a map of the world is rolled
a tremor the line of the shore
blue gaps and flecks for the highland

prenatally inserted
inside its fragile case
this axis of upright gait
unrolls, like a gift

of a world laid bare
where the outlines of dry land
show us the way to mend
coils linking body and soul

the ocean's mighty caress
in a half-named universe
has taken us over—and
an old wall map from holland

covers as it were our head
drawn into its funnel

❖

entire peoples also possess
a hard to conceal passion
for suicide. having blocked
ways, and ways out, and ways in,
respiratory restriction
creates its own place
inside a rolled-up map
when continents are coarse
to the touch—and not one state
can be guessed at, only a crack
in the cardboard or the paper

a rift traverses the heart
of some—better not look
which—country! just let it lose
its zigzags in the darkness
like undeciphered signs
of your own fate

maps and calendars and maps.
time and space. time
of diaspora and dissolution
in the short dictionary of rhyme
in the blockades of besieged speech

let's leave a few names behind,
the broken line of a frontier.
uncontoured, unconcerned by features
light streams from the plan, from the page
turning over us

some few of all the voices
I can hear: freed from the chorus
a nebulous stalk, it's a splinter
from woods exploded by the spring

some few of them over my head:
eyewash, a scumble of cloud.
on the historical tracks
some sort of halfway station

looming. a manuscript vault—
or, rather, no dome but a hillock.
within it a chasm, but in our talk
the blue tit cannot even find the space

to weave a nest. how can one live one's life
more meagerly?—and speechless cross
to an artificial gallery
made of fretworked bone and sky

all the spring walls crumble into powder
maps of the naked seas are being laid bare
lilac-yellowy flecks—
only the faces—neither drift nor alter
and the eyes open wide in an iconic
inverse perspective—breathe—their gaze distorted

violet florenskii has been studied. dark purple
rozanov banged shut. crossroad of Garden street
and Peagreen street. windows and people
in subdued semitransparent bodies
suffocate, go deaf
and shout—but sounds are soldered in a vessel

of light blue glass
no—colorless not light blue

news gets round. I see from the window:
a gray-haired poet, once a bloomsbury youth,
is crossing the street. above him
moves the diurnal moon—
sympathetic influence of the almost
hallucinated disc . . . saint Hieronymus
fondling a lion . . . but in all conscience this
never hung on any wall!
and news gets round as in sleep
bypassing brain and penetrating body
and skin responds at random
growing alternately tense and slackening

at the internal and external noise
extinguished in the sound of plainsong

tuned to contemplation
of the miraculous we are immersed
in radiant underwood and I do not
exist—but a harsh-lit forest
of pseudogothic pinnacles
playing its various chords lives on

shadow of cloud on the roof   traces
of flickering presence   the dead
or exited—under illumination
of threefold sevenfold light   cast
by a single second and sheer zero spring
that borders no summer

flight to egypt

almost the moment almost
the place, the dead center of crossed
wires in a gunsight—almost the place
but hard to wrest the spirit.
pursuit. and for some reason or other
glancing back to find
in april quattrocento air
and breath and rest on the road
to egypt. flight. the edge of the picture
shadowy and impenetrable

wellspring, an angel, an ass
a family fleeing beyond the frame—
all this to one side, but straight on
at the center—sheer caprice
of targeted antique ruins
collapsing bole of a column

and in symmetrical sculptures
purple vine tendrils snake
braiding a hot thigh.
pursuit. the attendant

guardian in a hurry
to be home stares at the last
visitors. through the summer
windows heat seeps inside
from late afternoon—in the gallery
in front of a shadowy picture
Three remain. we at the start
of an inapparent path
almost the moment almost
a radiant Map behind our shoulders

colorlessness. just infrets
of shrubbery amid the snows
and in the low sun a rosy
gathering of birch boles

but everything on the variegated way
blending into one band
colored yellowish-red
with the glide of light across a face
          All poems from this cycle are translated by Michael Molnar.

Yuri Arabov

YURI ARABOV was born in 1954 in Moscow. In addition to his poetry, he
is also well known as a filmmaker. He began publishing in 1987, and his
poems have appeared in numerous Soviet journals. He took part in the
"Crossing Boundaries" festival in San Francisco in 1991.

One Way to Overcome Slavery

We're the dying representatives of a dying profession. Even in Dickens's time
it was already ludicrous and demeaning to speak with poems. So in our day
the occupation's been primarily taken up by the members of the Soviet
Writers' Union, who occupy themselves with successfully fighting to raise the
pay for poetry to two and a half rubles a line—or even higher. Well, let
them be praised and honored for that. Recently I was overwhelmed when I
received more than 500 rubles for a thin selection of my poetry. I immediately
wanted to sing hosanna to the Moscow writers' organizations, but I caught
myself just in time.

The matter is that for quite some time now I've been thoroughly
convinced that to take money for poetry is absolutely unnecessary, although
not one of us, myself included, ever refused to accept the damned payoffs.
But Russia's been run down by all of our literary professionals (this con-
sciousness of the nation, these superintendents of the soul, and so on, who
cite Pushkin as their source). But they're not really selling inspiration; they're
attempting to palm off their own program. I'm talking about the better
ones among them, not the graphomaniacs and political zealots who keep
guard. But we have to understand and forgive them—with all of their ide-
ological declarations and the chicken coups in which survive the "individu-
alists" or "avant-gardists." Yet we, the so-called young, why are we any

worse? Why are we forced to deny ourselves even undercooked kielbasa when the preceding generation gobbled up caviar? But still . . . but still . . .

The friends who change things—especially those of you among us from the avant-garde—do some more thinking before it's too late. A miracle appeared in your trembling hands either by the will of fate or by accident, but with the help of which you may extract the slave from yourself even more quickly than predicted by the late Anton Pavlovich. No one but its own creator needs a rhymed poem, so it's really worthless. The Soviet ruble (that miser) or the Silver Fund, as it is called, compels us all to crawl before separate citizens and whole organizations which deep in their soul label us as vipers—and not as vipers that crawl but as vipers that speak. They're not right, these separate citizens. Because poetry is not a commodity, it's a path. It's no better than any other path (such as the religious), but it's preferable to many (such as the political). The soul grows with each new poem, so the reader owes nothing to the poet—and, likewise, the poet owes nothing to the reader. The reader's position may even be higher than that of the poet. Someone's work is appreciated only when the reader, independent of the poet, goes through an analogous spiritual journey in his or her own life— and then, suddenly, there's some kind of acknowledgment, that momentary mental handshake, the result of which is love. It doesn't need to be tied to anything. One doesn't need to propagandize the avant-garde anymore than one needs to propagandize socialist realism. The artist having been released from slavery with the help of his own work is broader and more multilayered than any "ism." Within him there should exist at least three levels: that pertaining to the avant-garde, to the real, and to the spiritual (i.e., that which is not made by hands). With these first two everything is more or less clear. They exist within each of us. But the third level is more complicated. It is already a quality of the nonslave.

Concerning my own poetry, I don't consider myself an avant-gardist, for I still value the creations of Leonardo, especially his mechanisms, more than I value my own saliva. Cultural tradition for me—it's not an empty sound—and from classical Russian poetry I most of all love these lines: "My blue bells, flowers of the steppes . . ." I honestly don't read that much recent writing, but the poetry I do read is that of my own generation.

Translated by John High and Julie Gesin.

I'm introducing it as a hunchback,
with a handbag around its neck

                      like a pelican,
but if you take a camel

              by the waist,
the hand will plunge through

                as if going through a volcano.

Sleep, my laziness, with a glass saw
sawing

              me in half.
I want to scratch my knee
but it happens my knee is not there.

Along the China Wall

                of my spinal chord
a fly is crawling, and I feel,

              its bare foot,
but, so that they don't call me a squabbler
I fall asleep without chasing it away.

The idiots bare with their studies,
chattering about Eternity

              with the lisp of Ilyich
but the non-idiots were born for laziness,
not all of them, but in any case, I was.
I could have slept

             through another ten centuries,
without undressing, spitting on shame,
on the sandpaper falling from my cheeks,
and on the snow lying on my tongue.

I'm impatient with discipline.
Human kind scares me.

It creates this noise
in my
      head.

And within it,
             like an old quarry,
are the remains of landslides and quotations.
How many Yulanovs' were there?
                          I don't remember.
I can't count.

I don't need either the devil,
                 that horn,
or the demon
          with the face of a rotten carrot.
I scratch . . .
        but this is not my leg,
this is,
      god dammit, what is it!

May the gun spit out the bullet,
so you'll forget your own name,
may the water
         be transformed into our skeleton,
and may they call this snow frost.

And may God, over his own stove
force the fire to burn the other way.
And the forest, shaking it off,
             head toward the East,
and the ashes will again sit at the desk.

I'm waiting, having disappeared, like glass
in the pond,
        all put together from car coils,

until the laziness turns into madness
and into death,
                    which is called its sister.

Translated by John High.

Initiation into the Circle of Poets

Henchmen comrades Yezhov, Yagoda, here
is my head on a plate like an ear
of corn. Surely some labor camp has a nice vacancy;
I know if I don't go, the vermin won't publish me.

For the years go by, all the finest days
always without Yazhov, without Yagoda always.
Whether riding by train with no pot to piss in
or flying the skies with a watchguard to listen,

people bug you with freedom, poke at you too
and each points an accusatory finger at you;
what kind of fate is this malignant doom?
When the guard isn't there, it's the boss convict goon.

Not everything is revealed here for not everyone
and the bride is not weightless on her own.
It's not the tree here that the lumberjack's shorn
nor is it a bird that our Father has borne.

And no one's sarcoma, not your critic unreined
injecting blue dye in your eyes in your veins,
not one bit a halfwit, not an imbecile's face
which isn't any worse than a psycho case.

Behind the grainy desk, watching the tornado
that flattens the landscape beyond his window,
Octoberist kid-Pavlik, parents turned in, commences
an essay entitled "How to Serve Prison Sentences."

Dear sweet silly fool!
For what perch do your drool?

Farrody, is it possible you didn't know,
never touched tea with unboiled H$_2$O.

Has the sky dropped lower than the soot in this pit?
It's not for us, standing up, to brush against it.
Look how like peelings stuck in the grater
the seagulls are clotted to the viscous water.

With the clack of knitting needles their feathers meander,
take the form of the mustache of a battalion commander.
Birds drawn with a child's innocent style:
two hands outstretched from a faceless watch dial.

Makarenko, I say! Do you hear me, Makarenko!
I'd have wiped out all gnats to the final mosquito,
if this upside down world weren't baptized in the sea
of a mud puddle by children, as though in a bidet.

And when we grow old and our tonsils fall out
and our shirts tear to bits and our pants have the gout,
we will crawl like Meresyov to the *New World Review*
and treat our company there to our brotherly stew.

Translated by Sara Dickinson and Forrest Gander.

Windy

When the moon smoking in the clouds
blows off the skin from the spring
water, then all
                    that can scare me—
asleep between two grains of ash—
is only the wind.

Only wind and the smoldering heat.
          A shallow water
crab scuttles into the deep, waving orange claws,
and a worm like the thin strip
of mortar between bricks,
                    petrifies.

Windy. Hot and windy.
Touch it with a twig
                    and the mirror dries out like a river.
The wind curls up
                    between propeller blades,
in the eye of a needle
                    it sucks itself in like a star.

When it stretches out,
                    through the spittle of burdocks,
it scoops into its bag a thrush.

If you brush against a bucket
                    at dawn,
milk will pour out
                    in the shape of an udder.
Between two vacuums
                    the wind takes shape
and names them.

Overhead, the ratty net
of constellations
                    where shivering winds reign
and are deposed, like duckpins
the cipher of love is bowled over
                    by the cipher of death.

From Rybinsk to Mongolia the wind pours.
Spokes of steaming
                    and rusty rye.
The wind blows in the brain
from some kind of petty
                    bourgeois power.

An aimless empty moon
whimsically considers seducing a revolver.
If bagels are stacked
                    in an endless chain,
a hurricane begins to churn inside them.

What lives within the wind?
                    Imaginary magnitudes,
shadows of oaks
                    whose trunks are ruined.
Vague anxieties,
                    consequences without reasons,
and those unincarnated windbags of the soul.

And outside the wind?
                    Everything else.
God, avoiding
        confirmations,
prefers, I suppose,
                    something other—
other landscapes,
                    and stirring backwaters.

Yes, it's windy, my friends.
Like open-mouthed catfish, deep
                    holes suck at the air.
And your scream
                    falls back into your lungs
after barely rising
                    to your larynx.

Translated by Sara Dickinson and Forrest Gander.

Thoughts on Formal Logic

Even when they were permitting,
                    it was clear they would ban.
But we puzzled whether to wear it
                    shorter or to the floor.
One of us blew up
                    and demanded assistance.
Then someone shouted in Finnish
                    what sounded like gogol-mogul.
But when they were banning,
                    it was clear what they would permit.

But someone didn't realize

          that the floor was planked

and guessed the creaking he heard

          was from new suede shoes

although he himself wore boots

          never anything else.

But when they permitted,

          it clearly wasn't over.

One admonished another for failing

          to acknowledge our Father in the
             monument

and a third went off the deep end

          and was lost to the enemy

mixing up polemics

          with conclusions and postulates.

But when they permitted,

          it clearly was not for long.

Crops undulated in wind

          and sparks crackled the oats.

Everybody seemed content;

          then someone wanted buckwheat,

and simultaneously he was struck

          perfectly speechless.

But when they allowed for eternity,

          someone asked, How come?

Since he refused to understand

          by his conscience or was stunned.

As he paused later in a tundra,

          slop in his mess tin froze over.

When they absolutely prohibited

          then the Greeks discovered wine,

the Spaniards blew their noses

          and the Turks closed the window a bit
             more

and only one of us, from Rostov,

          flung his medal at the posted
             militiaman

as though he'd never before

          seen such a thing.

Translated by Sara Dickinson and Forrest Gander.

A Monument

When I see how
the worker and the peasant woman
stand side by side for days on end
I'm slaughtered by insomnia.

Where is their daughter, cast in iron?
Where is their dismemberably metal son?
There stands the steel wife
and her husband fantastically armed.

She, with her fresh clean scarf
framing the face of a bloodless Aztec,
is naturally a Trotskyite,
while he is a pharmacy clerk with his brother-in-law.

This is
                    our common monument
built up over the years
in which the hammer has swung like a pendulum
and the sickle has tried those who fear.

This is
                    Adam and Eve
planting a family tree in stone.
                    The Trotsky-serpent tempts Eve
who, without trembling or shame,
feels for the snake
                    between her husband's thighs.

They stand at a cliff on which
only the brittle houses of the wild monks are built
and Zeus peeps out from a thunder-cloud,
this time named Frederick.

Stern Nord hits him with a ruler
and Zeus runs down like a battery.

We are no higher than that monument
and no lower

               than the horizon.

Why do I circle them unwillingly?
Why am I frightened by their confident bearing?
Snowdrifts in bedsores, ginger in the air.
Their feet gripping into granite
and into the sky.

I pity their rigid spines
and speeches, grinding on like tractors
since I am their orphaned son
and I want to go home.

    Translated by Cole Swensen and Aleksei Andreev.

Aleksandr Eremenko

ALEKSANDR EREMENKO, born 1950, was notoriously crowned "King of the Poets" by a convention of "unofficial" writers in Moscow in 1989. His work has been widely translated, and his first officially published book, *Models and Situations,* appeared in 1990, quickly selling out its initial printing of 150,000 copies.

Twelve Years in Literature

Having received my invitation to take the exams at the Institute of Literature in 1974, I bought a German grammar book and removed a naval tattoo from my right arm.

The first later turned out to be problematic; the latter amusing. Amusing because the situation in Moscow at the time resembled one in which—"every man's for himself." The stormy sea of literature swarmed with life jackets scattered across all sorts of rocky islets. My imagination's flagship—a three-masted frigate proudly named "Synthesis of Poetry, Philosophy and Science," was sinking before my eyes into the open ocean depths of that fundamental contradiction of socialism: planned production and uncontrollable demand.

And sadness filled my soul.

Sad as it is to realize, the expression "there has to be poetry" has been elevated in our midst to a methodological principle. One can hear it from a young author as well as from a venerable literary scholar. In conversations about poetry we constantly use this expression. At first glance this would seem trifling. But the incorrect premise brings an avalanche of misunderstandings in its wake. And thus, it turns out poetry already owes us something.

It owes us continuously, and it keeps on owing. Until we learn to say that "poetry *may be* this or that," and not merely say it but understand it

as a methodological principle—until then the bludgeon of literary scholarship
will shatter to pieces any attempts to revitalize the poetic language. As to
those critic-regulators, they'll go on with confidence driving the "flitting
canoes" of poetic images onto rocky islets and into fjords. And just as the
poetic image is essentially elusive (as when expressed by words, the Tao isn't
constant), so then does that very same poetic image untie the critic's hands
for all of his vulgar interpretations. There's a precise dependence here. And
the level at which poetry is discussed every five years deteriorates ceaselessly.
And God, the way they describe some of my poems: "scientific," "metallic,"
"modernist," "absurdist," "grotesque," or simply "those of a troublemaker."

Neither now nor later will I cite their names or publishing houses. It
isn't that I'm afraid to make enemies. It's rather from fear that I'll reduce
our general misfortune to one or another particular case. It'd be quite easy
to find the guilty railway switchman, to do him in and then rest under the
laurel leaves: The root of evil's been found out and uprooted. "The ideology
and psychology of stagnation" which Gorbachev referred to as "bureacraticism
and formalism" at the January plenary session resulted in a decline of the
criteria used in assessing creativity in the arts. And this is happening every-
where. It was he, the Editor, who announced to my friend when the latter
brought my translated poetry to the publishing house: "We will never print
your work, because you, along with Eremenko, are modernists." Quite a
construct! Isn't it? Simply from the point of view of formal logic?

Of course, some coordinates are needed. But where can we get them,
if we've forgotten overnight the old sensible idea of 'school.' After all, given
the unanimity of artistic methods, shouldn't the multifaceted creative per-
sonalities be permitted some concepts of their own? In other arts, the idea
of 'school' has remained and it works, whereas our long-suffering critics are
forced to this day to explain things in jargon. I nearly ended up under the
streetcar when I read the description "somewhat masterful" writer. As if he's
not yet a "master" but has a good head for business? Is that it? And when
there's no terminology, no concept of schools or movements which would
distinguish the searches for new art by stylistic criteria, the young poetry's
permitted to be enslaved to all kinds of opportunistic critics, each one of
whom can accuse with impunity anyone of anything you like: of pessimism,
of rootlessness, of elitism . . . even of inhumanity. One well-known poet
accused a young author in his seminar at a Moscow symposium of being
inhuman. This is convenient to do, when suggesting that a representative of
one school pay for another's tab. "Shura, pay for the kefir." And Shura pays.
Either with years of silence, or pseudocivic verselets. Only in our country
could such a vertiginous situation occur: the lag in the language that describes

poetry predicates a lag in poetry itself. I mean printed poetry, of course. That's why we're still unfamiliar with conceptual poetry, and with the primitive Smirnovian movement. They haven't built a podium for them yet.

But this is, as they say in Odessa, a conversation that "misses the money." After all, so far we've been talking about the tactics of rejection and the suppression of published poetry. This is a tactic used with confidence by the keepers of burrows and islets mentioned before. And who needs their burrows anyway? "What can one steal from a pauper?" No one wants their spiritual baggage or their (security) guard stripes any longer. And yet they're still trembling over their baggage, some of them probably afraid of a raid from the NTR,[1] others of the classic pogrom thugs. And I mean this quite literally. One such "lover of pearly-white toothed poetry" announced that I and my metaphors were capable of committing patricide. That is the logic of a young professional editor. This is the level which one is forced to deal with them on. They jealously protect their dock-tailed spirituality from NTR realities. They had welcomed the NTR before, because they had understood it as a cheap invasion of plastic spoons and TVs. But "the devil is not so frightening as he is attractive."[2]

Yes. My soul was saddened. Because at this point we'll have to speak of the saddest thing of all. Most certainly an author experiences many original sensations before he succeeds in being published. To be published—that's only half the trouble. The most shattering scenes are performed when you get ready to try to publish. It is here that you discover such play-acting, such unbridled cynicism and impunity, such characters, such a combination of ignorance and treachery, such rock-bottom human degradation, that only a writer of genius could describe it. Maybe I'm not right? Am I speaking too categorically? Then let him throw the first stone at me who has never once played the hypocrite, who has never been led by the nose at the editor's, who has never closed his eyes at overt baseness. This theatrical romance is an idyll compared with what goes on in our editorial and publishing practice. What goes on there, and I'm not afraid to make this assertion, is quite terrible—the corruption of the young author who's not yet firmly standing on his own two feet, the one encountering for the first time the sphere of life he's decided to dedicate himself to. But he doesn't suspect that life's laws of survival are specific and that certain of its moments are being painstakingly hidden from him. What's more, he may even attain certain successes, may even become famous, but at death still remain ignorant regarding those

1. Nayuchno-Tekhnicheskaia Revoliutsia, the Scientific-Technical Revolution.
2. An old Russian saying.

springs that move the apparatus he's come in contact with. In any case, the visible part of this apparatus is primitive. On the other hand, however, it's reliable. The author's young, pure, and sinless—the apparatus experienced. It's been layered and tested on hundreds of similar authors, and, despite its dirty brown coating, it works smoothly, its sins being so great that it cannot, fatally, work any other way: It cannot "reform" itself as they now say.

The author putting his manuscript with trembling hands on the editor's table wonders naively *whether* his poetry shows talent; being published would confirm his hopes. The apparatus (and this is true, my young author, it is true!) sees miles ahead, not yet even knowing your poetry, not knowing whether or not you are talented. And the question of your publication is a question of whether or not to move a pawn into that complicated game it plays not for life, but to the death. The author's gifted—the apparatus lacks all talent. The author's naive—the apparatus is cynical. The author is cynical—the apparatus is naive. The author is educated—the apparatus is illiterate. The author is illiterate—the apparatus is educated. It is regulated unerringly. There's a gray point on the scale where the author and the apparatus are equalized. In that case nobody gets anything from anybody. There's no conflict. But the more gifted the author, the more powerfully the apparatus repels him. And vice versa, the more mediocre, the stronger the apparatus attracts him. The genius isn't accepted at all, since the apparatus doesn't take him seriously. In other words, it doesn't notice him: He doesn't exist for it. In the same way that the apparatus doesn't exist for the genius. He doesn't notice it. The apparatus and the genius do not need each other (the genius simply creates new structures: Lomonosov—the university, Pushkin—"The Contemporary," Vissotski—the tape-recorded culture.)

Since our editorial and publishing activity has been turned upside down (the author exists for the publishers and not vice versa), the initiative has ended up in the publisher's hands. Literature has always lost when in such a juxtaposition. And the bureaucratic apparatus, "stagnating" (but I would say "closing up its ranks"), has displayed a tendency to merge into one of three roles: author, editor, publisher (in the role of the reviewer of the submitted manuscript). And so, having closed up its ranks successfully, it (the apparatus) begins to oppose everything that is alive in literature. It's well known that we don't train a sufficient number of specialists in editorial work. There are still a considerable number of editors, who, professionally, are poorly trained. Ninety-nine percent of reviews are written in very general terms—(Dear Irene, Your muse is too timid. Greetings, xxx). These people, unsure of their own competence, become the kind who never take risks. And one needn't speak of some mythical "censorship." Evil's not as attractive as some would like it to be. Working for years under the principle of—*"and what if something 'bad' were to happen,"* they've objectively put up a powerful barrier against young literature. It's a fact that the preceding generation of poets was shattered against this fortification. For decades the bureaucratic apparatus has gotten its own way, intentionally or not—by nodding its head upwards, saying: "Up there they won't let it pass." First of all, it's corrupted the larger part of our generation (those thirty- to thirty-five-year-olds). It laid itself out when it invented the "Aesopian" language, an even more outrageous occurrence precisely because it was developed by the generation following that of the 1960s. These poets learned to code their attitude toward negative phenomena so well that our "second bottom" disappeared all together—there wasn't anything left to decipher. Secondly, it bred a mass of immoral authors (on the one hand, those creating super patriotic slogans, on the other, those writing "insidious" fables). Thirdly, it clearly doublecrossed the samizdat press, which not only "did in" many minds but also split our youth on these grounds. Fourthly, it was the apparatus itself that generated a quasidissident mood, undermining the sense of civic activism, as it demonstrated brilliantly, the corruption of society within the literary process. Not having dared to gulp down boiling water during the 1960s, they're still blowing on it to this day.

They (the critics and editors as one) were cynical enough to pretentiously discuss for ten to fifteen years whether young poetry existed or not. My friends' poetry lay around in editorial offices for years—so there was no poetry. Recently selections and books have been published—and for three years there's been ceaseless discussions of what sort of poetry it is, black or white, right or left. So now these critic/editors will shuffle out another ten to fifteen names for another five years and then—they'll sleep through another generation, or ruin it. It's time—at least for those we still listen to, to stop the talking, time for them to simply help clean out, not just in articles but concretely, like a caretaker with a shovel—everything that impedes those who are really young. Those who are eighteen to twenty years old now! They like to talk about the so-called gray poetry which has "swelled out." Aesthetes. They're afraid of the gray poetry. Literature was always gray. And it always will be. This is a symptom of the fact that society is on a satisfactory level of cultural development and democracy. Forget about the gray, publish the real thing. But truthfully they're afraid of things far more attractive for their careers and salaries. One poet on the editorial board said that the suggested selection of authors couldn't be published: It'd be noticed in the West. He's afraid of the West? He's not afraid of the devil, or the West, East, North or South. . . . He's afraid that an enlightened public will stop listening to his inventions about how he drank vodka with the classics of Soviet poetry. Why wasn't this poet afraid in time to stop the tenth grade Komsomol organizer who murdered his friend in order to save his career? Wasn't it they who corrupted him with their hurrah-Komsomol poetry lacquering up literature? At the expense of the government. They're afraid of the West. Or of the snow man. But they're not afraid of each other, when they publicly announce that rock music is a manifestation of "satanism"?

Being raised themselves in an atmosphere of editorial arbitrariness, they've taught the youth to speak with the editors "on tiptoe," that is, to do everything through pull or networking. And so an author walks around the editorial offices for years, strikes up acquaintances with the masters and influential drinking buddies. Ingratiates himself. The author's embarrassed, somewhat afraid. That's why we can't find a worthy artistic expression for this theme. Perhaps in the film *Light Blue Mountains* something has been started. . . . After all, compared to the author, the apparatus possesses a greater "level of freedom": It's free to have the manuscript exterminated, free to place it on the list of planned publications and is then free to remove it from the list. And regardless of how the pages of newspapers and journals howl about gray poetry, or how they justify it, one has to agree with the staggering fact that the literary process depends not on the writer and enlightened critics but on particularly petty people, connected to the bureaucratic machine. These "particular" people determine and predict the level and tendencies of literature. This sounds wild, but it's fact. The enlightened critics will tell me, with a smirk—we know this. And we know many other things. In that case then, I'd respond, stop the striptease you've spread in the press in connection with the young poetry. At least stay silent. After all, it's not us who hammer on about the "tendencies," about the generations that have either "found" or "not found" themselves, "reflected" reality or "not." Right off I can give you ten names that would be an ornament to any, I repeat any, literature (for instance, N. Iskrenko, P. Smirnoff, Y. Arabov, A. Volhov, all of whom have recently made their presence known).

It's commonly said that young literature gets "untiring attention." There's no need for "untiring" attention, just give it attention. It is, after all, clear that all of these conferences, seminars, and commissions do not serve what's most important: discovery of talent. Certain organizers of the recent forum of creative youth in Moscow even attempted to reorganize it and pour it out into the old bureaucratic swamp. The same thing is being done with the Poetry Club. And if new forms of working with young people will be discovered there, it will have to be done through complete severance from the editorial/publishing bureaucracy. The way it exists now, the apparatus either demands complete submission or drags it into boycott. One must admit that the Writers' Union doesn't have the experience of working with youth. Facts—are a stubborn thing. And they talk about how, rare exceptions notwithstanding, all the books directing attention to themselves were marinated for an incredibly, disgracefully, criminally long time in the editorial offices. What we need is cardinal measures, ones that would guarantee a normalization board of reviewers—reviewers independent of the directorship of editors and publishers. We need a journal that would ensure glasnost when it comes to protecting the writers' rights. We need a legal, fully empowered organ—a Professional Committee of literary experts. But instead of this they offer us countless lithographical unions and mentor discussions on how one does not enter literature "in a huge wave" (all at once), how this is an intimate matter. And it will remain an intimate slow suicide of the author, if he finds himself opposed by this "huge wave."

My notes would be incomplete if I didn't mention here one other thing a young author encounters. This is my personal experience, so why not share it? Above I spoke about the idea of 'school.' Of course, these are unrealizable fantasies. In our midst even the concept of a movement doesn't survive. We don't have trends. What we have are antagonistic groupings. And they're by no means competing, oh no. . . . And the division in this case doesn't follow, alas, either an aesthetic or any other criterion. I don't know to what level glasnost has to be raised in our country so that some light is thrown, at least on the area of plotting, among circles surrounding literature. Maybe the present level is sufficient. I don't know. But any talk about a literary process in this day will remain childish if it avoids the problem.

I'm not that concerned about the theatrical underpinnings of the question. I'm writing about the young writer's fate. And I see how a certain circle of writers, critics, and poets, having proclaimed themselves as the shareholders of our national idea—promote a policy of persecution in literature. And so, they actively attempt to influence youth in their own interests. The fact that it costs them nothing to place both an outstanding bard and a popular woman singer on the same level—that's their personal problem. But the way in which they are turning the next generation into idiots, playing on their least attractive sensibilities, this is no longer a private matter. I don't know with what clever formula they're able to accommodate the contradiction between a Marxist worldview on the one hand and photocopies of astrological tables and similar literature on the other. I've observed how a young writer, entering the literary field, loses all sense of contradiction and inner conflict after falling under their influence for two to three years. And of course, loses his sense of creative contradictions as well. How quickly and expertly that young person was slipped a comfortable theoretical platform while still rocked about on the unstable deck of Moscow's cultural scene. And how afterwards that person, with a face left innocent of thought, settled comfortably upon that theoretical base: in one hand publications, in the other—a simplistic slogan. How quickly he stopped thinking and lost interest in everything— reducing all arguments to a hackneyed topic. What does this have to do with artistic work? Why, he's a member of a powerful clan, a fighter for an idea; and his existence then is justified. And the fact that he could be used at any moment like a pawn in a game, like a plug, like the simple squiggle of a signature under a petty denunciation, well that's . . . and some turn out to be still more ingenious: They strive actively to occupy positions in editing offices and publishing houses, under the cover of the more famous names, and quite openly and resolutely try to block those they don't want from the pages of the magazines. This type has appeared just recently. He may also write his "Twelve Years in Literature." These people are capable of anything. They've modeled themselves completely to the reigning atmosphere of cor- ruption, selling out. They've decided to influence the literary process both seriously and thoroughly. This isn't literature. It's a meat grinder. I don't know who gains from the schism. I only know that a talented person at the beginning of his career invariably encounters the situation in which in crude terms he's offerd the choice: *either or.* And his subsequent fate depends on it. And this is why the simple "knee-jerk social reflex" is frequently called the "civic duty" of literature. "The baker stitches the boots."[3] And it can't be any different when our writers occupy themselves with the problem of rerouting northern rivers, when the public prosecutor writes poetry and a poet practices herbal medicine.

Translated by John High with Katya Olmsted and Nina Genkin.

---

3. From a fable by Ivan Krylov.

A horizontal country.
Verticals moving by.
Here, the diagonal and its side always
exist as an immeasurable continuum.

At the house, a garden
square of a window.
Snow falls along the diagonals.
As for tomorrow, the snow will only be a heap
piled there . . . against the other side.

Satan is omniscient in fact
within the depth of the draftsman's tools.
Today's genius—is still a genius,
but he doesn't remember a fucking thing.

There's truth in everything
so drink up, friend.
At the house, a garden—making whatever noise it wants.
Who can understand its language
when awakening . . .

Translated by John High and Katya Olmsted.

And Schubert on the water, and Pushkin living on rations,
and Lermontov's eye grown accustomed to the darkness . . .
I've learned you, blissful swingsets
loafing about the illusive boundary line without a knife.

It's as if I were strung up in a public toilet
on a long vector which splashed in the heat of the moment.
And already I'm up to my elbow in that black swill
plunging deeper on up to the shoulder.

Translated by John High and Katya Olmsted.
The poem makes reference to Osip Mandelstam's "Solomnika" ("Straw") and Nikolai
Zabolotsky's "Vchera o smerti razmyshliaia" ("Musing Yesterday a Death").

Igor Alexandrovich Antonov,
your death isn't far off.
In other words, after a few eons
you'll fly over us like a light-emitting body.

A simple Moscow guy, you'll fly over us
complete, like a transfigured Buddha.
Rama Krishna, Kedrov, and Gagaren
each watching in amazement.

A long time now I haven't trusted my own heart,
yet I clearly remember where you
puked, having opened the small door—so cultured
and flowers growing through the asphalt!

Kali Yuga—there's the centrifuge.
So as not to spin out of orbit
we stand, clutching one another
at this remote reach of the Milky Way.

And when the infinite astral plan
converges with the earth's crashing,
you'll go like Christ through the beer halls
in your foreign bell-bottom jeans.

You'll go down among the drunks and the barnacles[1]
Go to those who don't have any legs at all.
And the one who refuses you
won't be able to call himself a yogi.

You'll walk up to a telephone in the middle of the night—
eyes practically crawling out of their orbits:
Igor Alexandrovich Antonov, as if one of the living
talks to the living!

---

1. A paraphrase of Mandelstam's line in his poem "Lamarck": "I'll go down to annelids and barnacles."—Trans.

And during the final incarnation,
gathering all of yourself into a fist,
may your impotent glow
strike down ignorance and darkness!

Your genius can't be measured.
From the southern mountains to the northern seas
you've infinitely paralleled yourself
with my immeasurable motherland.

Translated by John High.

Pieter Brueghel

A tavern
and behind it, the drunk tank
and above it, an iron weathervane.
Pieter was wandering down the road,
down the long, great road he came

just like on the globe, sliding
half-drunken, there goes Europe
and the caravan groping toward Lyon
and from there, hitching rides

and then by any means possible
and on; shitting in Anvers, pissing in France
while in the head, the promenade of the wind
and on the slopes, the rain razing the grasses.

Oh yes, his son is marching well.
Pieter is painting well.
In the Netherlands, a tangible boredom,
books being burned and everybody's pleased.

In Italy, the heat is unbearable,
and their paintings, inconceivable. It should be impossible
and yet there, and like nowhere else.
But can they paint like Pieter?

Farther south, more pepper,
more alcohol and Bosch.
While Pieter the younger dead drunk and asleep
under a cart in a field.

There he will sleep through the peace of four centuries
and there he will wake, shockingly sober
and from there he will walk
laughing, down the road, the railroad

past a garden exploding with produce
past the sauna-cafés
ah, past a hydrogen bomb
ah, past the whores at the harbor.

Translated by Cole Swensen.

Philological Verse

"A step sideways is an escape."
Probably restful though—
to be born on Earth
an armed guard and a Descartes.
Such a hussar of theorems!
Strolling around with
a loaded gun
and Spartan computers!

What a poet has perished
in the ship's regulations!
Why even one of
the assorted knives
aimed deep inside you
like a homemade laser,
is manufactured like delirium,
like your pet snake's ultimate hell.

And so language, having lost its essence,
brings the delirium of proverbs out
upon the dictionaries' sandbars,

like a Rome turned loose.
In my own barely living blood
electrolysis roams among
the unbearable trash,
we use in conversation . . .

Some kind of idiot
invented idioms,
one unable to bear the burden,
of the anchors' rasping,
and so that you and I have to talk
on different wavelengths.
The reader waits for a rhyme.
Well take it then, jerk. . . . [1]

A step sideways is an escape.
Look at things directly:
Breton was a surrealist,
while Pushkin was a mason.
And if it's a Dalai,
it's absolutely got to be a Lama,
and if it's the spaceship "Soyuz"
then it's—"Apollo" as well.

And if it's Bret, well then, it's Harte,
If you say Maria, then it's Remarque,
and if somebody's a buddy, then he's a king's buddy,
and if you say skiing, then it's got to be a lodge,
and if it's a crank, then it's a shaft,
an archipelago . . . step
just slightly to the side, and pardon me,
that's much too clever, by half.

    Translated by John High.

---

1. A reference to lines from Pushkin's *Eugene Onegin:* "The reader waits for a rhyme for a rose / Well here it is, grab it."—Trans.

To Hieronymus Bosch,
inventor of the projector

1.
I look at you from such deep graves,
that before my glance can reach you, it splits in two.
We'll hoax them now as always by playing a comedy:
that you were not there at all. And so, neither was I.
We didn't exist in the inaudible chromosomal bustle,
in this large sun or the large white protoplasm.
They're still accusing us of such senility,
standing watch with their upraised oars in a primeval soup.
We'll as always now again attempt to bring together
the bodies' trajectories. Here are the conditions of the first move:
if you illuminate the nearest stretch of road,
I'll call you a noun of the feminine gender.
Of course in this rubbish I'll find—plain as day—
the appropriate conflict, one corresponding to the assigned scheme.
So, floating up from the bottom, the triangle will forever stick
to its theorem. You still need to be proven.
We'll still have to drape over you some combination of morphemes
/ the morphine that has lost its way in the dazzling form of a wasp /
so that the bodies' possessors would recognize you in the appropriate
    shape
on every occasion. My glance has now returned to the first stanza.
I look at you from such deep . . .
The game continues—the move will grow out of me, like a gun port.
Take away the convoy. We're acting out a hoax.
I was sitting on a mountain, depicted where the mountain is.

I was sitting on a mountain, depicted where the mountain is.
Below me / if I spit—I'd hit /
the crowd of runners passing through an impenetrable and dark blue hell,
the numbers on their shirts wiggling like fine lice.
Behind my back a painted paradise rustled,
now it's trumpeting along the edge, now ringing so that you could hear it
    a mile away.
It was an angel that floated by, or it was a brand new clean street car,
like a cross-eyed little boy, with a metallic pipe in his mouth. . . .

And like an antenna, the empty hand will turn the altar
and the son who combined with himself there within
will wander on—lost in the wet and flabby aspens' structure,
like a paper hockey goalie unfurled by the wind.
Who today can pare down this language—folded over 2–3 times, complex &
yet simple—this meaning that's wound itself around the theorem's screw
with its length, width, height—this 3-fold horror
of a system built into the mind?
Here's a heavenly sign—hell's making progress,
concentric cold circles approaching us.
I look at you—and my glance bends,
biting its own tail, stomping on the nape of my neck with its boots.
And the last days are stuck in the bellowing tableau,
the running deer imprinted on frozen firewood.
Surfacing from the bottom—beneath the ice, go ahead, push apart the
    year-old ring
and it'll rejoin, bringing you to your knees,
where the three-dimensional well isn't worth a spit.
Archimedes up to his own knees in mud—the secant flatness of the
    Tatars.
A direct pistol shot does exist in this cross-eyed world,
but even it is no straighter than a straight intestine.
Just as a wolfhound would never strangle a desert wolf—
in the empty skies the skyscraper is scraping nothing but the sky.
And when /I forget the word/ your spine will end up
in this meat and grinder—
and then your gullet will sing for sure!

2.
A nightingale expands in the bushes.
A star spins over it.
Water's crammed into the marsh,
as an electrical transformer.

The moon flying over our heads.
A projector burning on the vacant lot
delineating this sector,
from where the angle's given.
        Translated by John High.

Afterword: Metamorphosis

MIKHAIL EPSTEIN

Since 1985, Mikhail Epstein's work on Russian, Soviet and world literature has appeared regularly in such leading journals as *Novymir* (New World), *Voprosy literatury* (Issues in Literature), *Rodnik* (The Spring, Latvia) and *Iskusstvo Kino* (Cinema Art), as well as the independent almanac *Zerkala* (Mirrors). Epstein's first major study, *Paradoxes of Innovation: On Literary Developments of the Nineteenth and Twentieth Centuries,* appeared in Moscow in 1988. This book, in which he presents some of his ideas on culturology, a Soviet approach to cultural studies, became a phenomenal success, selling out nineteen thousand in only two weeks. It established Epstein as one of the most important intellectual figures in the on-going process of cultural renewal in the Soviet Union. In 1989, Epstein emigrated to the United States. He is currently assistant professor of Slavic studies at Emory University.

As the century ends, we are amazed to find ourselves returning to its beginnings. The poetic currents that were formed in Russia at the beginning of the twentieth century—symbolism, acmeism, futurism—have unexpectedly reemerged as a new poetic triad: metarealism, presentism, conceptualism. This is not to say that those original movements have simply been renewed; rather, there has occurred an expansion of poetic boundaries, a restructuring of the figurative space of sign systems.

Symbolism and futurism delineated, in their time, two opposing means of relating the word to its signification. In the case of symbolism the signifier

Excerpted and revised by the author from the essay of the same title, originally published in *Paradoxes of Innovation: On Literary Developments of the Nineteenth and Twentieth Centuries* (Moscow, 1989). Translated by Anesa Miller-Pogacar.

is almost withdrawn, giving full precedence to the signified. This is a poetics of suprasignification through which the mythological nature of the image comes to indicate another world, a world that is eternal and whole. Futurism, on the other hand, was the world of the signifier itself, where the word, the "self-winding word" (Khlebnikov) *is* the authentic reality, rescinding everything otherworldly, everything beyond the bounds of its own phonetic properties. Between these two movements—or, rather, stylistic boundaries—there was located the realm of acmeism, which stood for the golden mean, for the customary and direct meanings of words.

Now we find before us another three poetic movements, arising at the same historical distance from the end of the century that the others did from its beginning. And it seems that in a like manner the new developments have transcended a flat, quasirealistic, social-realistic picture of the world, restoring the former breadth and depth of poetic space that once prevailed in our country. At the risk of oversimplification, we can nonetheless trace paths of succession from symbolism to metarealism, futurism to conceptualism, while presentism makes a new attempt to define the mean. Metarealism endeavors to return to the word the fullness of its figurative and transcendent meanings. To the same degree, conceptualism tries to wrench out of the word any meaning whatever, leaving an empty, echoing shell. Presentism, like acmeism before, strives to avoid Scylla and Charybdis, the excessive pretentiousness of archetype and the excessive banality of stereotype, by turning to the world of visible, tangible surfaces, which are the ultimate depth in their own right. Thus, we do observe a process of succession, but I describe it as such only to show more clearly the striking shifts and ruptures manifest within this very process. It is these changes that radically distinguish the end of the poetic century from the middle years; precisely for that reason the end becomes a link to the beginning.[1]

---

1. Elsewhere Epstein writes of the distinctiveness of the new generation as follows: "The new poetry arouses in the reader a feeling of aesthetic unease, a loss of orientation. There are many complaints of secret coding, extreme complexity. . . . This is not a matter, however, of a complexity in the language, but rather of the fundamental absence of any stable center, which used to be indentified with the lyric 'I.' All complexities would clear up when they could be correlated with the centered system of self-reference: 'I am thus-and-so. . . . I see the world as so-and-so.' No matter how demonically terrifying or cynically demoralized, fantastically cruel or naively dull-witted (as in the poetry of the early years of this century, the 1920s, the Oberiuty, and others), reference to the poetic 'I' nonetheless gave readers the happy chance of transforming themselves, of moving aside their own 'I' in favor of another's. But now there is no one with whom to identify. Poetry ceases to be a mirror for the self-infatuated ego; there remains only a murky blot of banalities left over from his last lyric sighs. Instead of a multiplicity of reflections, there is the crystalline structure of rock that leads the gaze away, not back to the self. A poetry of Structure has come to replace the poetry of the 'I.' At a certain decisive breaking point in

On Conceptualism

It is a sign of our time that notions defining the heterogeneity of literature have returned, along with the precept of competitiveness—"stylistic currents," "artistic directions," "poetic schools," and "creative collectives." These notions do not erase such customary, tenacious categories as the "literary process" and "authorial individuality," but they do mediate them, filling a vacant intervening area.

By the 1970s and early 1980s it was already impossible to contain the growing and essentially fertile stratification of our literature within a few ideological-stylistic currents. Deprived of the possibility of openly announcing themselves and defining their creative postitions, these currents often degenerated into short-lived groupings, brought together by mercantile or regional rather than properly artistic aspirations. Only very recently have some of the "submerged" currents of our literature begun to surface and are now being favored with the attention and interest of society. Among the most clearly defined, artistically intentional currents are conceptualism and metarealism; they are represented in the visual arts as well, but we will confine ourselves here to the sphere of poetry.

Virtually nothing has been written on conceptualism in our country, although representatives of this current have on several occasions presented their works before large audiences that not only heard them out but also discussed them with great interest. I recall a meeting one evening in particular: June 8, 1983, at the Central House of Art Workers. It was officially called "Stylistic Searching in Contemporary Poetry: On the Dispute over Metarealism and Conceptualism." At this event, for perhaps the first time since the 1920s, a vocal and theoretically formulated demarcation took place between two stylistic currents of our poetry. The process of artistic differentiation made itself clearly felt; without it the threat of stagnation and repetition of generalities hangs over literature.

What is conceptualism? We will attempt to explain the theory without making evaluations but, rather, by describing the principles that this stylistic current recognizes as pertinent to itself and by which it must therefore be judged. Almost any artistic work (with the possible exception of the purely ornamental or decorative) is conceptual insofar as there lies within it a certain conception, or the sum of conceptions, which the critic or interpreter draws

---

history, the 'I' revealed its unreliability, inauthenticity, it traitorously slipped away from responsibility, and responsibility was taken up by structure: social structures, sign structures, atomic, genetic."—AMP.

out. In conceptualism this conception is demonstrably separable from the live artistic fabric and even becomes an independent creation, or "concept," in itself. In place of a "work with a conception" we see before us a "conception as the work."

It would seem that there have been and are being produced in our country more than enough of such pseudo-artistic compositions from which the ideological formula protrudes like a bare stake from the back of a scarecrow. Precisely this break between the idea and the thing, the sign and reality, is created—but in this case with complete intentionality, as a stylistic principle— in the works of conceptualism. The petrification of language, which brings forth ideological chimeras, becomes nourishing soil for this process. Conceptualism is the workshop for making scarecrows, ideologically figurative formulas, which are hastily covered with a slovenly sackcloth of linguistic fabric.

> The outstanding hero—
> He goes forward without fear
> But your ordinary hero—
> He's also almost without fear
> But first he waits to see:
> Maybe it'll all blow over
> And if not—then on he goes
> And the people get it all.

Behind these lines by Dmitri Prigov we easily recognize the formula that lies at the basis of numerous pathetic works about the fearless, all-conquering hero and his slightly backward but devoted comrades in arms. The typical problem with such odic writings is how to reliably hide the formula behind the clothing of linguistic beauty so as to make it frighteningly similar to a live person. The poet-conceptualist, on the contrary, drags the formula out into the open from the sum of its aesthetic imprintings and changes of form, placing it as an independent fact before the reader's perception.

From this there develops a peculiar aesthetic (or, if you prefer, antiaesthetic) of tongue-tiedness. Since the detached formula turns out to be primary in relation to all of the "highly-low-artistic" (Zoshchenko) means of its embodiment, the more arbitrary, inorganic, and unsanitary the language, the better for demonstrating the self-sufficiency of the formula, it's extraneousness to art as such. Conceptualism in this sense comes forward as criticism of artistic reason, unmasking beneath the covering of lyrical soulfulness or epic picturesqueness the skeleton of an idea-engendering construct.

Here flows the beauty of the Oka
Through the beauty of Kaluga
The beauty of the people
Toasts its legs-arms in the sun

By day it's off to work he goes
To the beauty of his blackened lathe
And in the evening he comes back
Again to dwell by the Oka's beauty

Perhaps this is—just incidentally—
That same beauty we've expected
In a year, two at the most,
To save the world through beauty

How many lyric songs and pompous poems have been composed along these plot lines, stunning in their monumental simplicity! Prigov's concept is a generalization of numerous stereotypes free-floating in mass consciousness, from the idyllic-benevolent "beautification" of our native landscape to a parodic deflation of Dostoyevski's prophecy that "beauty will save the world." Conceptualism puts together a primer, as it were, of these stereotypes, removing from them the aura of creative mist, lofty animation, revealing their vulgar nature as signs called forth to stimulate the most elementary reactions of love and hate, "for" and "against." In so doing, they use minimal linguistic means to demonstrate the depletion and deadening of language itself, degenerated to the formulation of best-selling ideas. Tongue-tiedness turns out to be the alter ego of grandiloquence, the exposure of its quintessential emptiness. Conceptualism unequivocally reflects the reality of those conditions in which it arose and spread, or, more precisely, the apparent, empty "idealness" of those conditions. Much of what Prigov was writing about in the late 1970s and early 1980s is now openly discussed in publicistic literature; back then such ideas were kept quiet, and we must give the poet his due for his courage in having expressed them:

It doesn't matter that the dairy yield recorded
Is unequal to the dairy yield for real
Whatever's written down—is written on the skies
And if it doesn't come to pass in 2–3 days
Then in some few years it *will* soon come to pass
And in the highest sense it has already been

> And in the lowest sense it soon will be forgotten
> And in fact it's just about forgotten now

In these lines we see the characteristic conceptualist intergrafting of "journalistic" and "mystical" jargons: One grows over into the other ("written" in account books / "written" on the skies), revealing the very process of mystification as it takes place in everyday reality, which itself then turns into something loftily incomprehensible, portentously unavoidable—until what little that remains of actual reality is so negligible as to be easily forgotten. Many of Prigov's poems are constructed in precisely this way: They start out with some sort of ordinary, topical fact then wildly exalt it, raise it to the level of a rhetorically providential plan, while, along the way, exposing its basic typicality, its insignificance. Then they conclude with a rhythmic faltering, a weak gesture of some sort, or a muttering of the initial fact within the frame of workaday consciousness for which it doesn't matter how or of what one thinks or speaks—reality has already become so disembodied as to lose its significance and substance: "And in fact it's just about forgotten now."

Conceptualism draws upon the entirely respectable traditions of our national literature in the twentieth century: the poetry of the Oberiuty (D. Kharms, N. Oleinikov, early Zabolotsky, and others) and the prose of Mikhail Zoshchenko. Nevertheless, we must also note a shift of the stylistic system that the conceptualists have achieved in contrast to their predecessors. In the works of Zoshchenko or Oleinikov mass consciousness is personalized within a concrete social layer (the petty bourgeoisie, the NEPmen, [entrepreneurs of the early Soviet period when small-scale capitalistic ventures were allowed under the New Economic Policy, 1921–28], etc.) and in the image of a concrete protagonist, usually speaking in the first person. Conceptualism eschews this kind of localization, be it social or psychological. The structures and stereotypes that are brought into focus do not belong to any one concrete consciousness but, rather, to consciousness in general—the author's as much as the character's. For this reason conceptualist works cannot be placed in the category of humorous or ironic pieces in which the author maintains a certain distance between himself (or the realm of the ideal, which is the same thing) and the reality that he is mocking.

While it may be seen as either a strength or a weakness of conceptualism, the values of its world are uniform and admit of no privileged points of view whatsoever, no zones free from conceptualization. This is a world of objects from which the subject is absent, or else he with all of his acute existential misery falls into line with the rest of the objects fabricated by the

"existential" rubber stamps of language—as, for example, in Lev Rubin-
shtein's composition "Life is all around us," in which sayings of the following
type are set down in a series:

> "Life is not given to man in a hurry.
> He doesn't even notice it, but he's alive . . . "
>
> "Right . . . "
>
> ***
>
> "Life is given to man when he's barely alive.
> It all depends on the likes of his soul . . . "
> "Hold it!"
> "Gentlemen, by the way, the tea's getting cold . . . "
>
> ***
>
> "Three—four . . . "
> "Life is given to man for a lifetime.
> All our life we must remember this . . . "
> "All right, next . . . "

Various positions on life and sayings about life are used here as ready-made
objects placed by the author in his museum of linguistic models. The author's
own position is lacking, as something inappropriate, even impossible, quite
as if a tour guide in the process of showing us around a museum should
suddenly offer up his own personal possessions as part of an exhibit.

Rubinshtein has developed his own version of conceptualism, a much
more rigid version than Prigov's. Prigov's poems are monocentric, pronounced
by a single voice that sounds from the idiotic depths of the collective uncon-
scious, while still preserving a certain gravitational lyricality, a dull-witted
seriousness of worldview. Prigov intentionally reduces his poems to rhyme
scheming, graphomania à la Dostoyevski's Lebiadkin, beyond which emerges
the tragedy of entire generations condemned to tonguelessness, having swal-
lowed their own native tongue, like the "cannibaless Ellochka" [a character
in *The Twelve Chairs* (1928) by Ilya Ilf and Yevgeni Petrov], who shows that
cannibalism was at one and the same time "tonguebalism"—the destruction
of language down to its elementary signal systems [*tongue* and *language* are
a single word in Russian].

In Rubinshtein's works rhyme-scheming falls away like yet another final
mask with its frozen, aesthetic grimace, and the skeletal constructions of our
daily language are uncovered in their almost algorithmic predictability.
Rubinshtein writes his texts on cards, which he files through during public

readings like a bibliographer habitually, almost mechanically, filing through the card catalog (this is, in fact, Rubinshtein's profession); a system of summarization, of enumeration, prevails. Various linguistical misunderstandings and microdialogues arise, continually pointing to one final goal: to reveal that our words denote no one knows what, perhaps nothing, although they continue to be pronounced; the very habit of living boils down to this verbal persistence.

54.
—The air burst aloud . . .
55.
—What say? Allowed?
56.
—Not allowed, aloud.
57.
—But I heard "allowed." That sounds even better.
58.
—Maybe it's better, but I said: "The air burst aloud."
59.
—I already understood what you said, but "allowed" is still better.
60.
(Pause)

[Trans. Gerald J. Janacek]

This exerpt from the catalog "A Little Nighttime Serenade" (1986) is only a tiny snag in the endless linguistic red tape that Rubinshtein draws out, now tangling it in petty paradoxes, now untangling it in tawdry tautologies, but always reproducing with diplomatically dispassionate precision the tirelessness of our verbal practice, ambling through pauses from laugh to laugh, from banality to banality.

Rubinshtein is a master of displaying the tawdriness of tawdry speech formations, a certain lack of willfulness of our speech operations: No matter what is said, it all appears as merely an imitation of someone—no one— else's speech; it is not we who speak this way, this is how they speak "us." Conversations alongside of literature, penetrating judgments on life, everyday remarks—it's all drawn into a speech-engendering mechanism, stamping its clichés onto library file cards or punch cards. After hearing Rubinshtein's catalogs, one begins to perceive one's own utterance differently; they seem to become a continuation of these phraseological enumerations, they slough off dead layers one after the other, leaving them for catalogs yet to be written.

Thus, there occurs a *liberation from speech;* it must now begin anew from a source as yet unknown, from which first arose the Logos. Rubinshtein's texts undermine our faith in the independence of our own judgments; they open the door on another author standing behind them, thereby posing the difficult question of our linguistic identity. In order to speak for ourselves we must overcome "the Other" in ourselves, but this is not at all simple to do. The Other has already managed to say so much; all of our oral and written literature, teeming with self-repetition and multitudes of tautologies, all that has been accumulated over the millenia of "speaking man," belongs to him.

It would be superficial to reduce all the work of conceptualism to the level of a social criticism of language. Both Prigov and Rubinshtein deal not only with the newly formed linguistic "stamps" of the past few decades but also with the evaluative capability of language itself to stamp and register as it makes use of us, exploiting our speech organs for the production of "surplus value," or, better yet, surplus devaluation that fills up the world with ephemeral significances, pseudomeanings, ideological garbage. Conceptualism is a canal system, draining off all of this cultural garbage and scrap into cesspool texts where the garbage can filter out from the nongarbage— a necessary function for any developed culture. Conceptualism is the auto-representation and self-criticism of language, which, having lost the second dimension of being able to speak about itself, risks identifying itself with reality and proudly abolishing the latter—an entirely imaginable event, as our recent history shows with its rhetorical "achievements" [the whitewashing of reality through official proclamation in the Stalin and Brezhnev eras.— AMP]. The culture that does not allow its conceptions to be brought out into the open and changed into concepts, into the objects of conceptual art, is a one-dimensional culture, condemned to decay.

And finally there is the question of answerability, which readers unaccustomed to such texts love to pose to conceptualist artists. "Here you are," they say, "writing and writing, but, after all, those are *not* your words. What is it you yourself wish to say? What is your authorial position, where is your answerability for the word, without which there can be no serious art?" At this point one must recall that the realm of a writer's answerability is not some abstract authorial word but the object of concrete, writerly work. And if a writer, as in the case of Nikolay Gogol, Leskov and the *skaz* writers [an extreme technique of rendering dialectal and vernacular speech characteristics in literature.—AMP] of the nineteenth century, works with someone else's— or no one in particular's—word, then he answers for its precise reproduction, in the same way that the compiler of a dictionary answers not for the "sincere expression of his own convictions" but for the fullest possible representation of the laws and potentials of the language itself. It is, in fact, the position of compiler which appears more productive and therefore more morally responsible as regards contemporary conceptualist texts than does the position of a composer. The dictionary is a genre no less significant and responsible than a text consisting of the direct utterances of an author. If contemporary literature is becoming increasingly "dictionaric" (not scientifically but *creatively* dictionaric), then this has been conditioned by the laws of development of literature itself, which is entering upon the phase of self-description, self-interpretation. Conceptions are becoming concepts—artistic designs and objects of study; in this lies the essence of the conceptual revolution that places before art the need to analyze and criticize its own language.

On Metarealism

Along with conceptualism, another stylistic current has formed in our poetry since the beginning of the 1970s, which also long remained unknown to the broader reading public. It did not fit into the normative framework of the "middle" style [Epstein refers here to the three styles codified in Lomonosov's eighteenth-century poetic theory—AMP], which alone was acceptable to publishing houses and editorial boards by virtue of moderately combining characteristics of "live conversational" style and "high poeticality." Any attempt to disturb this balance met with an administrative-aesthetic protest. A decidedly low style, incorporating elements of street slang in the tawdry, literarily unpolished manner of plebian conversation, was classified as "hooliganism" [a typical Soviet pejorative term for almost anything from vandalism to swearing.—AMP] or provocation, calculated for shock effect. High style, conscientiously freed from conversationality and all marks of everyday life, oriented toward the most highly authoritative spiritual traditions, was regarded as "secondary" and "bookish." Poetry stays alive, however, precisely by going beyond the bounds of prevailing norms, through the counterbalances of its stylistic foundations. Establishing the middle style as a precept, in part conversational and in part literary, led to the dominance of mediocrity—a grayness that swallows up contrasts. The other two styles, the "low" and the "high," were pushed out into the realm of unofficial existence, where they both gained popularity with a single audience, primarily our youthful readership, which has been oriented toward alternative forms of artistic thought.

The stylistic current opposed to conceptualization and directed not toward simplification and primitivization but toward the greatest complexity of poetic language has become known in recent years as metarealism. Metarealism is not a negation of realism but its expansion into the realm of things unseen, a complication of the very notion of realism, revealing its multidimensionality, irreducible to the level of physical and psychological verisimilitude and including a higher, metaphysical reality, like that made manifest to Pushkin's prophet [Epstein refers here to one of Pushkin's best-known short poems, "The Prophet," which describes poetic inspiration in terms of a profound religious experience.—AMP] That which we are accustomed to calling "realism," narrowing the breadth of that concept, is the realism of only one reality, the social reality of day-to-day existence which directly surrounds us. Metarealism is the realism of multiple realities, connected by a continuum of internal passageways and interchangeabilities. There is a reality available to the vision of an ant or the wandering of an electron, a reality of which it has been said "there leads / the lofty flight of angels" [Pushkin's prophet again.—AMP], and all of these enter into the essence of Reality. The prefix *meta* would not be needed if realism were not understood in an abbreviated form. *Meta* merely returns to realism that which has been left out from the all-encompassing Reality, when it is reduced to any one of its many subspecies.[2]

Such a broadened and deepened contemplation of Reality appears in the works of Vladimir Aristov, Arkadii Dragomoshchenko, Nadezhda Kondakova, Viktor Krivulin, Olga Sedakova, D. Shchedrovitsky, Elena Shvarts, and other poets of both Moscow and Leningrad. Of particular significance for their work are the traditions of "sacred" and "metaphysical" poetry of the European Middle Ages, the Renaissance, and baroque and classical styles. The image is reborn in its archetypal significance, penetrating through the density of cultural overlayerings, to the mythological, originary basis. If conceptualism consciously reduces the image to its simplest ideological scheme, tearing from it the mask of artistry, then metarealism raises the image to the level of superartistic generalizations, giving it the generality and semantic dimensionality of myth. In both instances there is a noticeable pull toward the construction of supertemporal models of reality which lower the veils of history to reveal the stereotypes of mass consciousness or the

2. Metarealism, despite the similarity of the prefix, has little in common with surrealism, since it turns not toward the subconscious but to a supraconsciousness; it does not intoxicate but sobers creative reason. "Surrealistic images are like the images induced by opium . . ." (André Breton). The surrealists were repelled by soberly plebian, reasonable bourgeois reality and brought into it the whimsy of intoxicating dreams. Metarealism is repelled by the monstrous senselessness, the drunken haze and fogginess that has covered the historical horizon, and, for that reason, it calls in every way possible for an awakening, for an emergence from the hypnotic drunkenness of this single reality into a multidimensional perception of the world.—Epstein.

archetypes of collective unconsciousness. This generation, spiritually formed under the conditions of historical stagnation, cannot help but feel the retarded flow of time and respond with a heightened sensitivity to the eternal, recurring situations of being.

Instead of symbol or metaphor, the metarealists put forward a different poetic figure that is not easy to place in a traditional classification of tropes. This figure is close to that which the ancients understood as "metamorphosis": One thing is not simply similar or corresponding to another, which presupposes an indestructible border between them, the artistic predication and illusory quality of such juxtaposition; rather, one thing *becomes* the other. All of the similarities that poetry has loved to seek out—the moon with a frog, lightning with a photographic flash, birches with the keys of a piano (metaphors from the works of Esenin, Pasternak, and Voznesensky)—these are only the signs of metamorphoses that have not taken place and in the course of which things really, not apparently, exchange their essences. Metareal poetry seeks intently for that reality wherein metaphor is again revealed as metamorphosis, as an authentic intercommonality, rather than the symbolic similarity of two phenomena. Metarealism is not only metaphorical but also metaphysical realism, insofar as it is the poetry of that reality which is hidden within the metaphor, uniting its divergent meanings, the literal and the figurative.

> You will unfold in the expanded heart of suffering,
> wild rose,
>   oh,
>   wounding garden of earth's creation!
> The wild rose is white and whiter than any.
> He who will name you would out-argue Job.
> I am silent, I vanish in mind from the beloved gaze,
> not lowering my eye
> nor dropping my hands from the gate.
> The wild rose comes like a gardener, stern and heedless of
>   fear,
> with the crimson rose,
> with the hidden wound of care beneath its wild blouse.

In Olga Sedakova's poem "Wild Rose" there are neither similarities nor correspondences, but there is a continuous flow and transformation of essences. The wild rose is an image of all the world, in which a thorny path leads to the secret garden; suffering leads to salvation. The essence of the image begins to grow through its own broadened, transformed being; it does not refer to something other than itself: The nature of the wild, universal garden is revealed in the flourishing rose bush, simultaneously with the higher nature of the gardener, whose sufferings till the soil of the garden and turn a "hidden wound" into a "crimson rose." The precise position of the lyrical heroine is also poetically defined: She stands by the fence, awaiting a meeting that already transfixes her gaze and at any moment will sieze all of her being. The unfolding of the image—planting, the garden, the gardener (for whom the risen Saviour was mistaken, according to legend)—brings to mind the germination of a seed within which the future plant is already contained, through the organics of transformation, rather than the technique of comparison. All of Sedakova's poetry could be called, if we select for it the most concise single term, poetry of transformation.

The world of Ivan Zhdanov's poetry is also metareal, extended into the realm of the transparent, where pure prototypes of things are made manifest. Wind, mirror, memory, atmosphere, melting, reflection—these are the motifs that pass all through his writing, consistently disembodying the substance of objects:

> Does a house die, if afterwards there remain
> only smoke and space, only the immortal scent of habitation?
> How the snowfalls protect it,
> bending as before, above the roof
> that is long gone,
> parting at the point where the walls once stood . . .
> In dying, more like itself than in life.

The essence of a thing comes out in its return to the original, or predetermined, model; death utters the secret, all-clarifying word on life. Zhdanov is the master of depicting forms that seem already to have lost their substance but regain themselves in memory, in times of waiting, in the depth of a mirror or the shell of a shadow. Often the essence that has survived its own existence is singled out in a crisp formula. We are accustomed to the fact that a river has depth while objects have weight, but for Zhdanov "depth floats on the autumn water/and weight flows on, washing things away"; properties of things are more primary than the things themselves, and "flight flies without birds."

Zhdanov's poetry draws a fully visible, three-dimensional state of being for things that have faded away into their own reflection and then find themselves there with greater obviousness than in that passing state of being from which they came. The same act by which a thing sinks into the depth of its own essence brings this essence to the surface, where it appears to us: death is equal to resurrection.

The Scale of Poetic Styles

Within one and the same cultural situation conceptualism and metarealism fulfill two necessary and mutually supplementary tasks: they slough away the false, habitual, tenacious meanings of words while giving them a new polysemy and fullness of meaning. The verbal fabric of conceptualism is slovenly, artistically undervalued, and torn to rags, because one of the tasks of this current is to show the dilapidation and infirm helplessness of the vocabulary through which we make sense of the world. Metarealism creates a tall and solid verbal structure, seeking out the limits of transformation of things, of association in meaning; therefore, it turns toward eternal themes or eternal prototypes in contemporary themes, and it is saturated with archetypes: word, light, death, earth, wind, night. It draws upon nature, history, high culture, and art of various periods as the material for its creative works. Conceptualism, on the contrary, reveals the deceptiveness of all value designations; it is overtly associated with the themes of today, of the ephemeral, the communal lifestyle of mass consciousness, and the lower, vulgar forms of culture.

I wish to emphasize that metarealism and conceptualism are not so much closed groups as they are the poles between which contemporary poetry remains in motion: the stylistic boundaries between which there exist as many intergradations as there are poetic individualities. The most consistent and extreme metarealism is that practiced by Sedakova; a transparent and almost disembodied archetypal foundation emerges through her poetry. While sharing with Sedakova a striving for the eternal, "Platonic" prototypes of things, Zhdanov gives his image system dynamism by turning to contemporary realia. In such works as his "Radiator Rhapsody" a tense relationship is created between traditional and pure archetypes such as "water," "rose," and "Orpheus" and the incongruous elements whimsically inserted into this transparent world as kenotypes, the prototypes of a new age: "cast-iron gutters," "newspaper," and "can opener."

Farther along in the space of transition from metarealism to the opposite pole one finds the stylistic realm of such poets as Aleksandr Eremenko, Ilya Kutik, and Alexei Parshchikov. They are similarly drawn to the kenotypal level of contemporary civilization, abounding as it is in new objects and ideas whose origins were not assigned by prehistory and mythology but which demands an equally generalizing, structuring approach. In their poems such technicisms as "dual molecular spirals," "tactile contact," "hypothetical medians," and "Cronstein's construction" are used not as details of daily life in the era of the nuclear technological revolution but as the mysterious prototypes of a world that is to come, like the signs of an unknown civilization arising out of darkness, its eschatological indicators. While harking to the traditions of futurism with its taste for contemporaneity and the technological plasticity of objects, the new poetic lacks social-aesthetic aggressiveness and evangelical utopianism; delight in the future is excluded by an intent, visually gripping attention toward the present, toward data itself, the extent and endurance of objects. Such poetry cannot be considered futuristic; rather, it is *presentistic*—a poetry of presence, of the present (from the Latin *praesens*).

Presentism affirms the presence of an object, its visibility and tangibility, as the necessary and sufficient conditions of its meaningfulness. Between the extremes of poetic monism (the merging of object and sense) and dualism (their separateness) a medial approach to reality is sketched out, close to a phenomenological description. A poetic work is built as a succession of different views of the object, different ways of perceiving and inscribing it, which form in their totality the manifestations of its actual essence. Such is Parshchikov's "Catfish," the sum total of perceptions: in water and on land, waking and sleeping.

> For us, it's as if he's excavating a trench in the water.
> And above, surfacing—his wave explodes about him.
> Consciousness & skin compressed tightly together.
> He's like a black passageway leading from the moon's bedroom.
>
> So plunge your hand—into these underwater alleys
> beginning to speak with you, predicting futures on your palm.
> The kingfish thrashes about the sand, echoing,
> freezing up, like a key growing thick in a lock.
>
> [Trans. John High]

An object is the apparition of an object, the sum of its refractions through different visual media and signal codes. The thing is neither united with the idea nor opposed to it but is an idea itself, that is, in the ancient Greek meaning of the word, "appearance"—that which presents, "makes present" itself. Parshchikov expresses the principle of such a view of the world, which from within itself *is* the world: "I became the habitation for vision of all the planet." In this medial stylistic diaposon between the poles of metarealism and conceptualism we also find the poetry of Mikhail Aizenberg, Aleksandr Eremenko, Nina Iskrenko, and Tatyana Scherbina.

Moving farther along the stylistic scale, we eventually cross over into the realm of conceptualism, where the shift has been demonstrated above in the example of Prigov's work, in which all of reality, even its deeply archetypal layers, becomes the field of a conceptual game, albeit one conducted according to the rules of a more or less traditional, vaudevillian-idiotic rhyme-scheming. Farther on in the direction of the conceptualist limit we encounter Rubenshtein, the most extreme and consistent representative, with his use not even of words but of ready-made verbal blocks, formulas like catalog cards, points in a service manual or commands in a computer program.

From archetype through kenotype to stereotype through all the subtle shifts in the relation of idea and object, the broad field of image potentials is covered. Individual style is actualized not as a membership in one or another group or trend but as inclusion in the field itself, where the dialectic of the artistic image unfolds through an opposition that strives at one end toward myth, at the other toward concept. Metarealism and conceptualism, along with the intermediary zone between them that can be designated as presentism, together trace out new image formations, among which there remains adequate open space for yet another however greatly talented poet.

Translators

ALEKSEI ANDREEV lives in Moscow and works as an interpreter for Japanese and American delegations traveling to the Soviet Union.

ELENA BALASHOVA was born in Moscow; she now lives in Berkeley, California, where she works in the library of the University of California. She and Lyn Hejinian have been working together as translators since 1985, and a volume of their translations of works by Arkadii Dragomoshchenko has been published under the title *Description*.

IVAN BURKIN, poet and translator, is professor emeritus of foreign languages at San Francisco State University.

JEAN DAY is a poet and translator living in Oakland, California. She is the author of a number of books, including *A Young Recruit*.

SARA DICKINSON is a doctoral candidate in Russian literature at Harvard University.

FORREST GANDER lives in Providence, Rhode Island, where he teaches English and creative writing. He coedits Lost Roads Press with his wife, the poet C. D. Wright. He is a 1989 recipient of a National Endowment for the Arts Fellowship in poetry.

NINA GENKIN is a native Russian speaker living in San Francisco, where she is a high school teacher.

JULIE GESIN was born in Leningrad and moved to the United States twelve years ago. She is a writer, translator, and visual artist presently living in San Francisco.

PAUL GRAVES is a poet and translator living in New York City. He is translator (with Carol Ueland) of *Apollo in the Snow: Selected Poetry of Aleksandr Kushner.*

LYN HEJINIAN lives in Berkeley, California, where she is the coeditor and publisher, with Barrett Watten, of *Poetics Journal*. Her books include *Writing is an Aid to Memory, The Guard,* and *My Life*. In collaboration with Elena Balashova, she is translator of *Description*, a volume of poetry by Arkadii Dragomoshchenko.

BARBARA HELDT is professor of Russian at the University of British Columbia and is the author of *Terrible Perfection: Women and Russian Literature*.

JOHN HIGH is a founding editor of the *Five Fingers Review* and an editor of the Five Fingers Press publishing series. He studied at the Pushkin Institute in Moscow and has traveled numerous times to the Soviet Union. He is the recent recipient of a Fulbright award, and a National Endowment for the Arts fellowship, both given for his translation of contemporary Russian poetry. He teaches creative writing at San Francisco State University.

GERALD J. JANECEK is professor of Russian at the University of Kentucky. Translator of Andrei Bely's *Kotik Letaev* and *The First Encounter,* he is a specialist in Russian symbolism and futurism, as well as current avant-garde Russian poetry.

J. KATES is a poet and translator who lives in Fitzwilliam, New Hampshire. His translations of contemporary Russian poetry have appeared in publications in Ireland, New Zealand, and the United States. With Stephen A. Sadow, he is the translator of a collection by the Argentinian poet Ricardo Feierstein, *We, the Generation in the Wilderness.*

GARY KERN is translator of, among other works, *Before Sunrise,* by Mikhail Zoshchenko, and *Snake Train: Poetry and Prose by Velimir Khlebnikov.* He lives in Riverside, California.

MICHAEL MAKIN is assistant professor of Slavic languages and literatures at the University of Michigan and was formerly research fellow at New College, Oxford. He specializes in modern Russian poetry and has a book forthcoming on Marina Tsvetaeva.

ANESA MILLER-POGACAR is currently translating a collection of Mikhail Epstein's writings and editing an anthology of recent critical theory from the Soviet Union. She is a doctoral candidate in Russian literature at the University of Kansas.

MICHAEL MOLNAR lived in Leningrad from 1983 to 1985. He has published a study of Andrei Bely, and his translations of poetry by Arkadii Dragomoshchenko, Viktor Krivulin, Alexei Parshchikov, Lev Rubinshtein, and Elena Shvarts have appeared in various journals. He is now research assistant at the Freud Museum, London.

KATYA OLMSTED earns her living as a translator and as a sales representative for the Putnam Publishing Group. She studied at the Pushkin Institute in Moscow and received her B.A. in Russian studies from San Francisco State University.

MICHAEL PALMER is a poet and translator living in San Francisco. He is the author of *Notes for Echo Lake, First Figure,* and *Sun.*

PAUL SCHMIDT lives in New York City, where he is engaged in translating the collected works of Velimir Khlebnikov. The first two volumes, *The King of Time* and *Letters and Theoretical Writings,* are now in print.

COLE SWENSON is currently working on her Ph.D. in French and English literature at the University of California at Santa Cruz. Her book, *New Math,* was the recipient of a National Poetry Series award.

CAROL UELAND is assistant professor of Russian language and literature at Drew University. She is translator (with Paul Graves) of *Apollo in the Snow: Selected Poetry of Aleksandr Kushner.*

ANDREW WACHTEL is an assistant professor of Slavic languages and literature at Stanford University. Some of his translations of Soviet poetry appeared first in the *Berkeley Fiction Review.* He has translated Russian prose for a book entitled *Classic*

Russian Idylls. His translation of Daniil Harms's play *Elizaveta Bam* was performed in San Francisco in 1984.

DONALD WESLING teaches English literature at the University of California, San Diego. He has published two books on poetic forms. Having learned the Russian language in the 1980s, he spent three months at the Leningrad State University in 1988, conducting research on Soviet poetry.